기적의
영어
표현
암기북

기적의 영어표현 암기북

지은이 김수현
펴낸이 **최정심**
펴낸곳 (주)GCC

초판 1쇄 발행 2012년 2월 15일

2판 4쇄 발행 2015년 12월 15일

3판 1쇄 인쇄 2019년 2월 28일
3판 1쇄 발행 2019년 3월 2일

출판신고 제 406-2018-000082호
주소 10880 경기도 파주시 지목로 5
전화 (031) 8071-5700 팩스 (031) 8071-5200

ISBN 979-11-89432-98-0 13740

이 도서의 국립중앙도서관 출판예정도서목록(CIP)은
서지정보유통지원시스템 홈페이지(http://seoji.nl.go.kr)와
국가자료공동목록시스템(http://www.nl.go.kr/kolisnet)에서 이용하실 수 있습니다.
(CIP제어번호 : CIP2019006400)

www.nexusbook.com

바로바로
써먹는

기적의
영어

초보 맞춤형
우선순위
영어표현
총집합

표현
암기북

김수현 지음

넥서스ENGLISH

 # 머리말

영어에 익숙해지는 방법은 의외로 간단합니다.
자신의 일상을 영어로 옮겨 보는 것!

우선

1　반복되는 하루의 일과를 한글로 정리하고
2　이에 해당하는 영어 표현을 동사의 현재시제로 표현해 봅니다.

예를 들어,

나는 7시에 기상한다.
7시 50분에 집을 나선다.
8시 30분쯤 회사에 출근한다.

이를 영어로 옮기면 다음과 같습니다.(물론 이와 같거나 유사한 의미를 갖는 다른 표현들을
사용해도 좋습니다.)

I get up at 7.
I leave for work at 7:50.
I come to the office around 8:30.

반복되는 일과를 영어로 옮기는 과정이 끝나면,

3　일상생활의 특정 상황을 설정,
4　이에 필요한 표현들을 한글로 정리한 후
5　이것을 다시 영어로 옮겨 봅니다.

예를 들어,

송치가 있는 듯하다.
오늘은 반드시 치과에 간다.
오전에는 일이 바쁘다.
점심 먹고 가야지.

이를 영어로 옮기면 다음과 같이 될 것입니다.

I think I have a cavity.
I have to go to the dentist.
I'm busy this morning.
I'm going to the dentist after lunch.

이런 과정을 반복하다 보면 새로운 어휘 습득은 물론 영어 표현력이 빠르게 느는 것을 느낄 수 있습니다. 플래너에 그날 해야 할 일을 영어로 간단히 메모하는 습관 역시 영어에 익숙해지는 좋은 방법 중의 하나입니다. 스마트폰이나 컴퓨터의 언어 설정을 영어로 바꿔 사용하는 것 또한 훌륭한 방법이지요. 처음에는 대단히 불편하게 느껴지지만 몇 주 정도면 금방 익숙해질 것입니다.

〈기적의 영어표현 암기북〉은 이처럼 일상생활에서 반복되는 일이나 있을 법한 상황에서 필요한 표현들을 사전식으로 정리한 책입니다. 총 22개의 챕터에 인사 표현, 일상생활 표현부터 감정 표현, 학교·직장·여행지 등에서 쓰이는 표현 등을 다루고 있습니다. 늘 가까이 두고 영어로 말할 때 적극 활용해 보세요!

저자 김수현

 구성과 특징

Intro

09 의견의 대립

MP3를 들어보세요 03-U09

상대편과 옥신각신할 때 급기야는 "말이 안 통하는군요."라는 뜻의 You're ridiculous.
또는 You're full of nonsense. 같은 말이 나오기도 하죠. 상대편의 이해를 구하고
싶을 때는 이렇게 말해 보세요. Put yourself in my position. 바로 "입장 바꿔 놓고
생각해 보세요."입니다. 영화나 드라마에서도 자주 듣게 되는 말이죠.

원어민 발음 듣기 ☑□　회화 훈련 □□　듣기 훈련 □□

각각의 Unit은 간단한 머리말로 시작합니다. 해당 Unit의 주요 내용을
요약, 정리하여 무엇을 배워야 하는지에 대한 학습 목표를 한눈에 알 수
있습니다. 또한 그 Unit에서 알아야 할 대표적인 영어 표현, 문법에 대한
정보를 제공합니다.

Expressions

□ 약속해.	Promise me.
□ 약속할게.	I promise you.
	I'll promise.
	You have my word.
□ 한 가지만은 약속할 수 있어.	I can promise you one thing.
□ 약속은 지켜야지.	You should keep promises.
□ 약속이 있어.	I have a plan.
	I have an appointment.
	*appointment는 '병원 예약'이나 '업무 관련 약속'을 가리킬 때 주로 쓴다.

상황별 회화 표현 중에 일상생활에서 가장 많이 쓰이는 표현들을 우선
순위로 수록하였습니다. 표현 아래 *에는 문장에 활용할 수 있는 단어,
표현에 대한 설명 등을 추가하여 표현을 더욱 다양하고 정확하게 쓸 수
있습니다. 한글과 영어 표현을 동시에 수록하고 있어 내가 하고 싶은
말이 영어로 무엇인지 바로 알 수 있습니다.

> ※ **표현 아래의 *** 에서는 표현 속 단어의 대치어, 동의어, 반의어를
> 정리했습니다.
>
> → **대치어 표시** ex) *then → there(거기서)
>
> = **동의어 표시** ex) *ages = years
>
> ↔ **반의어 표시** ex) *high↔low

한 Unit이 끝날 때마다 〈Notes〉에 어려운 단어나 표현들을 정리하였습니다. 모르는 단어는 그냥 넘어가지 말고 바로 바로 외워 두세요. 어느샌가 어려운 표현도 척척 말하고 있는 자신을 발견하게 될 것입니다!

DIALOGUE

A I just want to say that I'm very sorry.
B Sorry doesn't make me forget what happened.
A I know. But I'm still hoping that you would forgive me and forget it.

본문에 실린 표현들을 활용하여 대화문을 구성하였습니다. 원어민이 직접 대화를 읽어 주어 더욱 생동감이 있습니다. 실제 대화에서는 표현을 어떻게 쓰는지 살펴보세요.

📖 별자리(star sign, constellation)

Aries/the Ram 양자리	Libra/the Scales 천칭자리
Taurus/the Bull 황소자리	Scorpio/the Scorpion 전갈자리
Gemini/the Twins 쌍둥이자리	Sagittarius/the Archer 사수자리
Cancer/the Crab 게자리	Capricorn/the Goat 염소자리
Leo/the Lion 사자자리	Aquarius/the Water Bearer 물병자리
Virgo/the Virgin 처녀자리	Pisces/the Fishes 물고기자리

해당 주제와 관련하여 필요한 정보나 추가 표현을 보너스로 넣었습니다. 별자리, 각종 요리법, 여행의 종류, 영화와 문학의 장르 등 실생활에서 더욱 유용하고 다양한 영어 표현들을 배워 보세요.

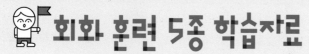

회화 훈련 5종 학습자료

〈기적의 영어표현 암기북〉의 5가지 학습자료들을 넥서스 홈페이지(www.nexusbook.com)에서
무료로 다운받을 수 있습니다.

원어민 녹음 MP3

195개 소제목별로 파일이 나뉘어져 있습니다. 미국인
성우가 normal speed로 녹음한 파일입니다. 원어민
발음을 확인해 보세요.

회화 훈련 MP3

원어민 음성을 듣고 따라 말해 볼 수 있도록 구성했습니다. 음성은 두 번 들려 줍니다.
두 번씩 따라 말해 보고 회화 훈련 □□ 에 ✔ 표시를 하세요. 회화 표현이 입에 붙을
때까지 반복해서 말하는 연습을 하세요.

듣기 훈련 MP3 & TEXT

주요 표현들을 MP3를 듣고 써 보는 딕테이션 훈련을
할 수 있습니다. '듣기 훈련 TEXT'를 보면서 '듣기 훈련
MP3'를 듣고 빈칸에 들어갈 말을 적어 보세요. 듣기
훈련이 어렵게 느껴진다면 해당 페이지의 내용을 한번
읽어 보고 다시 도전해 보세요.

쓰기 훈련 워크북

문제를 풀면서 책에서 공부한 내용을 확인해 보세요.
다양한 유형의 문제풀이를 통해 배운 내용을 복습할
수 있습니다. 틀린 문제는 꼭 책에서 내용을 다시 한번
확인하세요.

이 책의 100% 활용법

Step 1
주제·상황별
회화 표현
확인하기

195개의 주제, 상황별로 분류한 약 6,000개 회화 표현이 있습니다. 먼저 눈으로 표현을 익히고 읽어 보세요. 원어민 녹음 MP3를 들으며 정확한 발음을 확인하세요.

Step 2
회화 훈련

입에서 자연스럽게 영어회화가 나오도록 하려면 말하는 연습을 반복해서 해야겠죠? '회화 훈련 MP3'를 듣고 의미를 생각하면서 말하는 훈련을 합니다. 귀로 듣고 바로 입으로 따라 하는 것이 포인트! MP3를 들었을 때 의미가 잘 생각이 안 난다면, 책에서 오른쪽에 나오는 영어 표현을 손으로 가리고 왼쪽의 한글 뜻을 보면서 MP3를 들어 보세요. 한 문장당 3번 이상 말하는 연습을 합니다.

Step 3
듣기 훈련

쉬운 문장도 눈으로 TEXT를 보지 않고 귀로 들었을 때는 무슨 말인지 못 알아듣는 경우가 많습니다. 읽기 중심으로 학습하고 듣기 훈련을 소홀히 했을 때 나타나는 현상입니다. '듣기 훈련 MP3'를 듣고 영문 받아쓰기를 해 봅시다. 정답은 '듣기 훈련 TEXT' 자료 마지막 부분에 나와 있습니다.

Step 4
쓰기 훈련

'쓰기 훈련 워크북'에는 다양한 유형의 복습 문제들이 있습니다. 문제를 풀면서 책에서 공부한 내용을 다시 한번 복습하고 실력을 확인해 보세요. 입으로 말하기 연습을 하는 것도 중요하지만, 손으로 쓰는 과정을 거치면 기억에 더 오래 남습니다.

목차

Chapter 18

취미(Hobby)

Chapter19

교통(Transportation)

Chapter 20

각종 신고(Report)

Chapter 21

반려 동물(Animal companion)

Chapter 22

전화(Telephone)

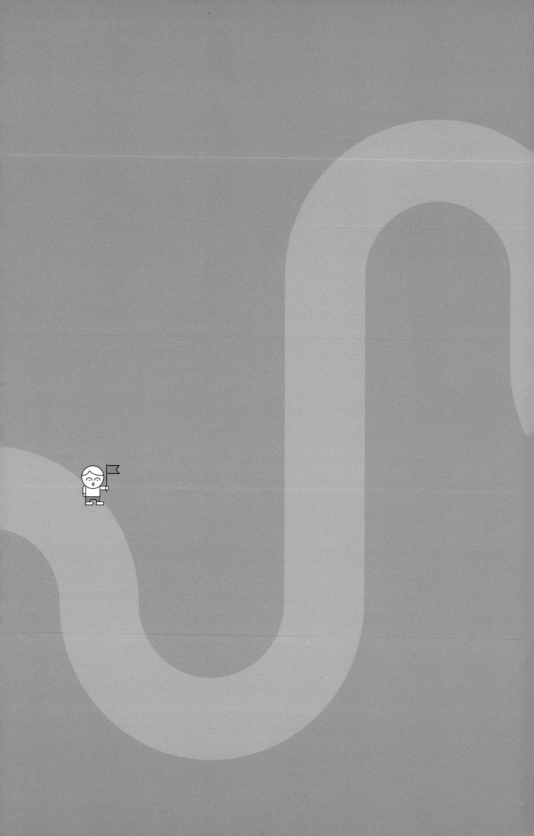

Chapter 01

인사 표현
Greeting

01 첫 만남, 인사하기

첫 만남과 재회, 우연한 만남 등에 따라 사용하는 표현들이 조금씩 다르니 구분해서 알아두어야 합니다. 특히 오랜만에 만났을 때는 '그동안 계속 못 만나 왔다'는 의미에서 have[has]+과거분사[현재완료]를 사용해야 하는 것도 잊지 마세요.

원어민 발음 듣기 ☑□   회화 훈련 □□   듣기 훈련 □□

□ 안녕하세요(안녕)!	Hello! / Hi!
	Hi, there!
	Good morning!
	*Good afternoon! 점심 인사 / Good evening! 저녁 인사
□ 처음 뵙겠습니다.	How do you do?
□ (좋은) 말씀 많이 들었어요.	I heard so many (great) things about you.
□ 만나서 반갑습니다.	(It's) Nice to see you.
	*nice=great, happy, glad
□ 이게 누구야!	Look who is here!
□ 오랜만이야.	Long time no see.
	It has been a long time.
	It has been a while.
	You're quite a stranger.
	I haven't seen you in ages.
	*ages=years, centuries
□ 다시 만나 반가워.	It's nice to see you again.
	Great to see you again.
	I'm so glad to see you again.
	*glad=happy, excited
□ 세상 좁다!	(What a) Small world!
□ 그동안 어디 있었어?	Where have you been?
	Where have you been hiding?
□ 지방에 있었어.	I was out of town.
□ 외국에 있었어.	I was in another country.
□ (회사 일로) 그동안 바빴어.	I have been busy (doing work).

□	우리 만난 적 있나요?	Have we met before?
		Haven't we met before?
		I think we have met (before).
□	파티에서 만난 것 같아요.	I think we have met at the party.
□	제가 아는 분 같은데.	Do I know you?
		I think I know you.
□	저를 아세요?	Do you know me?
□	낯이 익네요.	You look familiar to me.
□	저를 기억하세요?	(Do you) Remember me?
□	혹시 Ms. Kim 아니세요?	Aren't you Ms. Kim?
		Aren't you Ms. Kim by any chance?
		You are Ms. Kim, right?
□	너인 줄 알았어.	I thought it was you.
		I knew it was you.
□	다른 사람과 착각했어요.	I thought you were someone else.
		I took you for someone else.

DIALOGUE

A Aren't you Michael?
B Yes, I am. Do you know me?
A I'm Crystal from ABC high school.
B Crystal! Now I remember you. Very long time no see.
A So how have you been?
   Tell me everything about your life, girls, job, family….

A 너 마이클 아니야?
B 맞는데요. 저를 아세요?
A 나 ABC 고등학교 나온 크리스털이야.
B 크리스털이구나! 이제야 기억나네. 정말로 오랜만이다.
A 그래, 어떻게 지냈어? 그동안 살아온 이야기 다 해 봐. 여자, 직장, 네 가족들…….

Notes

stranger 낯선 사람, 오랜만에 만나는 사람   hide 숨다, 숨어 지내다   look familiar to ~에게 낯익다   by any chance 혹시, 우연히   I thought ~ ~인 줄 알았다(=I knew ~)   take A for B A를 B로 착각하다(잘못 보다)

02 안부 묻고 대답하기

서양에서도 서로의 안부를 묻는 것은 인간관계를 돈독히 하는 데 중요한 역할을 합니다. How are you?, How are you doing? 같은 안부를 묻는 질문과 I'm great.(잘 지내.), So-so.(그저 그래.) 같은 적절한 답변을 잘 알아두면 문화가 다른 외국인과도 깊은 교감을 나눌 수 있습니다.

원어민 발음 듣기 ☑☐　회화 훈련 ☐☐　듣기 훈련 ☐☐

▢ 어떻게 지냈어?

How are you?

How are you doing?

How is it going?

How is everything with you?

What's up?

What's new?

Anything new?

▢ 잘 지내.

I'm great.
*I'm great. = I'm good. / I'm fine.

Everything is going well.

Couldn't be better.

▢ 그저 그렇지 뭐.

So-so.

Not much.

Nothing special.

▢ 잘 지내지 못해.

Not so good.

▢ 항상 똑같지 뭐.

Same as always.
*always = usual

About the same.

Same old, same old.

▢ 그동안 어떻게 지냈어?

How have you been?

How have you been doing?

What have you been up to?

▢ 잘 지냈어.

I have been great.

▢ 잘 지내지 못했어.

I haven't been well.

▢ 가족은 어때?

How is your family?

18

□ 다들 잘 지내.	They are all good.	
□ 하는 일은 어때?	How is your work? *work = business	
□ 학교생활은 어때?	How is your school?	
□ 잘 되고 있어.	It is great.	
□ 늘 바쁘게 지내.	I'm always busy. (I'm) Busy as always. I don't have time to breathe. I keep myself busy.	
□ 좋아 보인다.	You look great! *great = wonderful, fantastic	
□ 안색이 별로다.	You don't look so good.	
□ 점점 젊어지네.	You're getting younger.	
□ 살 빠졌니?	Have you lost your weight?	
□ 전혀. 오히려 요즘 쪘는걸.	Not at all. I put on some weight lately.	
□ 요즘 운동하니?	Have you been working out?	

DIALOGUE

A So how is your work?
B Well, about the same. How about yours?
A I'm busy as always. I don't have time to breathe.

A 요즘 일은 어때?
B 뭐, 늘 똑같지. 네 일은?
A 나야 늘 바쁘지. 숨 쉴 틈도 없어.

📝 **Notes**

breathe 숨 쉬다 get+비교급 점점 ~해지다 lose weight 체중이 감소하다, 살 빠지다 put on weight 체중이 늘다, 살찌다(= gain weight) work out 운동하다, (기업이) 구조조정하다

03 날씨와 계절 관련 표현

외국인과 간단한 인사를 나눈 후 딱히 할 말이 없어 분위기가 어색해지는 때가
있었나요? 그럴 때는 It's a nice day, right?, It's freezing cold. 등과 같은 날씨나
계절 얘기를 해 보세요. 식상한 듯하지만 공감대를 이끌어내는 데는 최고입니다. 날씨나
계절을 말할 때는 가짜 주어 "it"을 사용하는 것도 꼭 기억하세요.

원어민 발음 듣기 ☑□   회화 훈련 □□   듣기 훈련 □□

□ 날씨 어때?
How is the weather?
What is the weather like?
How is it outside?

□ 오늘 날씨 좋다.
It's a nice day today.
*nice = great, fine, pleasant
The weather is great today.
What a lovely day today!

□ (오늘) 날씨 안 좋아.
It's a nasty day.
*nasty = dreadful, terrible
The weather is bad today.
The weather sucks.

□ 비가 오려나.
It looks like rain.
It's likely to rain.

□ 태풍이 오고 있어.
The typhoon is coming.
The storm is on the way.

□ 비가 내리고 있어.
It is raining.

□ 바람이 불고 있어.
It is windy.

□ 안개가 꼈어.
It is foggy.

□ 날씨가 너무 덥고 습해.
It is really hot and humid.
It is really muggy.

□ 날씨가 너무 추워.
It is freezing cold.

□ 길이 꽁꽁 얼어서 미끄러워.
The roads are frozen and icy.

□ 내일 날씨 어때?
How will the weather be tomorrow?
What will the weather be like tomorrow?

☐	일기예보에 따르면 ～	The weather forecast says…
		According to the weather forecast, …
☐	내일 흐릴 거래.	It will be cloudy tomorrow.
☐	내일 32℃까지 올라간대.	The temperature will go up to 32℃(degrees) tomorrow.
☐	내일 비가 올 확률이 70%래.	There is a 70% chance of showers tomorrow.
☐	이제 곧 봄이야.	Spring is just around the corner.
		*summer: 여름 / autumn: 가을 / winter: 겨울
☐	완연한 봄이네.	Spring is already here.
		Spring has clearly set in.
☐	전형적인 봄 날씨야.	It is typical spring weather.
☐	황사와 꽃가루 철이야.	It is the season of the yellow sand and pollen.
		*yellow sand = yellow dust
☐	곧 장마가 시작돼.	The rainy season is coming soon.
		The rainy season will start soon.
☐	나뭇잎이 붉게 물들었어.	The leaves are changing colors.
☐	요즘 일교차가 심해.	There is a big temperature gap these days.
☐	오늘 첫눈이 올 거래.	There will be the first snowfall today.
		We will see the first snow today.
☐	올 겨울은 눈이 많이 오네.	We have a lot of snow this winter.
☐	올 겨울은 한파가 온대.	There will be a cold wave this winter.
		We will have a cold wave this winter.
☐	올 여름은 폭염이 온대.	There will be a heat wave this summer.
		We will have a heat wave this summer.
☐	늦더위가 기승이네.	The lingering summer heat is severe.
		*a cold wave in spring: 꽃샘추위

📝 **Notes**

nasty 날씨가 잔뜩 흐린 suck 빨다, 아주 불쾌하다 muggy 찌는 듯이 무더운(=hot and humid) shower 소
나기 set in ~ 계절이 시작되다, 자리 잡다 snowfall 눈 내림, 강설량 lingering 질질 끄는, 좀처럼 사라지지 않는
severe 맹렬한, 기세등등한

04 친구 소개하기, 소개 받기

서로가 자신을 소개하거나 제삼자를 소개할 때는 동사 introduce(소개하다)와 This is ~.(이쪽은 ~입니다.)가 핵심적인 표현입니다. 처음 만나면 소개말과 함께 남녀노소 상관없이 악수를 나누는 것(shaking hands)이 보편적입니다.

원어민 발음 듣기 ☑☐   회화 훈련 ☐☐   듣기 훈련 ☐☐

☐ 크리스털, 이쪽은 수야.	Crystal, this is Sue.
☐ 제 친구 크리스털을 소개할게요.	I would like to introduce a friend of mine, Crystal.
	Let me introduce my friend, Crystal.
	I want you to meet my friend, Crystal.
	Everyone, this is my friend, Crystal.
	Everyone, meet my friend, Crystal.
☐ 제 소개를 할게요.	Let me introduce myself.
	Let me tell you about myself.
	Allow me to introduce myself.
☐ 꼭 한번 뵙고 싶었어요.	I have always wanted to meet you.
	I was looking forward to meeting you.
	We finally meet.
☐ 정식으로 인사한 적은 없네요.	I don't think we have been introduced formally.
☐ 뵙게 되어 영광입니다.	It is a great honor to meet you.
☐ 우리 친하게 지내요.	I hope we can be friends.
	I hope we get to know each other better.
☐ 성함을 여쭤봐도 될까요?	What's your name?
	Can I have your name?
	*Could I ~?나 May I ~?는 공손한 표현이다.
☐ 당신을 뭐라고 불러야 할까요?	What should I call you?
	How should I address you?
☐ 그냥 '수'라고 불러 주세요.	Just call me Sue.
	Sue is fine.

□ 어떤 일을 하세요?	What do you do (for a living)?
	What is your profession?
	What business are you in?
□ 연락처를 알려 주시겠어요?	Can I have your contact info?
	I would like to have your contact number.
□ 제 명함입니다.	Here is my (name) card.
	This is my business card.
	Let me give you my card.
□ 이 번호로 연락하시면 됩니다.	You can reach me at this number.
□ 언제든지 연락 주세요.	Call me anytime.
□ 근처에 오시면 들르세요.	When you are in the neighborhood, please stop by.
□ 언제든 환영입니다.	You are always welcome.
□ 그를 소개시켜 주실 수 있으세요?	Could you introduce me to him, please?
	If it is not too much trouble, please introduce me to him.
□ 언제 점심 식사 함께해요.	Let's have lunch together sometime.

DIALOGUE

A I don't think we've been introduced properly.
B Yeah, I'm Sue. You are…
A I'm Michael. Here is my name card.

A 우리 정식으로 인사한 적이 없는 것 같은데요.
B 맞아요. 저는 수입니다. 당신은…….
A 저는 마이클입니다. 여기 제 명함입니다.

Notes

get to know 알게 되다 **address** 주소, 호칭, ~라고 부르다 **profession** 직업, 전문직 **reach** 닿다, 연락을 취하다 **stop by** 잠깐 들르다 **sometime** 나중에 언제 **properly** 정식으로, 예의 바르게 **You are…** 상대의 이름을 유도해 낼 때 쓰는 표현(= What is your name?)

05 작별하기

사람 사이의 헤어짐은 돌아서면 그만이라고 생각하기 쉽지만 결코 그렇지 않습니다. Good bye.(잘 가.)라는 말과 함께 It was really fun.(정말 즐거웠어.), See you again.(다음에 또 보자.)라고 하거나, 참석하지 못한 사람에 대해서는 Say hello to ~.(~에게 안부 전해 줘.)라고 할 수 있겠죠.

원어민 발음 듣기 ☑☐   회화 훈련 ☐☐   듣기 훈련 ☐☐

☐ 안녕히 가세요(계세요).
(Good) Bye.
Bye-bye.
Later.
Take care.
So long.
Farewell.

☐ 좋은 하루 되세요.
(Have a) Good day.

☐ 이제 가야겠다.
I think I should go.
I'm afraid I have to go.
I have got to go.

☐ 이제 그만 갈까?
Are you ready to go?
Ready?

☐ 오늘 만나서 반가웠어요.
It was nice meeting you.

☐ 이야기 나눠서 좋았어요.
It was great talking to you.

☐ 오늘 정말 즐거웠어요.
I had a really great time today.
It was really fun.
It has been a real pleasure.

☐ 조만간 또 만나요.
See you again.
*again = soon, later, around
Let's meet real soon.
Let's do this again.

☐ 우리 조만간 이런 모임 또 가져요.
Let's have another get-together soon.

☐ 오늘 초대해 주셔서 감사해요.
Thank you for inviting me.
Thank you for having me.

24

☐ 오늘 와 주셔서 감사해요.	Thank you for coming. I appreciate your coming. I'm glad you came.
☐ 우리 연락하며 지내요.	Let's keep in touch. Stay in touch.
☐ 전화할게.	I will call you.
☐ 이메일 할게.	I will e-mail you.
☐ 우리 나중에 더 이야기해요.	Let's talk more later.
☐ 시간 될 때 놀러 오세요.	Come by when you are available. Visit us time to time.
☐ 가족에게 안부 전해 주세요.	Say hello to your family. Give my regards to your folks. *regards = best, love
☐ 운전 조심해.	Drive safely.
☐ 집에 도착하면 문자 줘.	Text me when you get home.
☐ 내가 태워다 줄까?	Would you like me to drive you home? Do you need a ride?
☐ 대리운전 불러 줄까?	Do you want me to call a driving service?
☐ 그럼 그때 보자.	See you then. *then → there (거기서)
☐ 다음번에는 아이들도 데려와.	Bring your kids next time.
☐ 떠나기 전에 너희들 봤으면 해.	Let's meet before I leave. I hope to see you all before I leave.

📑 **Notes**

I'm afraid ~ 안타깝게도 ~하다, ~해서 안타깝다 get-together 친구들끼리의 만남, 소모임 appreciate 고맙게 생각하다, 감사하다 available 이용 가능한, 여유가 있는 regards 안부(= best) folks 가족, 친지들 get home 집에 다다르다, 도착하다 ride 탈것, 교통수단 driving service 대리운전

Chapter 02

대화하기
Conversation

01 대화를 시작할 때

단도직입적으로 본론부터 말하기보다는 "있잖아.", "들어 봐." 등의 가벼운 표현으로 말을 시작하면 대화를 훨씬 부드럽게 이끌어갈 수 있습니다. 또는 Do you know ~?(~을 알아?)나 Guess ~.(~을 맞춰 봐.) 등 상대방의 관심을 끌 수 있는 표현들을 넌지시 던지는 것도 좋은 방법이죠.

원어민 발음 듣기 ☑□   회화 훈련 □□   듣기 훈련 □□

있잖아.	You know what? Guess what?
들어 봐.	Listen (to me). Check this out! Get this. I will tell you what.
주목해 주세요.	Everyone, pay attention. Everyone, listen (up).
안 들으면 후회할걸.	You've got to hear this. You don't want to miss this.
어제 무슨 일 있었는지 알아?	Do you know what happened yesterday?
어디서부터 시작해야 하나?	Where do I (even) begin? I don't know where to begin.
할 말이 있는데…….	I have something to tell you. Can we talk now?
우리 얘기 좀 해.	We need to talk. Let's talk. Let's go someplace to talk.
잠깐 시간 있어?	Do you have a minute? Got a second?
이야기할 시간 있어?	Do you have time to chat?

📑 **Notes**

check out 확인하다, 들어 보다 have got to ~해야만 하다 miss 놓치다, 그리워하다 minute 아주 잠깐의 시간 (=second) chat 잡담하다, 수다 떨다

28

02 대화를 진행하면서

대화를 이끌어갈 때는 eye contact(눈 맞춤)와 함께 상대방이 자신의 말을 잘 듣고 있는지 확인할 필요가 있습니다. 반대로 듣는 사람은 말하는 사람의 말을 경청하고 있다는 표현과 더불어 좀 더 이야기해 달라는 관심의 표현을 곁들일 수 있겠죠.

원어민 발음 듣기 ☑☐　　회화 훈련 ☐☐　　듣기 훈련 ☐☐

☐ 계속해.
Please continue.
Go on.
Keep going.
Keep talking.
Go ahead.

☐ 그래서 어떻게 됐어?
Then what?
What happened next?

☐ 듣고 있어.
I'm listening.
I'm paying attention to you.
I'm all ears.

☐ 내 말 듣고 있어?
Are you listening to me?
Are you paying attention to me?
Are you with me?
Are you following me?

☐ 경청합시다.
Let's listen.
Let's focus.
Let's pay attention.

☐ 어디까지 이야기했더라?
Where am I?
Where are we?

☐ 무슨 이야기 하고 있었더라?
What was I talking about?
Where were we talking about?

☐ 좀 더 이야기해 봐.
Tell me more.

☐ 좀 더 자세히 이야기해 봐!
Details! Details!

29

03 맞장구치기

네이티브들은 대화 중간 중간에 적절히 맞장구를 치는데 언어 습관이 다른 우리에겐 생소하게 느껴질 수 있습니다. "그래(요)?"라고 할 때는 Oh? 또는 Is that so?라고 하고, "맞아(요)."는 That's right.나 Exactly., 그리고 "설마 그럴 리가(요)."라고 할 땐 No way!나 You're kidding, right?라고 하면 됩니다.

원어민 발음 듣기 ☑☐   회화 훈련 ☐☐   듣기 훈련 ☐☐

그래요?	Oh?
	Yeah?
	Is that so?
	Is that right?
그래서요?	So?
	And?
어쩌라고요?	So what?
	I hear you.
정말이요?	Really?
	You don't say.
	(Are) You serious?
아마도. / 글쎄.	Well!
	Maybe!
	Probably.
	I'm afraid so.
맞아요. / 그러게요.	That's right.
	Exactly.
	You bet.
	I know.
	Tell me about it.
내 말이!	That's exactly what I'm saying.
	You read my mind.
	You took the word right out of my mouth.
설마 그럴 리가요.	No way!
	You're kidding, right?

I can't believe it.

Impossible!

☐ 그럼요. / 물론이죠.

That's true.

Of course.

Yes, indeed.

I agree.

I think so.

☐ 그래서 그랬군요.

That's why.

☐ 그렇게 된 것이구나.

That's what really happened.

☐ 말이 되네.

That explains a lot.

That proves it.

☐ 말도 안 돼요.

That is ridiculous.

Nonsense!

☐ 너무하네요.

That is too much.

That is crazy.

That went too far.

☐ 잘 됐어요.

Good for you!

How nice!

That is so great.

You must be happy.

☐ 안됐네요.

I'm sorry (to hear that).

That's too bad.

What a shame!

What a pity!

Bummer!

📝 **Notes**

serious 정말인, 심각한 read one's mind 마음을 읽다, 마음이 통하다 take the word right out of one's mouth ~가 하고 싶은 말을 바로 이해하다 kid 농담하다, 장난치다 indeed 물론, 정말로 prove 증명하다, 설명하다 ridiculous 말도 안 되는, 터무니없는(= absurd) go far 멀리 가다, 지나치다 shame 유감, 면목 없음 pity 딱함, 애석함 bummer 실망

04 간섭, 끼어들기

도중에 상대방의 말을 끊을 때는 간단히 Wait! 또는 Hold it right there!라고 하면
됩니다. 상대방의 말이 이해가 잘 안 될 때는 "뭐라고요?"라는 의미로 Sorry? 또는
Excuse me?라고 하죠. 또한 "나 아직 말 안 끝났어요."라고 할 땐 I'm not done
yet. 또는 I'm not finished.라고 합니다.

원어민 발음 듣기 ☑□   회화 훈련 □□   듣기 훈련 □□

☐ 잠깐! / 그만!	Wait!
	Hold it right there!
	Excuse me one second.
☐ 무슨 말을 하려는 거야?	What are you saying?
	What are you telling me?
	What are you trying to say?
	What are you getting at?
☐ 무슨 말 하려는지 알겠어.	I think I know what you're saying.
	I think I know what you are getting at.
☐ 무슨 뜻이야?	What do you mean?
	What are you suggesting?
☐ 무슨 말인지 통 모르겠어.	I don't understand.
	I don't understand a single word.
	I don't get it.
	I'm not following.
	I don't follow you.
☐ 뭐라고?	What?
	(I'm) Sorry?
	Excuse me?
	I beg your pardon?
	Come again?
	What is that?
☐ 다시 한번 반복해 줄래?	Can you repeat that?
	Can you explain that again?

□ 알기 쉽게 설명해 줄래?	Can you go over that again? Can you simplify that?
□ 헷갈려.	It's confusing. It makes me confused. I'm confused.
□ 굳이 말 안 해도 돼.	You don't have to say. You don't have to explain.
□ 나 아직 말 안 끝났어.	I'm not done yet. I'm not finished. I'm still talking. My lips are still moving.
□ 할 말 더 있는데.	I have more things to say. I want to say something more.
□ 말 끊지 마.	Don't stop me. Don't interrupt me.
□ 중간에 끼어들지 마.	Don't cut in. Don't break in.
□ 제발 내 말을 끝내게 해 주세요.	Please let me finish. Can't you let me finish?
□ 한창 뭐 하는 중인데요.	We're in the middle of something.
□ 빨리 말해 줄래요?	Can you talk fast? Can you be quick?
□ 천천히 말해 줄래요?	Can you talk slowly?
□ 또박또박 말해 줄래요?	Can you talk clearly?

📑 **Notes**

hold 잡다, 중지하다 get at 의미하다, 말하고자 하다 get it 알다, 이해하다 go over 다시 반복하다 simplify 알기 쉽게 단순화하다(= elaborate) confusing 헷갈리게 하는, 혼란스러운 don't have to ~ ~할 필요 없다 My lips are still moving. 입술이 여전히 움직인다(아직 말이 다 끝나지 않았다). interrupt 방해하다(= intrude) cut in 끼어들다, 새치기하다(= break in) in the middle of ~ 한창 ~ 중인

05 오해 풀기, 사과하기

대화를 나누거나 자신의 의사를 표현할 때에는 언제든지 오해의 가능성이 있습니다. 일단 오해가 생기면 거짓말을 하거나 어색하게 사태를 악화시키는 것보다 솔직 담백한 대화로 clear things up(오해를 풀다) 혹은 get things straight(확실히 짚고 넘어가다) 할 수 있도록 노력해야겠죠.

원어민 발음 듣기 ☑□   회화 훈련 □□   듣기 훈련 □□

□ (그건) 오해야.	That's a (huge) misunderstanding.
	It's a total mix-up.
	It's a total mess.
	You misunderstood me.
	You got me wrong.
□ 오해하지 마.	Don't misunderstand me.
	Don't get me wrong.
□ 그런 뜻은 아니었어.	I didn't mean it.
	I didn't mean to say it.
	I didn't mean to hurt your feelings.
□ 그런 의도는 없었어.	I didn't have that intention.
	I didn't say it on purpose.
□ 네게 한 말이 아니야.	I wasn't saying it to you.
	It wasn't meant for you.
□ 말이 허투루 나갔어.	It just slipped from my mouth.
	I was thinking out loud.
	You were not supposed to hear it.
□ 그냥 하는 말이었어. / 별 뜻 없었어.	It doesn't mean anything.
	It meant nothing.
□ 혼잣말이었어.	I was talking to myself.
□ 오해가 있는 것 같아.	I think we have a misunderstanding.
□ 오해 풀어.	Let's clear things up.
	Let's clear the air.
	Let's get things straight.

□ 어떻게 해야 네 오해가 풀릴까?	What can I do to make you feel better?
	What do you want me to do to clear things up?
	What should I do to get things straight?
□ 오해를 확대시키지 마.	Don't make a big deal out of this.
	Don't make a fuss out of this.
	*this → nothing (아무것도 아닌 일)
□ 툭 터놓고 얘기해 보자.	Let's have a heart-to-heart talk.
□ 솔직하게 말하지 그래?	Why don't you level with me?
□ 허심탄회하게 말할게.	I'll be completely honest with you.
	I'll level with you.

DIALOGUE

A I'm telling you. It's a misunderstanding.
B You were looking right at me when you said it.
A It didn't mean anything.
  What should I do to get things straight?

A 내가 장담하는데 그건 오해야.
B 네가 그 말을 할 때 나를 똑바로 쳐다보고 있었거든.
A 별뜻 없었어. 오해를 풀려면 내가 어떻게 해야겠어?

📝 Notes

misunderstanding 오해 total 완전히, 정말로 mix-up 혼란, 뒤섞임, 오해 mess 엉망진창 get ~ wrong ~를 잘못 이해하다, 오해하다 mean ~을 의미하다, ~할 의도가 있다 hurt one's feelings ~의 감정을 상하게 하다 intention 의도, 의향 on purpose 일부러(=purposely) slip from one's mouth 입에서 무심코 말이 흘러나가다 think out loud 무심코 말을 내뱉다 clear things up 오해를 풀다, 제대로 하다(=clear the air, get things straight) make ~ feel better ~의 기분을 나아지게 하다 make a big deal 일을 크게 만들다, 시끄럽게 하다(=make a fuss) heart-to-heart 마음으로부터, 솔직한 level with ~에게 솔직하게 털어놓다

06 말다툼

의도적이든 아니든 대화 중에 말다툼이 일어나는 경우가 있습니다. 지나치다 싶은 말에는 참지 말고 You crossed the line.(도가 지나치다.)이라고 경고하세요. 간단히 "입[말] 조심해."라고 말할 때는 Watch your mouth[tongue].라고 합니다.

원어민 발음 듣기 ☑☐   회화 훈련 ☐☐   듣기 훈련 ☐☐

□ 말이 지나치다.	It's too much. How can you say that? How can you talk to me like that?
□ 너 (넘지 말아야 할) 선을 넘었어.	You crossed the line. You are out of line. You went beyond. You went too far.
□ 나 기분 상했어.	You hurt my feelings.
□ 네가 상관할 바 아니야.	It's none of your business. You have no business here.
□ 넌 그렇게 말할 자격 없어.	You have no right to say that.
□ 말조심해.	Hey, watch! Watch your mouth. Be careful.
□ (그게) 내 탓이라는 거야?	Are you saying that it's my fault? Are you blaming me? So it's my fault.
□ 뭘 암시하는 거야?	What are you implying?
□ 말 빙빙 돌리지 마.	Stop beating around the bush.
□ 주제 바꾸지 마.	Don't change the subject.
□ 억지 부리지 마.	Don't twist my words.
□ (그렇게) 비꼬지 마.	Don't be (so) sarcastic.
□ 단도직입적으로 말해.	What's your point? Get to the point.

☐ 입 다물어!	Shut up!	
	Shut your mouth!	
	Zip it!	
☐ 그만해!	Stop it!	
	Cut it out!	
	Enough!	
☐ 거짓말 마!	Don't lie to me.	
	Stop lying.	
	You're a liar.	
☐ 네 말에 가시가 있어.	Your words have a sting.	
	You have a harsh tongue.	
☐ 내가 왜 이런 말을 들어야 해?	Why do I have to listen to this?	
	I don't need to listen to this.	

DIALOGUE

A Are you saying that it's my fault?
B I didn't say that, but….
A Stop beating around the bush. Get to the point.

A 네 말은 그게 내 탓이라는 거야?
B 그렇게 말하지는 않았지만…….
A 빙빙 돌려 말하지 말고 단도직입적으로 얘기해.

📑 Notes

cross the line 선을 넘다, 도가 지나치다(=be out of the line)   go beyond 도가 지나치다, 너무하다(=go too far)   imply 암시하다, 넌지시 의미하다   beat around the bush 변죽을 울리다, 핵심을 말하지 않고 딴소리만 하다   twist one's words 억지 부리다   sarcastic 비꼬는, 야유하는, 빈정거리는   zip 채우다, 닫다   cut out 그만하다, 관두다   sting 가시, 아픈 것   harsh 거친, 혹독한

07 비밀에 대해 말하기

Don't tell anyone.(아무한테도 말하면 안 돼.)이라고 말하면 더 빨리 퍼져나가는 비밀! 그래서 open secret(공공연한 비밀)이라는 말도 생겨났나 봅니다. 만약 비밀을 꼭 지키겠다고 다짐했다면 상대방에게 I won't tell anyone. 또는 I'll keep your secret.(비밀 지킬게.)이라고 말하세요.

원어민 발음 듣기 ☑☐   회화 훈련 ☐☐   듣기 훈련 ☐☐

☐ 비밀이야.	It's a secret.
	Hush!
	Shh!
☐ 완전 비밀이야.	It's top-secret.
☐ 극비야.	It's (strictly) confidential.
	It's (strictly) classified.
☐ 공공연한 비밀이야.	It's an open secret.
	Everyone knows the secret.
☐ 말 못해.	I can't tell you.
	I'm not supposed to tell you.
	I'm not allowed to say anything.
	I'm not at liberty to say this.
☐ 제발 말해 줘.	Please tell me.
	Please share it with me.
☐ 아무한테도 말하면 안 돼.	Don't tell anyone.
	Don't share this with anyone.
	You can't tell anyone.
	Keep it to yourself.
	Take it to your grave.
☐ 아무한테도 말 안 할게.	I won't tell anyone.
☐ 비밀 지킬게.	I'll keep your secret.
	My lips are sealed.
	You can trust me.
☐ 나 비밀 잘 지키잖아.	I can keep secrets.

□	비밀을 이야기할 사람도 없어.	I don't have anyone to tell. I have nobody to tell.
□	우리끼리 하는 말인데.	It's just between you and me. It's between us. It's our secret.
□	조용히 해. 누가 들을라.	Hush! Someone will hear you. Lower your voice. Keep it down.
□	비밀이(정보가) 샜어.	The secret is out. The information leaked out.
□	모두가 그것을 쉬쉬해.	Everyone hushes it.
□	비밀에 부치자.	Let's keep it a secret. *secret = private Let's keep it under our hat.

DIALOGUE

A It's just between you and me.
　We're going to have a new team leader today.
B What? Are you serious?
A Hush! Someone will hear you.

A 우리끼리 하는 말인데, 오늘 새로운 팀장이 온대.
B 뭐라고? 정말이야?
A 조용히 해. 누가 들을라.

📋 Notes

hush 쉬쉬하다, 쉿! strictly 엄히, 철저히 confidential 극비의, 기밀의(= classified) be supposed to ~하기로 되어 있다 be allowed to ~하도록 허용되다 be at liberty to ~ 마음대로 ~하다 share A with B A를 B와 나누다, 공유하다 take ~ to one's grave ~을 무덤까지 가져가다, ~을 아무에게도 말하지 않다 keep ~ to oneself ~을 스스로만 알다, 간직하다 seal 눈을 꼭 감다, 입(술)을 꼭 다물다, 비밀을 간직하다 leak out 바깥으로 새다, 누출되다 keep ~ under one's hat ~을 비밀로 하다

08 뉴스(소식) 전하기

새로운 소식이나 빅뉴스로 시작하는 대화는 언제나 흥미진진합니다. 소식을 전하기 전에 You wouldn't believe this.(들어도 믿기지 않을걸.)와 같은 표현으로 상대방의 호기심을 더욱 유발할 수도 있죠. 출처를 밝히고 싶지 않을 때에는 Someone told me ~(누가 그러던데 ~)로 이야기를 꺼내면 됩니다.

원어민 발음 듣기 ☑□ 회화 훈련 □□ 듣기 훈련 □□

☐ 빅뉴스가 있어.	Big news (for you)! I have big news for you.
☐ 깜짝 놀랄 만한 소식이 있어.	Surprise news (for you)! I have surprise news for you.
☐ 따끈따끈한 소식이야.	It's hot news.
☐ 좋은 소식과 나쁜 소식이 있어.	I have good news and bad news.
☐ 어느 것부터 들을래?	Which one do you want to hear first? Which one do you prefer?
☐ 들어도 믿기지 않을걸.	You wouldn't believe (this). You wouldn't believe your ears. You wouldn't believe what you hear.
☐ 새로운 소식 있어?	Any news? Anything new?
☐ 그 소식(이야기) 들었어?	Did you hear that? Did you happen to hear that?
☐ 누가 그러는데 ~	Someone told me… A little bird told me…
☐ 소문에 ~	Rumor says… There is a rumor (that)…
☐ 확실한 이야기야.	I heard from the horse's mouth.
☐ 나쁜 소식이 더 빨리 퍼져.	Bad news travels quickly.

📝 **Notes**

believe one's ears 누군가가 한 말을 믿다 happen to 혹시 ~하다 a little bird (정보의 출처를 밝히기 싫을 때) 풍문에 rumor 루머, 소문, 풍문 from the horse's mouth 정보 출처가 확실한

09 농담하기

적절한 유머는 대화가 잘 이어져 나갈 수 있도록 만드는 윤활유 역할을 합니다. 물론 그 정도가 심해 상대방이 자신을 놀리고 있다는 느낌이 들 정도로 불쾌감을 주어서는 안 되겠죠. 농담을 그만하라고 경고할 때는 Stop kidding around.(농담 그만해.) 또는 I'm not up for a joke.(농담할 기분 아니야.)라고 말합니다.

원어민 발음 듣기 ☑□   회화 훈련 □□   듣기 훈련 □□

□ 농담이야.	I'm kidding. *kidding=joking It is a joke.
□ 널 놀리는 거야.	I'm pulling your leg. I'm messing with you. I'm teasing you. I'm playing with you.
□ 농담이지?	You're kidding, right? You're pulling my leg, right? It was a joke, right?
□ 농담 그만해.	Stop kidding around. Enough with your jokes. It's not funny.
□ 농담은 그만하고 ~	Kidding aside, … Joking apart, …
□ 그만 좀 놀려 대.	Stop teasing me. Stop playing with me. Don't make fun of me.
□ 농담 아니야.	I'm not kidding. It's not a joke. I'm serious.
□ 농담이야 진담이야?	Are you kidding or what? Are you serious or what?
□ 농담 반 진담 반이야.	Half in joke. Half for fun.

41

□ 농담할 때가 아니야.	It's no time for a joke.
	Be serious.
	Get real!
□ 농담할 기분 아니야.	I'm not in the mood for a joke.
	I don't feel like joking around.
	I'm not up for a joke.
□ 농담으로 알아들을게.	I'll take it as a joke.
□ 그녀에게는 농담도 못 해.	She can't take a joke.
□ 그만 좀 웃겨.	Oh, stop!
	Stop making me laugh.
	Stop cracking me up.
□ 뭐가 그렇게 재미있어?	What's so funny?

*funny = hilarious

DIALOGUE

A Stop joking around.
  This is a serious matter.
B I know. I'm sorry.
  When I'm nervous, I make jokes.

A 농담 그만해. 이건 심각한 사안이야.
B 나도 알아. 미안. 나는 긴장하면 우스갯소리를 하게 돼.

Notes

pull one's leg 놀리다   mess with 장난삼아 가지고 놀다(= play with)   tease 놀리다, 괴롭히다   make fun of 놀리다, 괴롭히다   or what? 아니면 뭐야?   Get real! 정신 차려, 현실 감각을 가져!   be in the mood for ~할 기분이다   feel like ~할 것 같은 기분이다   be up for ~을 하려고 하다   take A as B A를 B로 받아들이다   crack up 박장대소하게 하다   hilarious 아주 웃긴

10 뒷담화

뒤에서 남의 흉을 보는 talking behind someone's back(뒷담화하기)은 죄책감을 느끼면서도 은근히 즐기게 되는 대화입니다. 하지만 Walls have ears.(벽에도 귀가 있다.)라는 사실을 절대 잊어서는 안 됩니다.

원어민 발음 듣기 ☑☐　회화 훈련 ☐☐　듣기 훈련 ☐☐

☐ 뒷담화하지 마. / 남 흉보지 마.
Don't talk behind someone's back.
Don't speak ill of others behind their back.
Don't criticize others behind their back.
Don't bad-mouth others behind their back.
Don't backbite someone.

☐ 뒤에서 그를 흉보다가 들켰어.
I got caught while backbiting him.

☐ 뒷담화하는 재미가 있지.
It's fun to criticize others behind their back.

☐ 그는 뒷담화가 심해.
He is a serious backbiter.
He always backbites others.

☐ 그들은 남 말 하기를 좋아해.
They are very gossipy.
They love (all kinds of) gossip.

☐ 벽에도 귀가 있어.
Walls have ears.

☐ 모두가 그녀를 흉봐.
Everyone criticizes her.

☐ 그녀는 평판이 나빠.
She has a bad reputation.
She has an ill name.

☐ 그는 왕따야.
He is being bullied.
He is picked on by others.
He is a loser.

☐ 할 말 있으면 내 앞에서 해.
If you have something to say, say it in front of me.

📑 Notes

talk behind one's back 누군가를 뒤에서 흉보다, 뒷담화하다(= speak ill of, criticize, bad-mouth, backbite) get caught 들키다, 잡히다　reputation 평판　ill name 악명, 나쁜 평판　be bullied 괴롭힘을 당하다(= be picked on)　loser 낙오자, 패배자

43

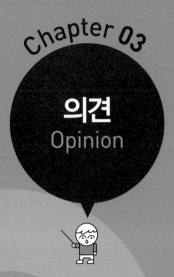

Chapter 03

의견
Opinion

01 의견 제시하기

자신의 의견을 제대로 표현하는 것은 대화에서 매우 중요합니다. 의견을 제시할 때는 I think... 또는 In my opinion... 등으로 말을 시작합니다. 의견을 제시하면서 정중하게 양해를 구할 때는 Can I say a word?(제가 한마디 해도 될까요?)라고 하면 되죠.

원어민 발음 듣기 ✔☐　회화 훈련 ☐☐　듣기 훈련 ☐☐

☐ 제 생각에는 ~	I think… In my opinion… My opinion is… If I may…
☐ 제가 보기에는 ~	As I see it… The way I see it…
☐ 제 관점에서는 ~	In my view… My point of view is…
☐ 좋은 아이디어가 있는데요.	I have an idea. Here's an idea. *idea = thought, suggestion
☐ 문득 떠오른 생각인데요.	An idea just came to my mind. An idea just crossed my mind.
☐ 한마디(몇 마디) 해도 될까요?	Can I say a word? Can I say a few words? I would like to say a word. I would like to say something. Mind if I say something?
☐ 제안을 하나 해도 될까요?	Can I make a suggestion? Can I say something?
☐ 충고 한마디 해도 될까요?	Can I give you a word of advice? Can I give you an advice?

📑 Notes

way 방법, 방식, ~하는 바　point of view 관점　come to one's mind 생각이 문득 떠오르다　cross one's mind 생각이 문득 스쳐 지나다　Mind if ~? ~해도 될까요?　make a suggestion 제안(제의)하다　a word of advice 충고 한마디　give ~ an advice ~에게 충고하다

02 확신과 결심에 대한 표현

확신을 나타내는 표현으로 I'm sure that ~(~은 확실해요)이 가장 흔하게 쓰입니다. 한편 "결심했어요.", "아직 결심이 서지 않았어요." 등은 과거에서부터 고민하여 현재 결심한 상태 또는 결심하지 못한 상태에 이르렀음을 표현해야 하므로 꼭 have[has]+과거분사[현재완료]와 함께 씁니다.

원어민 발음 듣기 ☑□　　회화 훈련 □□　　듣기 훈련 □□

□ ~은 확실해요.

I'm (pretty) sure that…
I'm (very) certain that…
I guarantee you that…
I'm (very) positive on…
There is no doubt about…

□ ~은 확실치 않아요.

I'm not sure that…
I can't guarantee you that…
I'm not positive on this…

□ 확실해? / 자신해?

Are you sure?
*sure = certain, positive, confident
Are you 100% sure about this?
(You) Swear?

□ 당연해요. / 물론이죠.

Absolutely!
Certainly!
Definitely!
Sure!
Positive!

□ 맹세해요.

I swear to god.
Cross my heart.

□ 두말할 필요도 없이 ~

Needless to say…

□ 저만 믿으세요.

Trust me.
You can count on me.
*count on = rely on
You have my word.

□ 저에게 맡기세요.

I'll take care of it.
I'll handle it.

47

	Leave it to me.
☐ 결심했어요.	I've made up my mind.
	I've finally come to the decision.
	My mind is all set.
☐ 많이 생각했어요.	I thought about it a lot.
	I gave it a serious thought.
	I considered all the options.
	*options = possibilities
☐ 결심(결정)하기 힘들어요.	It's very hard to decide.
	It's very difficult to make up my mind.
☐ 아직 결심이 서지 않았어요.	I haven't decided yet.
	I haven't made up my mind yet.
☐ 어떻게 해야 할지 모르겠어요.	I don't know what to do.
	I'm totally lost.
☐ 마음이 바뀌었어요.	I've changed my mind.
	I'm having a second thought.
☐ 다수(과반수)의 결정에 따를게요.	I'll follow the decision of the majority.
☐ 한번 해 봅시다.	Let's do it.
	Let's give it a shot.
	Let's go for it.
	Why don't we try?
☐ 후회하지 않아요.	I won't regret this.
	I won't look back.

📑 Notes

guarantee 장담하다, 보장하다 confident 확실한, 자신 있는 swear 맹세하다, 확신하다 cross one's heart 맹세하다, 확신하다 have one's word 약속하다, 믿어도 되다 take care of 돌보다, 해결하다 make up one's mind 결심하다, 결정하다 come to the decision 결심하다, 결정하다 give ~ a thought ~을 깊이 생각하다, ~을 심사숙고하다 second thought 재고, 다시 생각함 majority 대다수, 과반수 give it a shot 한번 해 보다, 부딪쳐 보다 go for it 사생결단으로 한번 해 보다 look back 돌아보다, 후회하다

03 예상과 가능성 표현하기

살다 보면 결과는 알 수 없지만 하고자 하는 일의 possibility(가능성)를 따져 보며 미래를 expectation(예견)하는 경우가 많습니다. 예상이 적중한 경우에는 My expectation is right.라고 하고, 빗나간 경우에는 It was unexpected.라고 합니다.

원어민 발음 듣기 ☑☐ 회화 훈련 ☐☐ 듣기 훈련 ☐☐

☐ ~로 예상해요. / ~로 기대해요.
I expect (that)…
I guess (that)…
We predict (that)…
My guess is…
My expectation is…

☐ 예상이 적중했어요.
My expectation is right.
My guess is correct.
It's just as I expected.
Just as I imagined.

☐ 바로 그거야! / 적중했어!
That's it!
Bull's eye!
Bingo!

☐ 예상이 빗나갔어요.
It was unexpected.
It's beyond our expectation.
I didn't expect this.

☐ 예상과 정반대예요.
It's contrary to my expectation.
It's quite opposite to my expectation.

☐ 어떻게 예상하세요?
What do you expect?
What's your outlook?

☐ 전망이 밝아요.
We have a bright future.
*future = prospect

☐ 전망이 어두워요.
We have a gloomy outlook.

☐ 예상을 못하겠어요.
I have no idea.
*idea = clue
I'm in the dark.

49

□ 얼마나 가능성이 있어요?	How much possibility do we have?
	How possible is this?
	Is there any possibility of this?
□ 성공 가능성이 높아요.	We have a high possibility to succeed.
	There is a high possibility to succeed.
	There is a high chance to succeed.
	*high ↔ low
□ 가망 없어요.	It's impossible.
	We have a zero possibility.
	There is no chance.
□ 가능성이 희박해요.	We have a fat chance.
□ 절망적이에요.	We're hopeless.
	We have no future.
	We're done.
□ 왠지 느낌이 좋아요.	I have a good feeling about this.
	I have a good hunch.
□ 왠지 불길해요.	I have a bad feeling about this.
	I have a bad hunch.

DIALOGUE

A It was very unexpected.
B Yeah, it's beyond our expectation.
A Do we have other options?
B There are a few. But I have a bad feeling about this project.
　　Let's drop it now.

A 예상 밖인걸?
B 나도 알아. 우리 예상이 빗나갔어.
A 다른 선택의 여지가 있나?
B 몇 가지 있기는 한데. 이번 프로젝트에 대해 왠지 느낌이 좋지 않아. 우리 이쯤에서 그만두자.

📋 Notes

predict 예측하다, 예견하다 expectation 기대, 예상 Bull's eye! 적중했어!, 맞혔어! bingo 맞았다, 맞혔다
beyond one's expectation ~의 기대를 벗어난 contrary to ~에 반대로(= opposite to) outlook 전망
(= prospect) gloomy 우울한, 암울한 clue 단서, 실마리 fat chance 매우 희박한 가능성 hopeless 희망 없
는, 절망적인 hunch 직감, 예감 drop 떨어뜨리다, 그만두다, 관두다

질문과 대답

의견을 주고받는 과정에서 질문과 대답은 필수적입니다. 하지만 질문에 답하고 싶지 않을 경우 I don't want to answer it.(대답하고 싶지 않아요.)이라고 분명하게 말하세요. 말문이 막힐 때는 Hmm. 또는 Let's see.라고 하며 생각할 시간을 버는 것도 좋은 방법입니다.

원어민 발음 듣기 ☑☐　회화 훈련 ☐☐　듣기 훈련 ☐☐

☐ 이것에 대해 어떻게 생각해요?	What do you think about this? What is your opinion on this? I would like to have your opinion. Let's talk about this. Any ideas?
☐ 다른 의견 있어요?	Does anyone have other opinions? Does anyone have other suggestions? Any other ideas? Any other suggestions? Any other comments?
☐ 추가(보충)하고 싶은 사람 있어요?	Does anyone want to add more? Anybody want to add something?
☐ 질문이 있으면 손드세요.	If you have any questions, raise your hand.
☐ 부끄러워하지 마세요.	Don't be shy.
☐ 마음껏 질문하세요.	Feel free to ask any questions. Ask anything.
☐ 주저 말고 질문하세요.	Don't hesitate to ask.
☐ 네, 질문 있어요.	Yes, I have a question. Yes, I want to ask something.
☐ 개인적 질문인데요.	It's (a) personal (question).
☐ 대답할게요.	I'll answer it. I think I can answer it.
☐ 그 점에 대해 설명할게요.	I'll explain it. I have an explanation for that.

☐ 자세히 설명할게요.	I will explain more in detail. I will tell you more details.
☐ 예를 들어 설명할게요.	I will explain with examples.
☐ 좋은 질문이에요.	Good question!
☐ 반가운 질문이네요.	Glad you ask.
☐ 왜 안 물어보나 했어요.	I thought you never ask.
☐ 대답하고 싶지 않아요.	I don't want to answer it. I'm not going to answer it. No need to answer it.
☐ 할 말 없어요.	I have nothing to say. No comment on that.
☐ 뭐라 말해야 할지 모르겠어요.	I don't know what to say. I'm speechless.
☐ 잠시만요.	Give me a moment. One second, please.
☐ (말문이 막혀서) 그게, 그러니까…….	Let's see…. Hmm. Well. What I'm trying to say is….

 Notes

suggestion 제안, 제시 comment 말, 의견 raise one's hand 손들다 shy 수줍은, 소극적인 feel free to 마음껏 ~하다 hesitate 주저하다, 망설이다 personal 개인적인, 사적인 in detail 자세히, 상세히 speechless 말로 표현할 수 없는, 말없이 잠자코 있는 moment 잠시, 잠깐

05 찬성과 반대

상대방의 의견에 전적으로 찬성 또는 반대할 때 totally, completely 등과 같은 부사를 쓸 수 있습니다. '적극 찬성'의 의미로 100%도 자주 쓰입니다. 반대할 때는 '미안하지만', '안타깝게도', '일리는 있지만', '이렇게 말하기는 싫지만' 등의 부드러운 표현과 함께 쓰는 것이 좋습니다.

원어민 발음 듣기 ☑□   회화 훈련 □□   듣기 훈련 □□

□ 당신 말이 맞아요.
You're (absolutely) right.
*right = correct

□ 일리가 있어요.
You have a point.
You've got a point.

□ 찬성해요.
I agree with you.
I'm with you.

□ 전적으로 찬성해요.
I agree with you 100%.
I'm with you 100%.
I couldn't agree with you more.
I totally agree with you.
*totally = completely, absolutely, entirely

□ 찬성하는 부분이 있어요.
I agree with you partly.
I don't disagree entirely.

□ 그건 말도 안 돼요.
You're wrong.
You're completely wrong about this.
That's ridiculous.

□ 반대해요.
I disagree.
I don't agree with you.

□ 미안하지만 찬성할 수 없어요.
I'm sorry but I can't agree with you.
I'm afraid I can't agree with you.
I hate to say this but I disagree.

□ 일리가 있지만 찬성할 수 없어요.
You have a point but I disagree.

□ 당신 말이 맞는다고 쳐요.
Let's say you're right.

□ 미심쩍어요.
I doubt it.
I have my doubt.

53

☐ 적극 반대해요.	I totally disagree.
	I couldn't disagree with you more.
	I'm strongly against it.
☐ 전 중립이에요.	I'm in the middle (position).
☐ 논란의 여지가 있어요.	It's debatable.
	*debatable = disputable
☐ 무작정 반대하지만 마세요.	Don't just say no.
☐ 반대를 위한 반대는 하지 마세요.	Don't say no for no.
☐ 그런 결론은 위험한데요.	That conclusion can be risky.
☐ 여론에 휩쓸리지 마세요.	Don't yield to the majority.
	Don't be overwhelmed by other people.

DIALOGUE

A You're absolutely right.
  I couldn't agree with you more.
B Thanks. But others think it's debatable.
A They have a point, too.
  Let's have another meeting soon.

A 네 말이 맞아. 전적으로 찬성(동감)이야.
B 고마워. 그런데 다른 사람들은 내 의견에 논란의 여지가 있다고 생각해.
A 그들 말에도 일리가 있지. 우리 조만간 또 다른 미팅을 갖자.

📝 Notes

absolutely 완전히, 전적으로 **have a point** 말에 일리가 있다, 동의하는 바가 있다(= have got a point) **partly** 부분적으로(= partially) **ridiculous** 말도 안 되는, 터무니없는 **debatable** 논란의 여지가 있는(= disputable) **risky** 위험스러운, 모험의 여지가 있는 **yield** 양보하다, 굴복하다 **majority** 과반수, 다수, 여론 **be overwhelmed** 압도당하다, 완전 주눅들다 **have a meeting** 미팅을 갖다, 미팅하다

06 의견 전달

누군가에게 의견이나 의사를 대신 전달해 달라고 부탁할 때는 Please tell him that ~.(~라고 전해 주세요.) 이라고 말하면 됩니다. 의견을 전달할 때는 인칭대명사를 구별해야 하는 번거로움이 있지만 익혀 두면 매우 요긴한 표현들입니다.

원어민 발음 듣기 ☑□   회화 훈련 □□   듣기 훈련 □□

□ 그에게 ~ 말씀 좀 전해 주세요.	Please tell him that… Could you tell him that…?
□ 그에게 이 메모 좀 전해 주세요.	Please give this message to him. Could you give this message to him?
□ 그가 불러요.	He is calling you.
□ 그가 당신을 찾아요.	He is looking for you.
□ 그가 당신과 이야기하고 싶어 해요.	He wants to talk to you. He wants to have a word with you.
□ 기다리라고 하네요.	He wants you to wait.
□ 금방 돌아오신다고 하셨어요.	He said he'll be right back.
□ 그를 대신해서 왔어요.	I'm here instead of him. I came here instead of him.
□ 그녀를 대신하여 말씀드립니다.	I'm telling you on behalf of her. I'm announcing this on behalf of her.
□ 그는 우리의 목소리예요.	He is our voice. He speaks for us.
□ 인터넷 게시판을 참조하세요.	Please check out the Internet (notice) board.
□ 커뮤니케이션에 문제가 있어요.	We have a serious communication problem. We don't communicate with each other. *communicate = talk

📑 Notes

have a word with ~ ~와 이야기하다   be right back 바로 돌아오다   instead of ~ ~을 대신해서   on behalf of ~ ~을 대신(대표)해서   speak for 대변하다   Internet (notice) board 인터넷 게시판

07 설득하기

대화 중에 상대방과 의견 차이가 생기면 상대를 설득하기 위해 Think again. 혹은 Please reconsider.라고 말합니다. 손익을 다시 한번 따져 보며 room for comprise(타협의 여지)를 찾기 위해서입니다. 이렇게 해서 서로에게 최상의 결론을 찾는다면 더할 나위 없이 좋겠죠.

원어민 발음 듣기 ☑□   회화 훈련 □□   듣기 훈련 □□

□ 재고해 주세요.	Think again.
	Think it over.
	Please reconsider.
	Why don't you think again?
□ 신중히 생각해 보세요.	Give it a serious thought.
	Think it over and over.
	Think twice.
□ 다시 생각해 볼게요.	I'll reconsider.
	I'll think again.
	I'll give it a second thought.
□ 마음속을 잘 들여다보세요.	Look inside of your heart.
□ 진정으로 원하는 것이 뭐예요?	What do you really want?
□ 제가 이야기하고 싶은 것은 ~	All I'm saying is that…
	My point is that…
□ 이익을 잘 따져 보세요.	Think carefully what you're going to get.
□ 모두에게 이익입니다.	It's good for all of us.
	It's the best for everyone.
□ 저라면 (단연) 그렇게 할 겁니다.	If I were you, I (definitely) would do that.
□ 먼 미래를 보세요.	Think about the future.
	Don't be short-sighted.
□ 일석이조입니다.	One stone, two birds.

📋 **Notes**

reconsider 재고하다   over and over 거듭, 다시 또 다시   second thought 다시 생각함, 재고   look inside 안을 들여다보다   short-sighted 근시안적인, 근시의   Kill two birds with one stone. 일석이조

08 제안의 수락과 거절

이번에는 상대방의 제안을 accept(수락하다)하고 refuse(거절하다)하는 표현을
알아봅시다. 수락할 때는 기쁜 마음으로 I'd love to. 혹은 Sounds lovely.라고
하고, 거절할 때는 정중하고 명확하게 I'm sorry but I have to say no.라고 말해야
오해가 없습니다.

원어민 발음 듣기 ☑☐   회화 훈련 ☐☐   듣기 훈련 ☐☐

☐ ~하실래요?	Would you like to...? Do you want to...?
☐ ~할지 궁금하네요.	I'm wondering if you could... I wonder if you can... *if = whether
☐ ~할까 생각 중인데요.	I'm thinking that...
☐ 같이 갈래요?	Would you like to come? Want to come?
☐ 저희와 함께 하실래요?	Want to join us?
☐ 좋아요, 그러죠.	Of course. Definitely. Certainly. Sure, why not? I'd love to. Sounds lovely. *lovely = great I'm in.
☐ 글쎄요, 생각해 볼게요.	Well, I'll think about it. Well, I have to think about it.
☐ 먼저 일정을 볼게요.	Let me check my schedule first.
☐ 지금 당장 답해야 해요?	Do I have to answer right now? Do you need my answer right now?
☐ 시간을 좀 주세요.	Give us some time.
☐ 사람들과 의논해 볼게요.	I need to talk to my people.

☐ 조만간 알려줄게요.	I'll let you know soon.
☐ 전화할게요.	I'll call you. *call → contact (연락하다)
☐ 해 보도록 할게요.	I'll try. I'll do my best.
☐ 미안하지만 거절할게요.	I'm sorry, but I have to say no. I have to pass. Sorry, but not this time.
☐ 너무 좋지만 안 되겠어요.	I'd love to but I can't. It's a tempting offer, but I can't accept it. Sounds great, but I can't. I wish I could.
☐ 다음에요.	Maybe next time. Maybe some other time. Maybe later. Rain check? Next time, I'm definitely in.

DIALOGUE

A Would you like to have a joint meeting next Friday?
B Sounds great, but I need to talk to my people first.
A Of course.
B I'll contact you very soon.

A 우리 다음 주 금요일 날 합동 미팅 할까요?
B 너무 좋죠. 그런데 우리 쪽 사람들과 먼저 이야기해 보고요.
A 물론이죠.
B 빠른 시일 내에 연락드릴게요.

📑 Notes

Would you like to ~? ~을 원하세요?, ~하고 싶으세요?(= Do you want to ~?) **wonder if** ~인지 아닌지 궁금하다(= whether) **give ~ time** ~에게 시간(여유, 말미)을 주다 **one's people** ~의 사람들, ~의 측근들 **do one's best** 최선을 다하다 **tempting** 끌리는, 매혹적인 **rain check** 후일의 약속, 다음 기회

09 의견의 대립

상대편과 옥신각신할 때 급기야는 "말이 안 통하는군요."라는 뜻의 You're ridiculous.
또는 You're full of nonsense. 같은 말이 나오기도 하죠. 상대편의 이해를 구하고
싶을 때는 이렇게 말해 보세요. Put yourself in my position. 바로 "입장 바꿔 놓고
생각해 보세요."입니다. 영화나 드라마에서도 자주 듣게 되는 말이죠.

원어민 발음 듣기 ☑□   회화 훈련 □□   듣기 훈련 □□

(조금도, 한 치도) 양보할 수 없어요.	I'm not going to concede. I'm not going to yield. I won't compromise. I won't budge an inch.
입장을 바꿔 놓고 생각해 보세요.	Put yourself in my position. *position = place, shoes Pretend you are me.
벽에다 이야기하는 것 같아요.	I feel like I'm talking to the wall. Am I talking to the wall?
말이 안 통하는군요.	I can't talk to you. You're full of nonsense. You're ridiculous.
감정적인 발언은 삼가 주세요.	Don't be so emotional. Leave your emotion out of this.
우린 최선을 다했어요.	We did our very best. We did whatever we possibly could. We reached our limit.
참을 만큼 참았어요.	We had enough. Enough is enough.
억지(고집) 부리지 마세요.	Don't be so stubborn. *stubborn = headstrong
당신만 힘든 것 아니에요.	You're not the only one who's going through a difficult time.

📑 **Notes**

concede 양보하다, 물러서다 budge an inch 아주 조금 움직이다, 〈부정〉 꼼짝도 안 하다 talk to the wall 벽에
다 말하다, 답답하다 leave A out of B A를 B에서 빼다, 제거하다 go through 겪다, 거치다

10 협상과 타협

융통성 있는 의사 전달로 해결되지 않을 일은 거의 없다고 합니다. meet halfway
(절충점)를 찾는 데 가장 중요한 것은 상반된 이해관계를 좁히는 것이지만, 때론 그
차이가 너무 커서 협상이 never-ending(끝없는)으로 지속되는 경우도 있습니다.

원어민 발음 듣기 ☑□   회화 훈련 □□   듣기 훈련 □□

☐ 협상합시다.	Let's talk.
	Let's meet halfway.
	Why don't we negotiate?
☐ 아직 타협의 여지가 있어요.	We still have time to talk.
	We still can negotiate. *negotiate = talk, compromise
	There is room for negotiation. *negotiation = compromise
☐ 타협의 여지가 없어요.	There is no room for negotiation.
	It's too late to negotiate.
☐ 협상의 진전이 없어요.	There has been no progress.
☐ 이러고 있을 시간 없어요.	We don't have time for this.
☐ 빨리 결론을 냅시다.	Let's conclude quickly.
	Let's settle quickly.
☐ 협상이 깨졌어요.	Negotiations broke down.
☐ 이해관계가 너무 상반돼요.	Both sides have very different ideas. *ideas = opinions
	They are looking at the totally different places.
	It's a never-ending story.

📝 **Notes**

meet halfway 절충점에 이르다, 타협하다   negotiate 협상하다, 타협하다(= compromise)   room 방, 공간, 여지
too ~ to ... 너무 ~해서 …할 수 없다   progress 진전, 진척   settle 문제를 해결하다, 결론 내다   break down (협
상 등이) 실패하다, 결렬되다   look at ~를 바라보다, 지향하다   never-ending 끝나지 않는, 한없는

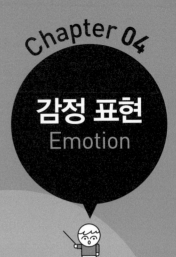

Chapter 04

감정 표현
Emotion

01 기쁨, 즐거움, 감동

사람의 감정을 나타내는 표현들 중 기쁨, 즐거움 등을 나타내는 표현을 배워 보겠습니다. 가장 일반적인 표현인 I'm so happy.(너무 기뻐.)에서부터 큰 감동을 표현하는 I'm so happy and that I could cry.(너무 기뻐서 울 것 같아.)까지 다양한 표현들을 익혀 보세요.

원어민 발음 듣기 ☑□   회화 훈련 □□   듣기 훈련 □□

□ 야호!	Yahoo! All right! That's it!
□ (매우) 기쁘다.	I'm (so) happy. I feel happy. *happy = delighted, glad, pleased I'm in paradise.
□ 그건 나를 기쁘게 해.	It makes me happy.
□ 신나. / 즐거워.	I'm excited. I'm thrilled. I feel awesome.
□ 기분 끝내줘.	Couldn't be happier.
□ 만족스러워.	I'm satisfied. I'm content.
□ 대만족이야.	I'm very satisfied. *satisfied = contented
□ 기쁨으로 가슴이 벅차.	My heart is full of happiness. My heart is overflowing with joy.
□ 꿈만 같아.	Is this a dream? I feel like dreaming. It's like a dream come true. I hope it's not a dream. Don't wake up.
□ 마음이 (마구) 설레.	My heart is beating (so fast). My heart is throbbing.

□ 너무 기뻐서 울 것 같아.	I'm so happy that I could cry.
□ 너무 기뻐서 말이 안 나와.	I'm so happy that I can't talk.
□ 구름 위에 있는 것 같아.	I'm on cloud nine. I'm floating on air. *floating = walking, treading
□ 입이 귀에 걸렸네.	You're smiling from ear to ear.
□ 요즘 싱글벙글하네.	You're all smiles these days.
□ 기쁨을 감출 수가 없어.	I can't hide my happiness.
□ 자꾸 웃음이 나와.	I keep smiling. I can't help smiling.
□ 너무 웃어서 배가 아파.	My stomach hurts. My sides hurt.
□ (웃다가) 오줌을 지렸어.	I pissed in my pants.
□ (웃다가) 오줌을 지릴 뻔했어.	I almost pissed in my pants.
□ 포복절도했어.	I held my sides. *held = split We rolled with laughter. *rolled = shook
□ 기분 좋아 보인다.	You look happy.
□ 뭐 기분 좋은 일 있어?	What are you so happy about? Any good news? Something good happened to you.
□ 뭐가 그렇게 재미있어?	What's so funny?
□ 좋은 소식은 함께 나누자.	Let's share the good news.
□ 웃음은 전염돼.	Laughter is contagious.

Chapter 04

감정 표현

📑 **Notes**

paradise 파라다이스, 천국 thrilled 신나는, 몹시 흥분되는 awesome 멋진, 최고의 overflow 넘치다, 벅차다
come true 실현되다 beat 때리다, 고동치다 throb 욱신거리다, 설레다 cloud nine (구름 위에 있는 듯) 기분이
매우 좋은 tread 밟다, 걷다 split 쪼개다 roll 구르다, 말다 contagious 전염성이 있는, 옳는

슬픔

'슬프고 눈물이 날 것 같은' 기분을 표현할 때 항상 sad만 써 왔나요? 슬픔이 아주 클 때 "가슴이 아프다.", "가슴이 찢어진다."라고 말하기도 하는데, 이것은 My heart hurts. 또는 My heart is broken.이라고 합니다. 이번에는 슬픔의 감정을 나타내는 다양한 표현들을 알아봅시다.

원어민 발음 듣기 ☑□　회화 훈련 □□　듣기 훈련 □□

□ (너무) 슬퍼.

I'm (so) sad.
I feel (so) sad.
*sad = miserable

□ 넌 나를 슬프게 해.

You make me miserable.

□ 너 슬퍼 보여.

You look sad.
Are you sad?
Why do you look sad?
Something's wrong?

□ 가슴(마음)이 아파.

My heart hurts.
It hurts my heart.

□ 가슴(마음)이 찢어져.

My heart is broken.
I feel heartbroken.
You break my heart.

□ 가슴에 사무쳐.

It touches my heart.
It went to my heart.
It came home to my heart.

□ 가슴이 뭉클했어.

I felt a lump in my throat.

□ (슬픔으로) 목이 메었어.

I was choked up.

□ (엉엉) 울고만 싶어.

I just want to cry (out loud).
I feel like crying (out loud).

□ 왜 울고 있니?

Why are you crying?

□ 눈물이 쏟아졌어.

Tears poured down my cheeks.

□ 와락 울음이 터졌어.

I burst into tears.
*burst into = break into

☐ 눈이 퉁퉁 붓도록 울었어.	I cried my eyes out.
☐ 아직도 눈물이 나.	I'm still in tears.
	It still brings tears to my eyes.
	My eyes all tear up.
☐ 너무 슬퍼하지 마.	Don't be so sad.
	Don't feel so sad.
☐ 실컷 울어.	Cry yourself out.
	Cry your heart out.
	Let it all out.
☐ 밤새 울었어.	I cried all night.
☐ 울다 지쳐 잠들었어.	I cried myself to sleep.
	I fell asleep while crying.

DIALOGUE

A Are you okay? You look sad.
  Something's wrong?
B (Bursting into tears) My friend died last night.
A Oh, I'm so sorry. How did it happen?

A 너 괜찮아? 슬퍼 보인다. 무슨 안 좋은 있어?
B (와락 울음을 터뜨리며) 어젯밤 친구가 죽었어.
A 저런, 이를 어째. 어쩌다 그런 일이 일어났어?

📝 Notes

miserable 슬픈, 불행한, 비참한 heartbroken 슬픔에 잠긴, 비탄에 젖은 touch 감동을 주다, 사무치게 하다
lump 덩어리 throat 목, 목구멍 be choked up 목이 메다 pour down 쏟아져 내리다 burst into 와락 터지
다, 터져 나오다 tear up 눈물이 글썽글썽하다 cry out 실컷 울다, 엉엉 울다 let out 내놓다, 드러내다

03 우울함, 외로움

depressed, blue, down 등은 '울적한' 기분을 나타내는 형용사들입니다. 특히 the blues 하면 '울적한 기분', '무거운 기분'을 뜻하죠. 월요일에 특히 몸과 마음이 축 처지는 '월요병'을 Monday blues라고 부르는 것도 그 때문입니다.

원어민 발음 듣기 ☑☐   회화 훈련 ☐☐   듣기 훈련 ☐☐

□ (많이) 우울해.	I'm (very) depressed.
	I feel (very) depressed.
	I'm heavy-hearted.
	I'm (so) blue.
	I have the blues.
	I feel down.
	I'm in a melancholy mood.
□ 우울해 보여.	You look depressed. *depressed = melancholy, down, blue, heavy-hearted
□ 날씨 탓인가.	Maybe it's (because of) the weather.
□ 컨디션이 별로야.	I don't feel good.
	My condition isn't so good.
	I'm under the weather.
□ 아무것도 재미없어.	Nothing interests me.
	I lost interest in life.
□ 모든 게 시들해.	Everything is dull to me.
	Everything is trivial to me.
□ 늘 기운이 없어.	I always feel tired.
	I'm groggy all the time.
□ 노력하면 뭐 해.	Why all the trying? *trying = troubles, efforts
	What for?
	Why bother?
□ 시원섭섭해.	I feel relieved, but sad at the same time.
□ 달콤 쌉싸름해.	It's bittersweet.

66

□ (너무) 허전해.	I feel (so) empty. *empty = hollow, vain My life is (so) empty.
□ (너무) 외로워. / 쓸쓸해.	I'm (very) lonely. I feel (so) lonely.
□ 혼자 있기 싫어.	I don't want to be alone. I don't want to be left alone.
□ 소외된 느낌이야.	I feel (so) isolated. *isolated = alienated
□ 방치된 느낌이야.	I feel (so) neglected.
□ 누군가와 이야기 나누고 싶어.	I want to talk to someone. I need someone to talk to.
□ 월요병이야.	It's Monday blues.
□ 사춘기야.	It's teenage blues.
□ 명절 증후군이야.	It's holiday blues. *holiday → party (파티)

DIALOGUE

A Maybe it's the weather.
  I feel a little depressed today.
B Speaking of depression, nothing interests me these days.
A You are the one who is depressed.
  You've got to cheer yourself up.

A 날씨 탓인가. 오늘 약간 울적하네.
B 울적하다는 이야기가 나와서 말인데. 나 요즘 아무것도 재미가 없어.
A 우울한 사람은 정작 너구나. 기운 내야지.

Notes

depressed 우울한, 울적한 heavy-hearted 마음이 무거운, 울적한 melancholy 우울한 dull 재미없는, 시들한
trivial 사소한, 별 중요성을 못 느끼는 groggy 피곤한, 기운 없어 휘청거리는 relieved 안도하는, 한숨 돌리는 left
alone 혼자 남겨진 isolated 고립된, 소외된(=alienated) neglected 방치된, 혼자 남겨진 speaking of ~
~ 이야기가 나와서 말인데 cheer oneself up 스스로 기운을 북돋우다, 힘내다, 용기 내다

04 낙담, 후회

원하는 바가 잘 되지 않아 낙담하거나 실망하여 급기야 후회를 거듭하는 일이 종종 있습니다. "실망이야.", "절망적이야.", "후회스러워."와 같은 말을 어떻게 표현하는지, 그리고 후회(~했어야 했는데, ~하지 말았어야 했는데)를 나타내는 should (not) have+과거분사는 어떻게 활용하는지 살펴보겠습니다.

원어민 발음 듣기 ☑□　회화 훈련 □□　듣기 훈련 □□

□ (매우) 실망이야.

I'm (very) disappointed.
It's (very) discouraging.

□ 실망스럽겠다!

You must be disappointed.
*disappointed = discouraged
It must be disappointing.
I think I understand your disappointment.

□ 나를 실망시켰어.

You disappointed me.
You let me down.
You crushed my hope.
You burst a bubble.

□ 절망적이야.

It's hopeless.
It's disastrous.
I'm desperate.
I'm giving up all hope.

□ 죽고만 싶어.

I just want to die.

□ 나 자신에게 실망스러워.

I disappointed myself.
I let myself down.

□ 실망하지 마.

Don't be so disappointed.

□ 실망시키지 마.

Don't you ever disappoint me.
*disappoint = discourage
Never ever let me down.

□ 후회스러워.

I feel regret.
I feel remorse.
I'm regretful.
*regretful = remorseful

☐ 후회되겠다. / 안타깝겠다.	You must be regretful.
	I think I understand your regret.
☐ 가슴을 치며 후회해.	I'm beating my chest.
☐ 모든 게 끝장이야.	It's all over.
	It's done.
	It's the end.
☐ 네가 할 수 있는 일은 없어.	There's nothing you can do.
☐ 난 끝났어.	I'm finished.
	I'm through.
	I'm screwed.
	I'm dead.
☐ 이제 어쩌지?	What am I going to do?
	What should I do?
☐ 헛수고만 했어.	I did it for nothing.
	It's all vain efforts.
☐ 달리 방법이 없어.	There is no other way.
☐ 그쯤은 예상했어야 했는데…….	I knew better.
	I should have known better.
☐ 좀 더 심사숙고했어야 했는데…….	I should have considered well.
	I should have given a deep thought.
☐ 난 낙오자야.	I'm a loser.
	I'm a total failure.
☐ 절호의 기회를 놓치다니.	I lost a golden opportunity.
	*golden = rare
☐ 다시 기회가 올까?	Will I have a second chance?
	I wonder if there's another chance.
	I hope there's another chance.

📋 **Notes**

let ~ down ~를 실망시키다 **burst a bubble** 거품을 터뜨리다, 희망을 깨다 **disastrous** 절망적인 **remorse** 후회, 양심의 가책 **beat one's chest** 가슴을 치다, 후회하다 **be over** 끝나다, 끝장나다, 종결되다 **screwed** 엉망이 된, 망친 **vain effort(s)** 헛수고 **loser** 패배자, 낙오자 **golden opportunity** 황금 같은 기회, 절호의 기회

05 위로, 격려

슬픈 일을 겪고 있는 사람에게 진심이 담긴 위로와 격려는 큰 힘이 될 수 있습니다.
I'm so sorry.(정말 안됐네요.), It's nothing.(아무것도 아닌 일이에요.), Don't blame
yourself.(자책하지 마세요.) 등의 표현을 사용해 보세요.

원어민 발음 듣기 ☑☐   회화 훈련 ☐☐   듣기 훈련 ☐☐

☐ 정말 안됐네요.	I'm so sorry. *so = very I'm so sorry to hear that. I feel so sorry for… I feel pity for… *for 뒤에는 무엇 때문에 안 됐는지가 나온다.
☐ 어떻게 견디고 계세요?	How are you holding up? It must be tough for you.
☐ 포기하지 마세요.	Don't give up. Keep trying.
☐ 다 잘될 거예요.	Everything will be fine. *fine = okay, all right
☐ 과거는 과거예요.	(What's) Done is done. The past is the past. The past is in the past.
☐ 다 잊어버리세요.	Forget about everything.
☐ 아무것도 아닌 일이에요.	It's nothing. It's not a big deal. It's no biggy.
☐ 자신을 과소평가하지 마세요.	Don't underestimate yourself. You are (much) more than that.
☐ 자책하지 말아요.	Don't blame yourself. Don't be so harsh on you.
☐ 당신 탓이 아니에요.	It's not (entirely) your fault.
☐ 천천히 생각하세요.	Take things slowly.

☐ 한숨 자면 기분이 나아질 거예요.	Take a nap and you will feel better.
☐ 내 어깨를 빌려 줄게요.	I'll give you my shoulder.
	You have my shoulder.
☐ 기운 내세요.	Cheer up!
	Pep up!
	Perk up!
	Chin up!
	Hang in there!
	Brace yourself up.
	Pull yourself together.
☐ 세상이 끝난 것이 아니에요.	It's not the end of the world.
	The world is not ending.
☐ 시간이 약이에요.	Time will cure you. *cure = heal
☐ 좋은 날이 올 거예요.	Good days will come.
☐ 쥐구멍에도 볕들 날이 있어요.	Every dog has his day.
☐ 내일은 또 다른 날이잖아요.	Tomorrow is another day.
☐ 다른 기회가 올 거예요.	You'll have a second chance. *second = another
☐ 긍정적인 면을 보세요.	Look on the bright side.
	Try to be positive.
	Think positively.
☐ 응원할게요.	I'll cheer for you. *cheer = root
☐ 당신을 위해 기원할게요.	I'll pray for you.
	I'll cross my fingers.
☐ 나중 일은 나중에 걱정해요.	Worry next time next time.

📝 **Notes**

hold up 견디다, 지탱하다 underestimate oneself 스스로를 과소평가하다 blame oneself 자책하다 be harsh on ~ ~에게 혹독하게 대하다 chin up 기운 내다 hang in there 버티다, 견디다 brace oneself up 기운 내다, 분발하다 pull oneself together 기운을 찾다, 냉정해지다 cross one's fingers 기원하다

06 불쾌함, 화남

기분이 나쁘고 화나는 감정은 기쁨이나 즐거움만큼 격한 감정들이죠. 단순히 I feel bad.(기분 나빠.), I feel unpleasant.(불쾌해.), I'm so angry.(열 받아.)뿐 아니라 Steam is coming out of my ear.(머리에서 김 나네.), It drives me crazy.(돌아 버리겠네.)와 같이 다양한 표현 방법이 있습니다.

원어민 발음 듣기 ☑☐   회화 훈련 ☐☐   듣기 훈련 ☐☐

☐ 기분 나빠.	I feel bad.
	I feel terrible.
	I feel awful.
	It's offensive.
☐ 불쾌해.	I feel unpleasant.
	I feel uncomfortable.
☐ 역겨워.	It's disgusting.
	I feel disgusted.
	You disgust me.
☐ (아주) 열 받아. / 화나.	I'm (so) angry.
	I'm mad.
	I'm furious.
	I'm pissed.
	I'm steamed.
	I'm fuming.
	You make me sick.

☐ 열 받게 하지 마.

Don't make me angry.
*angry = mad, furious, pissed

☐ 생각할수록 열 받네.

The more I think, the more I get angry.

☐ 머리에서 김 나네.

Steam is coming out of my ear.

☐ 뚜껑 열리네.

It blew my lid.
It flipped my top.

☐ 돌아 버리겠어.

It makes me crazy.
It drives me nuts.
*nuts = mad, insane
I could go crazy.

72

□ 스트레스 받아.	(So) Stressful.
	I'm stressed out.
	It gives me stress.
□ 가슴이 답답해.	I feel choked up.
	I feel frustrated.
	I could explode.
□ 바람 좀 쐬어야겠어.	I need fresh air.
	I'll go and get some fresh air.
□ 내가 기분 나쁘게 했어?	Did I do something to make you feel uncomfortable? *uncomfortable = unpleasant
□ 농담할 기분이 아냐.	I'm not in the mood for joking.
□ 왜 나한테 화풀이야?	Why are you taking your anger out on me?
	Don't take your anger out on me.
□ 걔 (화나서) 펄펄 뛰고 있어.	He is jumping up and down.
□ 걔 (화나서) 얼굴이 시뻘개졌어.	He turns (all) red. *red → blue : 시퍼레지다
□ 그는 노발대발하고 있어.	He is in hot anger.
□ 그는 격노했어.	He hit the ceiling. *hit the ceiling = hit the roof
□ 그녀는 걸핏하면 화를 내.	She easily gets angry.
	She is quick-tempered.
	She is hotheaded.
□ 화를 참을 수가 없어.	I can't control my anger.
	I have an anger management problem.
□ 더 이상은 못 참아.	That's it.
	I've had enough.
	I can't take it anymore.

📝 Notes

offensive 기분 나쁜, 비위에 거슬리는 disgusting 역겨운 furious 매우 화나는, 열 받는(= pissed, steamed)
fume 연기를 내다, 노발대발하다   blow 날리다, 날아가다   flip 홱 젖혀지다   nuts 미친, 머리가 돈(= insane)
choked up 목이 메이는, 답답한 frustrated 좌절감을 느끼는 take ~ out on someone ~을 누군가에게 쏟아
내다, 화풀이하다 ceiling 지붕, 천장 hotheaded 성질이 급한 anger management 화를 다스리기

07 (상대방에 대한) 비난

상대방에 대한 가벼운 질책이 불가피한 상황이 있습니다. 그럴 때는 Snap out of it!(정신 차례!), You're so naïve.(순진하기는.), Grow up!(철 좀 들에), I knew it.(그럴 줄 알았어.)과 같이 말할 수 있습니다.

원어민 발음 듣기 ☑□   회화 훈련 □□   듣기 훈련 □□

☐ 정신 차려.	Snap out of it.
	Focus!
	Concentrate!
	Collect yourself.
☐ 꿈 깨.	Wake up!
	Dream on!
	Get real!
	Reality check!
☐ 어리석기는!	You're foolish.
	Such a fool!
☐ 무식하기는!	So ignorant!
☐ 몰상식해.	You have no common sense.
☐ 너 이상해.	You're eccentric.
	*eccentric = weird
☐ 나잇값 좀 해.	Act your age.
☐ 네가 몇 살인지 알아?	How old are you?
☐ 주제를 알아야지.	(You should) Know your place.
☐ 철 좀 들어.	Grow up!
☐ 내가 뭐랬어.	I told you (so).
☐ 내가 경고했지.	I warned you.
	I was trying to warn you.
☐ 그럴 줄 알았어.	I knew it.
☐ 내 말은 절대 안 들으니까.	You never listen to me.

□ 네 탓이야.	It's all your fault.
□ (잘못을) 인정해.	Admit it.
□ 네가 책임져.	It's your responsibility.
	You're responsible for it.
□ 순진하기는!	You're naive!
□ 무신경하기는!	So insensible!
□ 평소에 생각이 없어.	You don't think.
	Use your head.
□ 넌 항상 투덜거려.	You always complain.
□ 넌 피도 눈물도 없어.	You're cold-blooded.
	You're heartless.
□ 재수 없는 소리 마.	Don't jinx me.
	Don't jinx things.
□ 넌 재수 없는 녀석이야.	You're bad luck.
□ 똑같은 말을 반복하고 있잖아.	You're saying the same thing over and over.
	You're like a broken record.
	You're singing the same song.
□ 몇 번이나 말해야 알아들어?	How many times do I have to tell you?
□ 건방져.	You, smart ass.
	You're acting fresh.
□ 뻔뻔해.	Some nerve!
	You're shameless.
□ 우는소리 하지 마.	Don't be such a crybaby.
□ 조용히 해 주세요.	Would you please keep it down?
	Keep it down, please.
□ 지금 몇 시인 줄 알아요?	Do you know what time it is?

Chapter 04 감정 표현

📝 **Notes**

snap out of ~에서 벗어나다, 제정신을 차리다　eccentric 상식을 벗어난, 이상한, 괴상한　naive 순진한, 세상물정 모르는　jinx 불길한 것; 불행을 가져오다　broken record (고장 난 레코드처럼) 같은 이야기를 반복하는 사람　fresh 주제 넘는, 건방진　nerve 뻔뻔스러움, 철면피　keep it down 조용히 하다

08 (자신에 대한) 불평, 불만

스스로에게, 혹은 자신의 삶에 대해 투덜투덜 불평, 불만을 늘어놓는 경우가 있습니다. 간혹 일이 너무 풀리지 않을 때 Life is unfair.(삶은 불공평해.), Why me?(왜 하필 나야!)와 같은 말을 하고 싶을 때도 있고요. 불평, 불만에 대한 다양한 표현들을 알아보겠습니다.

원어민 발음 듣기 ☑□   회화 훈련 □□   듣기 훈련 □□

□ 삶은 불공평해.	Life is unfair.
□ 왜 하필 나야!	Why me?
□ 머피의 법칙이야.	It's Murphy's law.
□ 안 될 일은 역시 안 되는 법이야.	Anything that can go wrong will go wrong.
□ 시간 낭비만 했어.	It's a waste of my time. What a waste of my time!
□ 일진 사나운 날이야.	I had a bad day. What a bad day!
□ 복도 지지리도 없지.	So unlucky. *unlucky = unfortunate
□ 내 삶이 마음에 안 들어.	I'm not so happy about my life.
□ 사람들 간섭이 싫어.	I don't like people interrupting my life.
□ 사람들이 나를 대하는 방식이 싫어.	I don't like the way people treat me.
□ 너무 피곤해.	I'm so tired. I'm so exhausted.
□ 넌더리가 나.	I'm sick and tired (of it). I'm fed up (with it).
□ 나 바보 아닌데.	I'm not a fool. I'm not stupid.
□ (내 욕을 하는지) 귀가 간지러워.	My ears are burning.

📝 **Notes**

go wrong 잘못되다, 잘 안 되다   treat 대하다, 대접하다   exhausted 지친, 탈진한   be fed up with ~에 넌더리가 나다

76

09 싸움

시비가 붙어 급기야 싸움으로 번질 때 You're dead.(너 죽었어.)나 You want a piece of me?(한 판 붙자.) 같은 말을 하죠. 다음 표현들은 직접 쓰기보다 누군가가 나에게 시비를 걸 때 대비용으로 알아두면 좋습니다.

원어민 발음 듣기 ☑☐ 회화 훈련 ☐☐ 듣기 훈련 ☐☐

□ 뭘 쳐다보는 거야?	What are you looking at?
□ 왜 시비야?	What's the matter with you?
	What's your problem?
	Are you picking a fight with me?
□ 일부러 그랬지?	You did it on purpose, right?
□ 내가 만만해?	You think I'm an easy target.
□ 먼저 사과해.	Apologize to me, first.
	You owe me an apology.
□ 멍청한 놈!	You, idiot! *idiot=jackass, jerk, asshole
□ 네까짓 게 뭐라고.	Who do you think you are?
□ 한판 붙자!	Let's do this.
	You want a piece of me?
	You want to take me?
□ 너 죽었어.	You're dead.
	You're dead meat.
	You have a death wish.
□ 천벌 받아라! / 꺼져 버려!	Go to hell!
□ 소리 지르지 마.	Don't yell at me.
	Don't raise your voice at me.
□ 경고한다.	I'm warning you.

📑 Notes

pick a fight 시비를 걸다   on purpose 일부러, 고의로   easy target 쉬운 목표, 만만한 상대   owe 빚지다
dead meat 죽은 목숨(몸)   death wish 죽음을 바라는 마음   raise one's voice 목소리를 높이다, 소리 지르다

77

10 긴장, 초조

긴장하고 초조하면 가슴이 두근거리고(heart is pounding) 식은땀이 나면서 (sweating) 가만히 있지 못하고 서성거리거나(hovering) 손톱을 물어뜯고(biting nails) 다리를 떨기도(shaking legs) 합니다. 화장실을 자주 가고 싶게 만드는 것도 긴장과 초조함의 증상이라고 하네요.

원어민 발음 듣기 ☑☐   회화 훈련 ☐☐   듣기 훈련 ☐☐

☐ 긴장돼.

I'm nervous.
*nervous = anxious
It's nerve wrecking.

☐ 떨려.

I'm shaking.
I have the jitters.

☐ 긴장하지 마.

Don't be anxious.
*anxious = nervous

☐ 실수하면 어쩌지?

What if I make a mistake?

☐ 생각하고 싶지도 않아.

I don't (even) want to think about it.

☐ 식은땀이 나.

I'm (cold) sweating.

☐ 안달복달하지 마.

Don't fret (yourself).

☐ 그런다고 달라지는 것은 없어.

Worry doesn't change a thing.

☐ 가만히 못 있겠어.

I can't just sit and do nothing.

☐ 가슴이 두근거려.

My heart is pounding.

☐ (긴장되서) 화장실 가고 싶어.

I want to go to the bathroom.
I have to pee.

☐ 담배 피우고 싶어.

I want to smoke.
I need nicotine.

☐ 커피라도 마셔야겠다.

I want some coffee.
I need caffeine.
I could use some coffee.

☐ 너무 긴장한 것 같다.

You look very nervous.
You look too tense.

□ 마음을 느긋하게 가져.	Try to relax. Try to be calm. Learn how to relax.
□ 잠시 다른 생각을 해 봐.	Think something else for a while. Put it away from your mind.
□ 손톱 깨물지 마.	Don't bite your nails. Stop biting your nails.
□ 그만 서성거려.	Stop hovering. Would you quit hovering?
□ 다리 떨지 마.	Don't shake your legs.
□ 눈 깜박이지 마.	Don't blink your eyes nervously.
□ 시계 그만 봐.	Stop watching the clock.

Chapter 04 감정 표현

DIALOGUE

A Why hasn't the result come out yet?
   I'm nervous to death.
B It will come out very soon.
   Please stop hovering. It gives me a headache.
A I can't. I need caffeine.
   Want some?

A 왜 아직도 결과가 안 나오지? 나 긴장돼 죽겠어.
B 금방 나올 거야. 제발 그만 좀 서성거려. 내 머리가 아프다.
A 서성거리지 않을 수가 없어. 커피라도 마셔야겠다. 너도 마실래?

📑 Notes

nerve wrecking 긴장되는, 진땀 나는 the jitters 신경과민, 안전부절못함 fret 애태우다, 조마조마해 하다 pound 두드리다, 두근거리다 pee 오줌 싸다 nicotine 니코틴 caffeine 카페인 could use + 명사 ~하면 좋겠다 tense 긴장된, 팽팽 put away 치워두다, 밀쳐두다 hover 정처 없이 서성거리다 blink 눈을 깜박이다

11 두려움, 놀람

두렵거나 무서운 감정은 형용사 scared, afraid, frightened 등으로 표현합니다.
너무 놀라 "충격 먹었어."라는 말은 I'm shocked. 또는 It's traumatic.이라고 하면
됩니다. 놀라서 "심장이 멎는 줄 알았어."는 I thought my heart stopped.라고 하고,
"눈이 휘둥그레졌어."는 My eyes were popped.라고 합니다.

원어민 발음 듣기 ☑☐   회화 훈련 ☐☐   듣기 훈련 ☐☐

(너무) 무서워.	I'm (so) scared. I'm afraid. I'm frightened. I'm terrified.
쇼크 받았어.	I'm shocked. It's shocking. It's traumatic.
섬뜩해.	It's spooky.
소름 끼쳐.	I've got some goose bumps. It gives me goose bumps. It makes my hair (all) stand.
멍해.	I'm stunned. I'm numbed. It stuns me. *stun=numb
너무 무서워서 꼼짝도 못하겠어.	I'm so scared and I can't move.
무서워하지 마.	Don't be scared. *scared=afraid, frightened
큰일 날 뻔했다.	It was close. It was a close call.
웬 날벼락이야.	That was quite unexpected. *unexpected=sudden That was out of the blue.
심장이 멎는 줄 알았어.	I thought my heart stopped.

▢ 눈이 휘둥그레졌어.	My eyes were popped.
	I was pop-eyed.
▢ (너무 놀라) 뭐라고?	What?
▢ 방금 뭐라고 했어?	What did you say just now?
▢ 믿을 수가 없어.	It's unbelievable.
	I can't believe it.
	No way.
▢ 내 귀를 믿을 수가 없어.	I can't believe my ears.
	*ears→eyes(눈)
▢ 무슨 일이야?	What's wrong?
	What happened?
▢ 분위기가 왜 이래?	What is going on here?
▢ 세상에! / 하느님 맙소사!	Oh, (my) God!
	Oh, (my) goodness!
	Oh, dear God!

DIALOGUE

A I was so scared and I couldn't even move.

B Yeah. It happens.

   When you're terrified, it stuns you.

A I thought my heart stopped, too.

A 너무 무서워서 움직일 수조차 없더라.

B 맞아. 그럴 수 있어. 끔찍할 정도로 무서우면 멍해지지.

A 내 심장도 멎는 줄 알았어.

📝 **Notes**

traumatic 정신적 충격을 받은 **spooky** 소름 끼치는, 섬뜩한 **goose bump(s)** 소름(=flesh) **stun** 어리벙
벙하게 하다, 멍하게 하다 **numb** 무감각하게 하다, 멍하게 하다 **close call** 아슬아슬한 순간, 아찔하게 위험한 순간
unexpected 예상치 못한, 갑작스러운 **pop-eyed** 눈이 휘둥그레진 **go on** 〈진행〉 ~이 일어나다

12 창피, 당황스러움

당황스러울 때 가장 많이 쓰이는 표현은 embarrassed 혹은 embarrassing입니다.
주어가 '사람'인 경우 embarrassed, '사물'인 경우 embarrassing을 쓰면 됩니다.
창피해서 어쩔 줄 몰라 하는 사람에게 Nobody thinks that way.(아무도 그렇게
생각하지 않아. / 너만 그렇게 생각하는 거야.)라고 말해 준다면 훨씬 위로가 되겠죠.

원어민 발음 듣기 ☑☐　회화 훈련 ☐☐　듣기 훈련 ☐☐

☐ 창피해! / 황당해! / 부끄러워!	I'm ashamed. *ashamed = embarrassed, blushed It's embarrassing.
☐ 혼란스러워! / 헷갈려!	I'm confused. It's confusing. It confuses me.
☐ 어찌할 바를 모르겠어.	I don't know what to do.
☐ 자존심 상해.	It hurts my pride.
☐ 얼굴을 들 수가 없어.	I can't hold up my head.
☐ 똑바로 쳐다볼 수가 없어.	I can't (even) look at you. I can't (even) look at your eyes.
☐ 쥐구멍에라도 들어가고 싶어.	I want to crawl into a mouse hole.
☐ 사라져 버리고 싶어.	I want to disappear.
☐ 창피해 할 것 없어.	Don't be ashamed.
☐ 부끄럽지도 않니?	Aren't you ashamed? *ashamed = embarrassed
☐ 언제까지 피하기만 할 거야?	Stop avoiding me.
☐ 아무도 그렇게 생각하지 않아.	Nobody thinks that way.
☐ 누가 생각이나 했겠어?	Who would've thought?
☐ 누가 상상이나 했겠어?	Who would've imagined?

📝 **Notes**

ashamed 창피한, 부끄러운　embarrassing 난처한, 쑥스러운　confused 혼란스러운　pride 자신감, 자존심
disappear 사라지다, 종적을 감추다　avoid 피하다, 회피하다

13 귀찮음, 성가심

귀찮고 짜증날 때 You're annoying me.(귀찮아.), Stop bothering me.(성가시게 굴지 마.) 하고 상대방에 쏘아 줄 때가 있습니다. 혼자 있고 싶을 때는 Leave me alone.(내버려 둬.)이라고 명확하게 자신의 의사를 전달할 필요가 있죠.

원어민 발음 듣기 ☑☐ 회화 훈련 ☐☐ 듣기 훈련 ☐☐

□ 귀찮아. / 짜증나.

You're annoying (me).

You're irritating (me).

It annoys me.
*annoy = irritate

□ 꺼림칙해.

It bothers me.
*bother = bug

It's bothering me.

□ 성가시게 굴지 마.

Stop bothering me.
*bothering = bugging

Don't bother me.

Get off my back.

□ (짜증스럽게) 또 뭐야.

Now what?

□ 날 좀 내버려 둬.

Leave me alone.

I want to be alone.

□ 상관하지 마.

It's none of your concern.
*concern = business

Mind your business.

Stay out of it.

□ 간섭하지 마.

Don't interrupt me.

Stop interfering.

□ 꺼져.

Go away.

Beat it.

Get lost.

Buzz off.

□ 내 사생활이야.

It's my privacy.

이래라저래라 하지 마.	Don't tell me what to do.
	Don't try to control me.
	Don't say "do this or do that."
	Don't push me around.
	*push = boss
내 일은 내가 알아서 해.	I can take care of myself.
	I know what I'm doing.
제발 노크해.	Would you please knock?
	Knock first, please.
밤에 전화하지 마.	Don't call me late at night.
(이렇게) 불쑥 찾아오지 마.	Don't burst into my house (like this).
	*burst into = barge in
	Don't show up at my door like this.
잔소리하지 마.	Don't nag at me.
	Stop giving me a lecture.
조용히 해.	Just be quiet.
	Stay quiet.
나중에 이야기하자.	Let's talk some other time.
	Can we talk later?

DIALOGUE

A Don't show up at my door like this.
 Call me first.
B I called, but you didn't answer the phone.
 I'm sorry to bother you.

A 이렇게 불쑥 찾아오지 마. 전화를 먼저 해.
B 전화했는데 네가 안 받더라고. 성가시게 굴어서 미안해.

Notes

bother 꺼림칙하다, 고민하게 하다 get off one's back 남을 괴롭히는 일을 그만두다 stay out of ~에 참견하지 않다 interfere 간섭하다 push ~ around ~를 몰아대다, 맘대로 조정하려고 들다(= boss ~ around) burst into 난입하다, 갑자기 뛰어들다(= barge in) show up 모습을 드러내다, 나타나다 nag 잔소리하다

14 그리움

나이가 들수록 예전 생각이 많이 떠오릅니다. 그럴 때 절로 나오는 말이 Good old times!(그때가 좋았지!)나 It brings me back to ~.(옛날 ~ 생각난다.)입니다. 보고 싶은 사람이 있으면 I miss her.(보고 싶어.)이나 I'm dying to see her.(보고 싶어 미치겠어.)와 같은 말도 하게 되죠.

원어민 발음 듣기 ☑☐　회화 훈련 ☐☐　듣기 훈련 ☐☐

□ 옛날이(그때가) 좋았는데.　　　Good old times!
　　　　　　　　　　　　　　　Those were the times!

□ 행복한 날들이었어.　　　　　(They were) Happy days.

□ 아름다운 추억이야.　　　　　It was a beautiful memory.

□ 십대 때 생각이 나게 하는구나.　It brings me back to my teens.
　　　　　　　　　　　　　　　It reminds me of my teens.

□ 시간을 되돌릴 수 있다면.　　　I wish I could turn the clock back.

□ 네가 (너무) 보고 싶어.　　　　I miss you (so much).

□ 네가 보고 싶어 죽겠어.　　　　I'm dying to see you.

□ 그녀는 많이 변했겠지.　　　　She must have changed a lot.

□ 우린 그곳에 가곤 했어.　　　　We used to go there.

□ (전에) 여기 와 본 적이 있어.　I have been here (before).

□ 첫사랑이었어.　　　　　　　It was my first love.

□ 첫 직장이었지.　　　　　　　It was my first job.

□ 누구나 처음은 잊지 못해.　　　We all remember our first.

□ 평생 그녀를 잊지 못할 거야.　I'll never forget her.

□ 어디서 본 듯해.　　　　　　　It looks very familiar to me.
　　　　　　　　　　　　　　　It's déjàvu all over again.

📝 **Notes**

remind A of B A에게 B를 연상시키다, 생각나게 하다　turn back ~을 되돌리다　be dying to ~ ~하고 싶어 죽겠다　must have+과거분사 ~했음에 틀림없다　used to 〈과거〉 ~하곤 했다　familiar 익숙한, 친근한　déjàvu 데자뷰 현상, 경험이 없는 것을 이미 경험한 것으로 느끼는 착각

15 걱정, 근심

걱정과 근심이 지나치면 단순히 I'm worried.(걱정돼.)를 넘어 I'm sick to worry.(걱정돼 미치겠어.), I couldn't sleep a wink.(한숨도 못 잤어.)와 같은 말을 하곤 합니다. 그럴 때 Don't worry.(걱정 마.)나 You're not alone.(넌 혼자가 아니야.) 등의 말로 상대방을 위로해 주면 어떨까요?

원어민 발음 듣기 ☑☐   회화 훈련 ☐☐   듣기 훈련 ☐☐

걱정돼.	I'm worried.
	I'm concerned.
	I feel uneasy.
	He makes me sick.
걱정하지 마.	Don't worry.
	Stop worrying.
	Don't trouble yourself.
	No sweat!
그 사람 괜찮을까?	Is he going to be okay?
	*okay = all right
걱정돼 미치겠어.	I'm sick to worry.
	Worrying is killing me.
한숨도 못 잤어.	I couldn't sleep a wink.
넌 걱정이 지나쳐.	You worry too much.
무슨 걱정(근심) 있어?	What are you worried about?
	Something troubling you?
걱정은 무슨…….	Nothing.
	Nothing's troubling me.
	Nothing concerns me.
사실은 걱정이 있어.	In fact, I'm in trouble.
말 못할 고민이야.	I can't tell anyone.
말해 봐. 들어 줄게.	Tell me.
	Try me.
아무도 도와줄 수 없어.	No one can help you.

□ 너는 혼자가 아니야.	You're not alone.
□ 주변에 도움을 청해.	Get some help.
□ 조심해!	Watch out!
	Heads up!
	(Be) Careful!
□ 나중에 후회할 텐데.	You're going to regret this.
	You don't want to do this.

DIALOGUE

A Something troubling you?
B No, nothing.
A What is it? Tell me. I could be a help.
B (Smiling) Thanks, but no.

A 무슨 걱정 있어?
B 아니야. 걱정은 무슨……
A 뭔데? 말해 봐. 내가 도움이 될지도 모르잖아.
B (웃으며) 고맙지만 됐어.

Notes

concerned 걱정스러운, 염려하는 uneasy 불안한, 걱정되는, 거북한 trouble oneself 고민하다, 걱정하다
sleep a wink 깜빡 자다 get help 도움을 청하다 heads up 조심해, 경계해

16 의심

어떤 일에 대해 의심이 들 때 It's strange.(뭔가 이상해./의심이 가.)라고도 하고, 비슷한 표현으로 I can smell a rat.(뭔가 수상해./낌새가 이상해.)이라고 말하기도 합니다. 결국 의심이 사실로 드러난다면 나를 속인 상대를 향해 "거짓말쟁이야!", "위선자!"와 같은 말로 비난할 수 있습니다.

원어민 발음 듣기 ☑□   회화 훈련 □□   듣기 훈련 □□

☐ 이상해. / 의심이 가.	It's strange. *strange = odd, doubtful I doubt it. It doesn't make (any) sense.
☐ 그의 동기가 의심스러워.	I'm suspicious of his motive.
☐ 냄새가 나. / 수상해.	I can smell it. I can smell a rat.
☐ 그 사람을 신뢰할 수가 없어.	I can't trust him.
☐ 궁금해.	I'm curious. I wonder why… *why 뒤에는 무엇이 궁금한지를 쓴다.
☐ 그가 나를 배신하다니.	He betrayed me. He stabbed me in my back.
☐ 감히 그녀가 나를 배신하다니.	How could she betray me? How dare she betray me?
☐ 너는 의심이 많아.	You're very skeptic. *skeptic = skeptical You're such a doubting Thomas.
☐ 넌 아무도 안 믿잖아?	You don't trust anyone, do you?
☐ 그녀를 어떻게 믿어?	How could you trust her?
☐ 물증이 없어.	There's no (physical) evidence. There's no smoking gun.
☐ 나를 시험하는 거야?	Are you testing me? Is this a test?

□ 제발 날 믿어 줘.	Please trust me.	

*trust = believe

Have faith in me.

□ 넌 입만 열면 거짓말이야.	You lie when you open your mouth.
□ 넌 거짓말쟁이야.	You're a liar.
□ 넌 위선자야!	You have two faces!

You're such a hypocrite!

□ 넌 가면을 쓰고 있어.	You're wearing a mask.
□ 그녀의 의도가 뭘까?	What's her intention?
□ 그녀가 정말 원하는 것이 뭘까?	What does she really want?

DIALOGUE

A How could you betray me again?
B I didn't. Please trust me.
A You stabbed me in my back once, didn't you?
B It was a total misunderstanding.

A 어떻게 또다시 나를 배신할 수 있어?
B 배신한 거 아니야. 제발 믿어 줘.
A 전에도 내 등에 칼을 꽂은 적이 있지 않아?
B 그건 완전 오해였다니까.

📋 Notes

make sense 말이 되다, 사리에 맞다, 이해가 되다 betray 배신하다, 등돌리다 stab 찌르다, 상처 주다 skeptic 의심이 많은(= skeptical) doubting Thomas 확실한 증거 없이는 믿으려고 하지 않는 사람 physical evidence 물증, (손에 잡히는) 확증 smoking gun (총에서 나오는 연기로 총이 발사됐음을 알 수 있는 것처럼) 확실한 증거, 결정적 증거 two faces 두 얼굴, 위선자 hypocrite 위선자

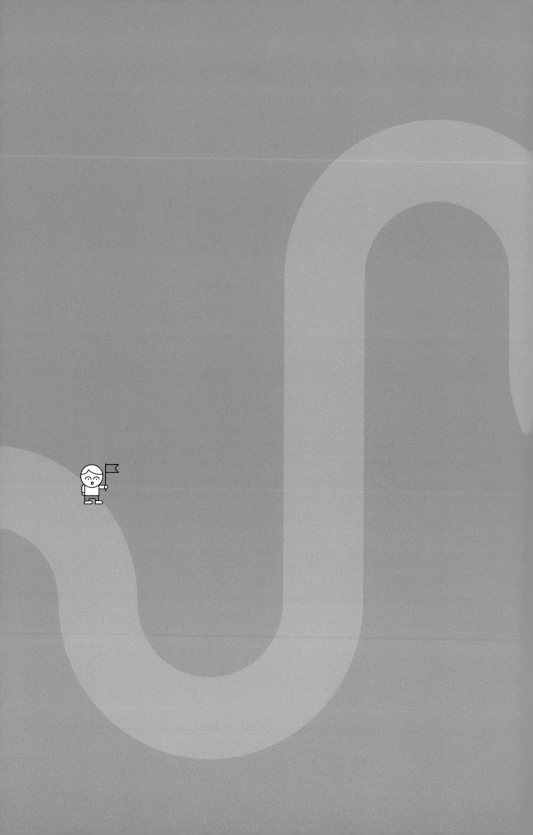

Chapter 05

대인 관계
Relationship

01 감사 표현

감사하는 마음을 전하는 표현할 때 보통 Thank you. 또는 I appreciate it.이라고
합니다. 무엇에 대해 감사하는지를 구체적으로 표현할 때는 Thank you for ~. 혹은 I
appreciate ~.와 같이 뒤에 감사의 대상을 말합니다.

원어민 발음 듣기 ☑☐ 회화 훈련 ☐☐ 듣기 훈련 ☐☐

▢ 매우 감사합니다.	Thank you very much.
	Thanks a lot.
	Thanks a million.
	Many thanks (to you).
	A thousand thanks (to you).
	I couldn't thank you enough.
▢ 여러모로 감사합니다.	Thank you for everything.
▢ 신세만 졌어요.	You're always kind to me.
	*kind = generous
▢ 어떻게 감사해야 할까요?	How can I thank you?
▢ 어떻게 감사드려야 할지 모르겠어요.	I don't know how to thank you.
▢ 별말씀을요!	No problem!
	No, not at all.
	Don't mention it.
	You're (quite) welcome.
▢ 제가 좋아서 했는데요, 뭐.	It was my pleasure.
	The pleasure is (all) mine.
▢ 감사하다는 말씀 전해 주세요.	Please say many thanks to him for me.
▢ 감사의 표현을 하고 싶어요.	I want to express my appreciation.
	*appreciation = gratitude
▢ 감사의 표시예요.	It's a token of my appreciation.
▢ 이러지 않으셔도 되는데.	You don't have to.
	You shouldn't.

02 축하, 축복

Congratulations!는 축하할 때 가장 널리 쓰이는 표현입니다. 간단히 Congrats! 라고도 하죠. 무엇을 축하하는지 덧붙이고 싶을 때는 Congratulations on ~ 뒤에 그 내용을 말하면 됩니다. 이때 전치사 on 뒤에는 명사나 동명사만을 쓸 수 있습니다.

원어민 발음 듣기 ☑☐　회화 훈련 ☐☐　듣기 훈련 ☐☐

Chapter 05 대인 관계

☐ 축하해요.	Congratulations! Congrats!
☐ 정말 잘됐어요.	(It's) Good for you. (I'm very) Happy for you. (It's) Great to hear.
☐ 정말 대견해. / 네가 정말 자랑스러워.	I'm very proud of you. You make me proud. That's my girl.
☐ 취업을 축하해요.	Congratulations on your (first) job.
☐ 결혼을 축하해요.	Congratulations on your wedding.
☐ 승진을 축하해요.	Congratulations on your promotion.
☐ 생일을 축하해요.	Happy birthday (to you).
☐ 오래오래 사세요.	Have a long healthy life!
☐ 늘 건강하세요.	Be healthy. Take good care of yourself.
☐ 부자 되세요!	Be rich! Make a fortune!
☐ 행운을 빌어요!	Good luck (to you)!
☐ 즐거운 성탄절 보내세요!	Merry Christmas!
☐ 즐거운 명절 보내세요!	Happy holidays!

📑 Notes

congrats 축하합니다(congratulations의 줄임)　promotion 승진　take good care of oneself 스스로를 건강하게 잘 돌보다　make a fortune 부자가 되다, 큰 재산을 모으다

93

03 칭찬하기

칭찬이 가진 긍정적 효과는 누구나 공감할 것입니다. Good job!(훌륭해!), Keep doing it.(계속 그렇게만 해.) 같은 칭찬의 말을 들으면 누구든지 기분이 으쓱해지고 스스로에 대해 뿌듯함을 느낍니다. 다양한 칭찬의 표현을 알아 두고 많이 사용해 보세요.

원어민 발음 듣기 ☑□   회화 훈련 □□   듣기 훈련 □□

□ 잘하고 있어.

(You're) Doing great.
So far so good.

□ 계속 그렇게(만) 해.

(Just) Keep doing it.

□ 잘했어. / 훌륭해.

Good job!
Great work!
Nicely done!
Well done!

□ 아주 훌륭해.

Excellent!
Superb job!
*superb = splendid

□ 최고야.

You're the best.
It's the best ever.
Perfection!

□ 그에 대한 칭찬이 자자해.

Everybody praises him.
Everyone speaks highly of him.

□ 그는 칭찬받을 만해.

He deserves praise.

□ 그는 믿음직해.

He is reliable.
He is trustworthy.

□ 그의 말에는 무게가 있어.

His words have weight.

□ 그녀는 경험이 많아.

She has many experiences.

□ 그녀는 세상사를 잘 알아.

She knows the world.
She has been around.

□ 그녀는 인맥이 넓어.

She has many connections.
She has many strings to pull.

그녀는 매너가 좋아.	She is well-mannered.
	She has excellent manners.
	*manners = etiquettes
	She always acts properly.
그녀는 윗사람에 대한 예의가 발라.	She respects elders.
	He knows how to treat elders.
그는 성품이 온화해.	He is sweet and gentle.
	He is a sweet and gentle soul.
그는 사람들과 잘 어울려.	He makes friends easily.
	He gets along with people.
모두가 그를 존경해.	Everyone respects him.

DIALOGUE

A How am I doing so far?
B You're doing amazingly great.
A Thanks. I'll keep doing my very best.

A 저 지금까지 어떻게 하고 있는 것 같아요?
B 아주 훌륭히 잘 하고 있어.
A 감사합니다. 앞으로도 계속 최선을 다해 노력할게요.

📋 Notes

so far 지금까지 keep -ing 계속 ~하다 superb 아주 훌륭한, 뛰어난(=splendid) speak highly of ~를 칭찬하다 deserve ~할 자격이 있다, ~할 만하다 know the world 세상을 알다, 세상 돌아가는 물정을 알다 be around 여기저기 돌아다니다, 경험이 많다, 세상을 잘 알다 connection(s) 인맥, 관계 well-mannered 매너가 좋은, 태도가 올바른 etiquette 에티켓, 예의범절, 매너 get along with ~와 잘 어울리다, 금방 친구가 되다

04 양해와 부탁

앞사람이 천천히 걷거나 길을 막고 있을 때 말없이 좁은 틈을 비집고 지나가기보다는 Excuse me.(실례합니다.) 또는 Can I get by?(지나가도 될까요?)라고 한마디 하는 것이 상대방의 기분을 상하게 하지 않을 겁니다. 양해를 구하거나 부탁하는 표현에는 어떤 것이 있는지 알아보겠습니다.

원어민 발음 듣기 ☑□   회화 훈련 □□   듣기 훈련 □□

☐ 실례할게요.	Excuse me.
	I'm sorry.
☐ 실례지만, ~ / 죄송하지만, ~	Excuse me, but…
	*excuse = pardon
	I'm sorry, but…
☐ 금방 돌아올게요.	I'll be right back.
☐ 잠깐만 기다려 주세요.	Give me one second.
	Could you wait for a second?
	Mind if you wait for a second?
☐ 그를 잠깐 빌려도 될까요?	Can I borrow him for a second?
	I need him for a second.
☐ (길에서) 지나갈게요.	Excuse me.
	Can I get by?
	Let me get by.
	Passing through.
☐ 문 좀 잡아 주세요.	Hold the door, please.
☐ 부탁이 있어요.	I have a favor.
☐ 부탁해도 될까요?	Can I ask you a favor?
	Could you do me a favor?
☐ 무리한 부탁인 줄 압니다만, ~	I know it's too much, but…
☐ 간청할게요.	I'm begging you.

📝 **Notes**

borrow 빌리다, 꾸다 get by 지나가다, 통과하다 pass through 지나가다, 통과하다 hold 잡다, 붙들다 ask a favor 부탁을 청하다 do a favor 부탁을 들어주다 beg 간절히 부탁하다

05 사과와 용서

"~해서 미안해."라는 표현은 I'm sorry for ~. 혹은 I'm sorry that ~.의 형태로 씁니다. 용서를 구할 때는 Please forgive me.(용서해 줘.) 혹은 Please accept my apology.(내 사과를 받아 줘.)라고 말하죠. '화해하다'라는 의미로 자주 쓰이는 표현인 make up도 같이 기억해 두세요.

원어민 발음 듣기 ☑☐   회화 훈련 ☐☐   듣기 훈련 ☐☐

☐ 정말 미안해.	I'm so sorry. *so = very, really, terribly, deeply I owe you an apology.
☐ ~해서 미안해.	I'm sorry for… I'm sorry that…
☐ 내가 얼마나 미안한지 넌 모를 거야.	You have no idea how sorry I am.
☐ 내가 제정신이 아니었나 봐.	I must have gone crazy. I must have been mad. I must have been out of my mind.
☐ 그땐 나도 내가 아니었어.	I wasn't myself then.
☐ 요즘 내가 내가 아니야.	I haven't been myself lately.
☐ 마음 상하게 할 생각은 없었어.	I didn't mean to hurt you. I didn't mean to hurt your feelings. Hurting you is the last thing I would do.
☐ 나도 내가 왜 그랬는지 몰라.	I don't know why I did that.
☐ 내가 지나쳤어.	I was too much. I went too far.
☐ 용서해 줘.	Please forgive me. Please accept my apology.
☐ 깨끗이 잊어 줘.	Please forget it. Please forget everything.
☐ 용서해 주기를 바라지도 못하겠어.	I don't expect you to forgive me.
☐ 다시는 이런 일 없을 거야.	It won't happen again.

□ 맹세해.	I swear (to God).
	Cross my heart.
□ 우리 화해하자.	Let's make up.
	Let's drop it.
	Why don't we let it go?
□ 내가 보상할게.	I'll make it up for you.
□ 방해해서 미안해.	(I'm) Sorry to interrupt.
	*interrupt = interfere
□ 갑자기 전화해서 미안해.	(I'm) Sorry to call you out of the blue.
	Sorry to call you suddenly.
□ 걱정을 끼쳐 죄송합니다.	(I'm) Sorry to make you worry.
□ 부담 드려 죄송합니다.	(I'm) Sorry to be a burden.
□ 나한테 사과해.	You owe me an apology.
□ 그걸 지금 사과라고 하는 거야?	Is that an apology?

DIALOGUE

A I just want to say that I'm very sorry.
B Sorry doesn't make me forget what happened.
A I know. But I'm still hoping that you would forgive me and forget it.

A 정말 미안하다고 말하고 싶어.
B 미안하다고 말해서 있었던 일이 전부 잊혀지는 것은 아니야.
A 나도 알아. 그래도 네가 나를 용서하고 지난 일은 잊기를 바라.

📄 Notes

go crazy 미치다, 정신 나가다 be out of one's mind 제정신이 아니다, 정신 나가다 the last thing 절대 하지 않을 것, 절대 하고 싶지 않는 일 go too far 지나치다, 과하다 swear 맹세하다 cross one's heart 맹세하다, 약속하다 make up 화해하다 let ~ go ~을 그만두다 make it up for ~ ~에게 보상하다 interfere 간섭하다 be out of the blue 난데없이, 갑작스럽게 burden 짐, 부담

06 약속

일반적으로 '약속하다'라는 의미로 쓰이는 동사는 promise입니다. 그러나 친구들과의 만남 같이 '계획'을 의미하는 약속이라면 plan을 쓰는 것이 더 알맞습니다. '저녁 약속'이나 '저녁 회식'은 dinner plan이라고 쓰면 됩니다.

☐ 약속해.

Promise me.

☐ 약속할게.

I promise you.

I'll promise.

You have my word.

☐ 한 가지만은 약속할 수 있어.

I can promise you one thing.

☐ 약속은 지켜야지.

You should keep promises.

☐ 약속이 있어.

I have a plan.

I have an appointment.
*appointment는 '병원 예약'이나 '업무 관련 약속'을 가리킬 때 주로 쓴다.

☐ 선약이 있어.

I've already made a plan.

I already have a plan.

I have a previous appointment.

☐ 일주일 전에 한 약속이야.

The plan was made a week ago.
*made=set

☐ 지금 와서 취소할 수 없어.

I can't cancel it now.

It must be rude to cancel it now.

☐ 시간 있어?

Do you have time?

☐ 언제 어디서 만날까?

When and where should we meet?

☐ 7시에 신촌에서 만날까?

How about Sinchon at 7?

Let's meet around Sinchon at 7.

☐ 시간(장소)를 바꿔도 될까?

Can we change the time(place)?
*change=switch

Mind if I change the time(place)?

☐ 10분 늦을 것 같아.

I'm going to be there 10 minutes late.

☐ 무슨 일 있으면 전화 줘.	Call me when something's up.
☐ 늦으면 전화해.	Call me when you are late.
☐ 나 좀 일찍 도착했어.	I came a little early. I got here a bit early.
☐ 늦어서 미안해.	I'm sorry I'm late. I'm sorry to have kept you waiting.
☐ 나 바람맞았어.	I was stood up.
☐ 기다릴게.	I'll wait for you. I'll be waiting for you.
☐ 천천히 와.	Take your time. You don't need to be in a hurry.

DIALOGUE

A Do you have a plan after work?
B Yes, actually I do. Why do you ask?
A Well, I had a plan but it was canceled.
   I thought maybe we could have dinner together.

A 오늘 퇴근 후 약속 있어?
B 응, 있어. 왜?
A 나도 약속이 있었는데 취소돼서. 함께 저녁이나 할까 했지.

 Notes

have one's word 약속하다　appointment 〈격식〉 약속　previous 사전의, 이전의　set 정하다, 확정하다
rude 무례한, 불손한　switch 바꾸다, 전환하다　something's up 어떤 일이 생기다　be stood up 바람맞다
be in a hurry 급하다, 서두르다

07 손님 초대

상대방을 집 등에 초대할 때는 Would you like to come? 또는 I'd like to invite you to ~.라고 말합니다. 편한 사이라면 간단하게 Want to join us? 또는 Come and visit us.라고 말하기도 하죠. 초대를 받고 온 손님에게는 Make yourself at home.(내 집처럼 편히 계세요.)이라고 말하는 것도 잊지 마세요.

원어민 발음 듣기 ☑☐   회화 훈련 ☐☐   듣기 훈련 ☐☐

☐ 오실래요?	Would you like to come?
	Want to join us?
	Come and visit us.
	I'd like to invite you to…
	*to 뒤에는 초대하는 목적이나 장소가 나옵니다.
☐ 꼭 오셔야 해요.	You have to come.
☐ 와 주시면 영광입니다.	It would be a great honor to have you.
	It would be a great honor if you come.
☐ 초대해 주셔서 감사합니다.	Thank you for inviting me.
☐ 와 주셔서 감사합니다.	Thank you for coming.
☐ 언제든지 환영합니다.	You're always welcome.
	You're welcome anytime.
☐ 집들이 오실래요?	Would you like to come to our housewarming party?
☐ 내 생일 파티에 올래?	Want to come to my birthday party?
☐ 몸만 와.	Just bring yourself.
☐ 옷 주세요.	Let me get your jacket.
☐ 앉으세요.	Please have a seat.
☐ 내 집처럼 편히 계세요.	Make yourself at home.
	Make yourself comfortable.
☐ 집처럼 생각하세요.	Consider it as your home.

📑 Notes

housewarming (party) 집들이   bring oneself 선물이나 음식 등을 가져오지 않고 방문하다. 몸만 오다
comfortable 편안한, 안락한   consider A as B A를 B로 여기다

08 절친함

가까운 사이라는 의미로 "우리 친해요."는 We're close.라고 표현합니다. 친한 친구임을 나타낼 때는 He is my best friend., We went to school together., We've been friends for 10 years.와 같이 표현할 수 있습니다.

원어민 발음 듣기 ☑□   회화 훈련 □□   듣기 훈련 □□

□ 우린 (아주) 친해. 가까워.

We are (very) close.

□ 그는 나의 가장 친한 친구야.

He is my best friend.

□ 너희는 얼마 동안 친구였어?

How long have you been friends?

□ 우린 십년지기 친구야.

We've been friends for years.
It's been many years.

□ 고등학교 이후로 계속 친구야.

We've known each other since high school.
We've been friends since high school.

□ 우리는 학교를 같이 다녔어.

We went to school together.

□ 우리는 떼려야 뗄 수 없는 사이지.

We're inseparable.
We're soul mates.

□ 그는 (나에게) 가족이나 마찬가지야.

He is (like) family (to me).

□ 우린 비밀이 없어.

We don't keep secrets from each other.
We don't have any secret.

□ 그녀는 나에 대해 다 알아.

She knows everything about me.

□ 그녀는 나를 항상 도와줘.

She always helps me.

□ 그녀는 항상 내 곁에 있어 줘.

She always stands by me.
She is always there for me.

□ 우리는 서로를 북돋아 줘.

We support each other.

□ 그녀의 부탁은 절대 거절 못해.

I can't say "NO" to her.

□ 우정은 영원해.

Friendship lasts forever.

□ 우리는 서로가 동등하다고 생각해요.

We believe we're equal to each other.

09 냉대, 무시

상대방에게 존중받지 못하는 것만큼 기분 나쁜 일도 없을 겁니다. '냉대하다', 즉 '차갑게 대하다'는 영어로 be cold to someone이라고 합니다. 이 외에도 look down on(~를 깔보다), ignore(무시하다), leave ~ out(~를 따돌리다) 등도 많이 쓰입니다.

원어민 발음 듣기 ☑☐   회화 훈련 ☐☐   듣기 훈련 ☐☐

□ 그들은 나를 냉대해.

They are cold to me.
They're giving me a cold shoulder.

□ 그들은 나를 무시해.

They're ignoring me.

□ 그는 다른 사람 의견을 무시해.

He ignores other's opinion.

□ 그들은 아는 척도 안 해.

They don't even say "hi" to me.

□ 그들은 내 말을 못 들은 척해.

They pretend not to hear me.

□ 그들은 나에게 말도 안 해.

They don't even talk to me.

□ 그는 답장이 없어.

He never replies.
He never writes me back.

□ 그들은 나를 없는 사람 취급해.

They act like I'm not there.

□ 그들은 나를 깔봐.

They look down on me.
They think I'm an idiot.
I'm nobody to them.

□ 그는 내게 반말을 해.

He talks down to me.
He speaks rudely to me.
*rudely = impolitely

□ 그들은 나와 눈도 안 마주쳐.

They don't make an eye contact with me.
They don't even look at my eyes.

□ 그들은 나를 완전히 따돌려.

They leave me entirely out of their conversation.
I'm completely left out.

📑 **Notes**

cold shoulder 냉대, 경시   act like ~처럼 행동하다, 가장하다   look down on ~를 깔보다, ~를 업신여기다
talk down 반말하다, 함부로 말하다   leave ~ out ~를 따돌리다, ~를 소외시키다

10 반어적, 빈정거리는 표현

'잘했다'는 의미의 Nice job!이나 Nice work! 같은 말도 상황에 따라 반어적으로 빈정거리거나 비꼬아 말하는 표현으로 쓰일 수 있습니다. 그러니 칭찬의 말이라도 때와 장소를 잘 가려서 써야 하죠. 말의 억양과 뉘앙스를 잘 살펴서 상대가 칭찬하는 것인지 비꼬는 것인지 구분할 수 있도록 하세요.

원어민 발음 듣기 ☑□ 회화 훈련 □□ 듣기 훈련 □□

□ 그렇게 빈정거리지 마.	Don't be so sarcastic.
□ 그는 항상 빈정거려.	He always makes sarcastic remarks.
□ 그의 빈정거림이 신경에 거슬려.	His sarcasm gets on my nerves.
□ (빈정거리며) 재미있네. / 웃기네.	(It's) Funny.
	That is interesting.
□ 계속 말해 봐. 그렇게 되나 보자.	Keep telling yourself.
□ (빈정거리며) 잘했네!	Nice job!
	*job = work
□ (빈정거리며) 잘됐네!	Terrific!
□ (지각한 사람에게) 일찍도 왔네!	You're early!
□ 꼴좋다! / 싸다!	It serves you.
	It serves you right!
□ 무슨 큰일이라고.	Big deal!
□ 누가 신경 쓴다고.	Who cares?
□ 신경도 안 쓰면서 (쓰는 척하기는).	Like you care.
□ (아무도 모른다는 의미로) 누가 알겠어?	Who knows?
□ (비꼬듯이) 너 잘났다!	So you're perfect.
□ 나한테 퍽이나 좋겠네.	How good for me!
□ (놀란 척하며) 아이쿠, 이게 웬일이야!	What a surprise!
□ (네 뜻대로 해서) 이제 만족해?	You happy now?

Chapter 06

외모
Appearance

01 잘생김, 예쁨

아름다움을 평가하는 기준은 저마다 다르지만 보편적인 기준에서 '잘생긴 외모'와 관련된 표현들을 모았습니다. 남성의 경우 He is full of testosterone.(남성미가 넘쳐.), He's tall.(키가 커.), 여성의 경우는 She is pretty.(예뻐.), She is gorgeous.(아름다워.), She is slim.(날씬해.) 등을 들 수 있겠죠.

원어민 발음 듣기 ☑□   회화 훈련 □□   듣기 훈련 □□

□ 그는 잘생겼어.

He's (so) handsome.

He's good-looking.

He has a handsome face.

□ 그는 정말 멋져.

He's so dreamy.

He's so cool.

He's a hunk.

□ 그는 남성미가 넘쳐.

He is masculine.
*masculine = manly

He is full of testosterone.

□ 그는 키가 커.

He is tall.

□ 키가 얼마나 돼?

How tall are you?

What is your height?
*in centimeters, in inches 같은 길이 단위를 덧붙일 수도 있다.

□ 그는 체격이 좋아.

He's well-built.
*well-built = well-cut

He has a great frame.
*frame = body

He is an athlete.

He is stout.

□ 그는 어깨가 딱 벌어졌어.

He has broad shoulders.

He is broad-shouldered.

□ 그는 근육질이야.

He is (very) muscular.

□ 그는 이목구비가 뚜렷해.

He has fine features.

□ 그는 목소리가 좋아.

He has a good voice.

He has a smooth voice.

☐ 그의 걸음걸이가 멋있어.	I like the way he walks.
☐ 그녀는 피부가 적당히 탔어.	She looks great tanned. She looks good with a tan.
☐ 그녀의 거무스름한 피부가 건강해 보여.	She looks healthier with a tan.
☐ 그녀는 예쁘게 생겼어.	She is pretty. She has a pretty face.
☐ 그녀는 아름다워(매력적이야).	She is beautiful. *beautiful = attractive She is gorgeous. She is stunning. She is breathtaking. She is lovely. She is charming. She is such a beauty. She is such a turn-on.
☐ 그녀는 자연 미인이야.	She is a natural beauty.
☐ 그녀는 귀여워.	She is cute. *cute = adorable She is such a cutie. She is as cute as a button.
☐ 그녀는 섹시해.	She is sexy. *sexy = glamorous She is a bombshell.
☐ 그녀는 여성미가 넘쳐.	She is feminine. *feminine = womanly
☐ 그녀는 날씬해. / 그녀는 몸매가 좋아.	She is slim. *slim = slender She is in good shape. She looks fit.
☐ 넌 어떻게 그렇게 날씬하니?	How do you keep in shape? How do you keep fit?
☐ 그녀는 체격이 아담해.	She is small. *small = tiny, petite

□ 그녀는 몸매가 여성스러워.	She has feminine curves.	
	She has a great shape.	
□ 그녀는 다리가 길어.	She has long legs.	
□ 그녀는 머릿결이 좋아.	She has sleek hair.	
	*sleek = silky	
□ 그녀는 머리가 단정해.	Her hair is well-gloomed.	
□ 그녀는 긴 생머리야.	She has long and straight hair.	
	Her hair is long and straight.	
□ 그녀는 피부가 고와.	She has silky skin.	
	She has soft and smooth skin.	
□ 그녀는 피부가 하얘.	She has light skin.	
	*light = fair	
	She is light-skinned.	
	She is fair-skinned.	
□ 그녀는 눈이 예뻐.	She has beautiful eyes.	
	*beautiful = gorgeous	
□ 그녀는 웃는 얼굴이 예뻐.	She has a great smile.	
	I like the way she smiles.	
	What a smile!	

DIALOGUE

A You look great tanned.
  Look healthier and sexy.
B Thanks. I used to prefer light skin, but not anymore.

A 적당히 탄 것이 너무 보기 좋다. 더 건강하고 섹시해 보여.
B 고마워. 예전엔 흰 피부를 선호했는데 지금은 아니야.

Notes

dreamy (남자가) 멋있는, 근사한 hunk 멋진 남자 masculine 남자다운, 사내다운 testosterone 테스토스테론(남성 호르몬) frame 몸의 골격 athlete 건장한 체격의 사람 stout 몸이 튼튼한 feature(s) 이목구비, 생김새 turn-on 흥분시키는 것, 흥분제 bombshell 아주 매력적이고 섹시한 여자 be in good shape 몸매가 좋은 keep in shape 몸매를 유지하다 curves 여성의 곡선미 sleek 매끄러운, 윤기 있는

02 못생김

'못생긴', '다리가 짧은', '뚱뚱한'과 같은 표현은 상대적으로 '못생긴' 외모를 묘사하는 말입니다. 특히나 여성들에게 이런 말을 하는 것은 실례일 수 있으니 몸무게나 얼굴에 난 티끌만 한 freckles(주근깨), pimples(여드름)를 지적하는 것도 삼가는 것이 좋겠죠.

원어민 발음 듣기 ☑□   회화 훈련 □□   듣기 훈련 □□

☐ 그는 못생겼어.	He isn't good-looking.
	He is ugly.
☐ 그는 키가 작아.	He is short.
☐ 그는 땅딸막해.	He is nuggetty. *nuggetty = stumpy
☐ 그는 멀대같이 커.	He is lanky.
☐ 그녀는 다리가 짧아(허리가 길어).	She has short legs.
	She has a long waist.
☐ 그는 어깨가 좁아.	He has narrow shoulders.
☐ 그녀는 너무 말랐어.	She is too thin. *thin = skinny, bony
☐ 그녀는 피골이 상접했어.	She is all skin and bones.
☐ 그녀는 통통해.	She is chubby. *chubby = overweight, plump
	She is a bit overweight.
☐ 그는 뚱뚱해. / 비만이야.	He is too fat.
	He is overweight.
	He is obese.
☐ 그는 이중 턱이야.	He has a double chin.
☐ 그는 뻐드렁니야.	He has buckteeth.
☐ 체중이 얼마나 돼?	How much do you weigh?
	What is your weight? *in kilos, in pounds 같은 무게 단위를 덧붙일 수도 있다.
☐ 그는 배가 나왔어.	He has a beer belly.
	He is potbellied.

Chapter 06

외모

□ 그는 대머리야.	He is bald.	

He is bald.
*bald = baldheaded

He is thin on top.

He has a receding hairline.

□ 그녀의 머릿결이 푸석해.　　He hair is very dry.

□ 그녀의 머릿결이 푸석해.

Her hair is very dry.

□ 그녀의 머리는 부스스해.

Her hair is messy.

□ 그녀는 머리숱이 적어.

She has thin hair.
*thin = fine

□ 그녀의 피부는 거칠어.

She has rough skin.

□ 그녀의 얼굴은 주근깨투성이야.

Her face is covered with freckles.

□ 그녀의 얼굴은 여드름투성이야.

Her face is covered with pimples.

□ 그녀의 얼굴엔 주름이 많아.

Her face is all wrinkled.

DIALOGUE

A I think I'm too fat.
B No, you're not.
　　You're a bit overweight. That's all.

A 나 너무 뚱뚱한 것 같아.
B 아니, 안 그래. 너는 약간 과체중일 뿐이야.

📝 **Notes**

nuggety 키가 작고 뚱뚱한, 땅딸막한(= stumpy)　bony 뼈가 앙상한, 여윈　chubby 토실토실한, 포동포동한
overweight 과체중의　obese 뚱뚱한, 살찐, 비만의　beer belly 볼록 튀어나온 배, 술배　potbellied 배가 볼록 튀
어나온　thin on top 머리가 빈, 대머리의　messy 엉망인, 지저분한　wrinkled 얼굴에 주름진, 주름이 많은　thin
hair 숱이 적은 머리, 가느다란 머리

03 개성, 분위기

잘생기고 못생긴 것과 상관없이 개성 있는 외모와 분위기를 가진 사람들이 있습니다. 그런 사람들은 double tooth(덧니)나 baldhead(대머리)가 기막히게 잘 어울려 오히려 매력 포인트가 되기도 합니다. 이렇게 외모에서 풍기는 분위기를 나타내는 표현을 살펴보겠습니다.

원어민 발음 듣기 ☑□   회화 훈련 □□   듣기 훈련 □□

☐ 그녀는 보조개가 귀여워.	She has cute dimples.
☐ 그녀는 덧니가 귀여워.	She has a cute double tooth.
☐ 그는 대머리가 잘 어울려.	He looks good with a baldhead.
☐ 그녀는 작은 눈에 애교가 있어.	She has charm in her small eyes.
☐ 그녀는 체격이 작지만 귀여워.	She is small but cute.
☐ 그는 재미있게 생겼어.	He has a funny face.
☐ 그는 둥근 얼굴이 어려 보여.	He has a roundish face and looks young.
☐ 그는 콧수염이 잘 어울려.	He looks good with his mustache.
☐ 그는 주걱턱이 그런대로 귀여워.	His spoon-like chin is kind of cute.
☐ 그는 잘생긴 편은 아니지만 매력적이야.	He's not handsome but attractive. *handsome = good-looking
☐ 그는 지적이야.	He looks intelligent.
☐ 그는 부유해 보여.	He looks rich. *rich = wealthy
☐ 그녀는 우아해.	She looks elegant. *elegant = graceful
☐ 그녀는 중성적이야.	She is an androgynous. She has androgynous features.
☐ 그는 무서워 보여.	He looks scary.
☐ 그는 후덕해 보여.	He looks generous.
☐ 그는 고전적이야.	He looks classic.
☐ 그는 도시적이야.	He has an urban image.

Chapter 06

외모

□ 그는 촌스러워.	He is rustic.
□ 그녀는 청순가련해 보여.	She looks pure and innocent.
□ 그녀는 얼굴에 개성이 없어.	She has a forgettable face.
□ 그녀는 나이 들어 보여.	She looks old for her age.
□ 그녀는 어려 보여.	She looks young for her age.
□ 그녀는 어떻게 생겼어?	What does she look like?
□ 그의 외모를 묘사해 봐.	Describe what he looks like. Can you describe what he looks like?
□ 그의 모습이 누군가를 떠올리게 해.	He reminds me of someone else.
□ (~랑 닮았다는) 그런 말 많이 들어.	I get that a lot.
□ 그는 그 영화배우를 꼭 닮았어.	He looks just like that actor. *actor → actress(여자 배우)

 Notes

look good with ~이 잘 어울리다   roundish 둥근, 둥그스름한   spoon-like 숟가락(주걱) 모양의
androgynous 중성적인, 양성적인   rustic 소박한, 촌스러운, 촌뜨기의   remind A of B A에게 B를 연상시키다

04 성형 수술

'미용 성형 수술'은 cosmetic plastic surgery라고 합니다. 부위별로 구분하여 '코 수술'은 nose job, 요즘 유행하는 '양악 수술'은 chin job, '주름 제거 수술'은 face-lifts라고 합니다. 성형 수술이나 미용 시술에 대한 표현을 알아봅시다.

원어민 발음 듣기 ☑☐ 회화 훈련 ☐☐ 듣기 훈련 ☐☐

□ (미용) 성형 수술 했어.

I had (cosmetic) plastic surgery.
I went through plastic surgery.
I got a nip and tuck.

□ 코 수술 했어.

I had a nose job.
I had my nose done.
*nose job → eyes job(눈 수술)

□ 양악 수술 했어.

I had my chin done.

□ 주름 제거 수술 했어.

I had face-lift.

□ 쌍꺼풀 수술 했어.

I had my double-eyelid done.

□ 보톡스 맞았어.

I got Botox.
I got facial Botox injections.

□ 박피했어.

I got facial peeling.

□ 점을 뺐어.

I removed moles.
*remove=get rid of
I had moles removed.

□ 지방 흡입 했어.

I had liposuction.

□ 다크서클 제거 수술 했어.

I removed a dark circle on my face.

□ 가슴 확대 수술 했어.

I had breast implants.

□ 그녀는 성형 수술로 아주 달라 보여.

She looks quite different after plastic surgery.

📖 Notes

go through 과정을 거치다, 겪다, 경험하다 nip and tuck 미용 성형 수술 job 성형(외과) 수술 chin 아래턱 peel (껍질 등을) 벗기다 mole 얼굴의 점, 사마귀 liposuction 지방 흡입술 implant 이물질의 체내 삽입

113

05 차림새

옷을 잘 입는 사람을 흔히 '패션 감각이 있다'고 표현합니다. 이것을 영어로는 '~에 취향이 고급이다'라는 뜻의 have great taste in ~이나 '~에 안목이 있다'는 의미인 have an eye for ~로 표현합니다. 옷 외에도 화장이나 액세서리, 구두, 가방 등의 소품들에 대해 어떻게 말할 수 있는지 표현들을 알아봅시다.

원어민 발음 듣기 ☑☐   회화 훈련 ☐☐   듣기 훈련 ☐☐

☐ 그는 패션 감각이 있어(옷을 잘 입어).	He has great taste in fashion.
	He has an eye for fashion.
	He has a remarkable sense of fashion.
	He's trendy. *trendy = fashionable, stylish
☐ 그는 옷을 못 입어.	He has a bad sense of fashion. *a bad 대신 no를 쓰면 "그는 패션 감각이 없어."의 의미이다.
☐ 그는 옷차림이 구식이야.	His fashion is so out of style.
	His fashion is so outdated.
☐ 그녀는 옷차림이 너무 튀어.	She is dressed too sexually.
	She wears loud clothes.
	Her fashion always sticks out.
☐ 그는 옷차림이 수수해.	He is dressed simply.
	He wears comfortable clothes.
☐ 그는 옷차림이 단정해.	He's dressed neat and tidy.
	He's neatly dressed.
☐ 그는 정장 차림을 좋아해.	He likes to dress up.
	He always suits up.
	He enjoys wearing suits.
☐ 그는 캐주얼 차림을 좋아해.	He likes casual clothes. *like = wear
	He enjoys wearing casual clothes.
☐ 그녀는 화장을 잘해.	She puts on make-up well. *put on = wear
	She looks great in make-up.
☐ 그녀는 화장이 자연스러워.	She wears light make-up and looks natural.

114

☐ 그녀는 화장을 못해.	She's not good at wearing make-up.
☐ 그녀는 화장이 너무 진해.	She puts on thick make-up. *thick = heavy, too much
☐ 그녀는 액세서리를 잘 해.	She looks great with (fashion) accessories.
☐ 그녀는 액세서리를 잘 할 줄 몰라.	She doesn't know how to wear accessories.
☐ 그녀는 큰 가방이 잘 어울려.	She looks great with a big bag.
☐ 그녀는 하이힐이 잘 어울려.	She looks great in high heels.
☐ 그는 최신 유행을 따라.	He follows the latest fashion. *fashion = trends He takes fashion trends seriously.
☐ 난 유행에 신경 쓰지 않아.	I don't follow the latest fashion.
☐ 난 내 나름의 패션 스타일이 있어.	I have my own fashion style. I like the way I dress.
☐ 난 색깔을 잘 맞춰.	I try to match the colors of my clothes.

DIALOGUE

A You don't seem to care about trends.
B That's right. I don't follow the latest fashion.
  I have my own fashion style.

A 너는 유행 같은 거 별로 신경 안 쓰는 것 같다.
B 맞아. 난 최신 유행을 따르려고 하지 않아. 내 나름의 패션 스타일이 있거든.

📑 **Notes**

remarkable 놀랄 만한, 대단한 a sense of fashion 패션 감각 trendy 유행의, 유행의 첨단을 걷는 사람 be out of style 유행이 뒤떨어지다, 구식이다(= go out of style) outdated 시대에 뒤떨어진, 구식의 loud 요란한, 눈에 띄는(튀는) stick out 두드러지다, 튀다 neat and tidy 깔끔하고 단정한 dress up 차려입다 suit up 정장 차림을 하다 latest 최신의 match colors 색깔을 맞추다

Chapter 07

성격
Personality

01 개혁적인 성격

애니어그램(enneagram)에서 나누는 아홉 가지 인간의 성격 유형에 대한 표현들을 배워 보겠습니다. Reformer(개혁가)로 알려진 1번 유형은 목표가 뚜렷한 a man of principle(원칙주의자)로 self-control(자기 절제)을 잘하고 perfection(완벽주의)을 추구하는 사람입니다.

원어민 발음 듣기 ☑□ 회화 훈련 □□ 듣기 훈련 □□

□ 그녀는 끈기(고집)가 있어.

She is persistent.
*persistent → tenacious(집요한)

□ 그녀는 인내심이 있어.

She is patient.

□ 그녀는 항상 노력해.

She always tries hard.

□ 그녀는 절대 포기하지 않아.

She never gives up in the middle.
She does her best.

□ 그는 옳고 그름을 잘 따져.

He always tells what is right and wrong.

□ 그는 합리적이야.

He is reasonable.

□ 그는 개혁적이야.

He wants to try new things.
He wants to change things.

□ 그는 원칙주의자야.

He is a man of principle.
He wants to follow principles.
He thinks rules are very important.

□ 그녀는 목표가 뚜렷해.

She has a clear goal.
She has a clear sense of purpose.

□ 그녀는 자기 절제를 잘 해.

She is self-controlled.
*self-controlled = moderate

□ 그녀는 완벽주의자야.

She is a perfectionist.
She wants to be perfect.

□ 그는 카리스마가 있어.

He is charismatic.
He has charisma.

□ 그는 남을 지배하려고 해.

He can be a control freak.

02 다정다감한 성격

Helper(조력가)로 알려진 2번 유형의 사람은 warm-hearted(다정다감)하고 social (사교적인)인 성격의 소유자로 남을 돕는 것을 무척 좋아합니다. 늘 energetic (에너지가 넘치는)해서 여러 사람들과 다양한 관계 맺기를 즐기는 사람이죠. 남을 기쁘게 하는 데서 true meaning of life(진정한 삶의 의미)를 찾는다고 합니다.

원어민 발음 듣기 ☑☐　회화 훈련 ☐☐　듣기 훈련 ☐☐

☐ 그녀는 남을 도와주는 것을 좋아해.	She likes to help other people.
	She feels good when she helps people.
☐ 그녀는 사교적이야.	She is social.
	She is quite a social person.
☐ 그녀는 활동적이야.	She is proactive.
	She is a dynamic person.
☐ 그녀는 에너지가 넘쳐.	She is energetic.
	She is filled with energy.
☐ 그녀는 이타적이야.	She is altruistic.
	She puts other people before herself.
☐ 그는 사려 깊어.	He is considerate.
	*considerate = thoughtful
☐ 그는 사람을 좋아해.	He likes people.
	He is a people person.
☐ 그는 친구와의 관계를 중요시해.	He thinks friendship is very important.
☐ 그는 다정다감해.	He is sweet.
	He is such a sweetheart.
	He is warm-hearted.
☐ 그는 다른 사람의 의견을 존중해.	He respects other people's opinions.
☐ 그는 남을 기쁘게 해.	He makes other people happy.

Chapter 07

성격

📝 Notes

social person 사교적인 사람　be filled with ~로 가득 찬　put ~ before oneself 자신보다 ~를 우선시하다
people person 사람들과 어울리는 것을 좋아하는 사람　warm-hearted 마음이 따뜻한

03 성공 지향적인 성격

Achiever(성공 지향적 인물)인 3번 유형은 progressive(진취적)하고 성취욕이 강합니다. 어떤 일이든 달려들어 성공시키려고 애쓰는 active doer(도전적이고 실천적인 인물)라고 할 수 있죠. 하지만 지나치게 성공에 집착한다면 workaholic(일 중독자)이 되거나 full of vanity(허영)에 빠질 수도 있습니다.

원어민 발음 듣기 ☑☐   회화 훈련 ☐☐   듣기 훈련 ☐☐

☐ 그는 진취적이야.

He is progressive.
*progressive = aggressive

☐ 그는 성취욕이 강해.

He wants to feel a sense of achievement.
He looks for something very fulfilling.

☐ 그는 성공 지향적이야.

Success in life is very important to him.
He always pursues success.

☐ 그는 화술이 뛰어나.

He has excellent verbal skills.

☐ 그녀는 적응력이 뛰어나.

She is highly adaptable.

☐ 그녀는 경쟁심이 강해.

She is competitive.

☐ 그녀는 질투심이 강해.

She can be extremely jealous.
She is a jealous type.

☐ 그녀는 실천적이야.

She is a doer.
She acts first.

☐ 그는 추진력이 있어.

He is driven.
He has the drive.
He is a real go-getter.

☐ 그는 자신의 이미지에 신경 써.

He is sensitive about his image.
He is sensitive about what other people think.

☐ 그는 허영이 심해.

He is so vain.
He is full of vanity.

☐ 그는 일 중독자 같아.

He can be a workaholic.
He has no (personal) life.

120

04 낭만적인 성격

4번 유형의 사람은 전형적인 낭만주의자입니다. 개인의 감정에만 신경 쓰는 경향이 있기 때문에 흔히 이들을 Individualist(개인주의자)라고 하죠. 하지만 artistic (예술적인)한 기질이나 천부적인 심미안을 갖고 있어 예술계에서 활동하기에 적합하다고 합니다.

원어민 발음 듣기 ☑□   회화 훈련 □□   듣기 훈련 □□

□ 그는 낭만적이야.

He is romantic.

He is romantic with a capital R.

He likes to do something romantic.

□ 그는 명상을 즐겨.

He enjoys meditating.
*meditating = contemplating

□ 그녀는 창조적이야.

She is creative.

She has a creative mind.

□ 그는 직관력이 뛰어나.

He is highly intuitive.
*intuitive = perceptive

□ 그는 심미안이 있어.

He has an eye for beauty.

□ 그녀는 예술가적 기질이 있어.

She is artistic.

□ 그녀는 감상적이야.

She is quite sentimental.
*sentimental = emotional

She is melodramatic.

□ 그녀는 매사에 예민해.

She is sensitive.

□ 그는 감수성이 예민해.

He is impressionable.

□ 그는 쉽게 상처 받아.

He gets easily hurt by people.

□ 그는 사교성이 떨어져.

He is not social.

He doesn't know how to socialize with people.

□ 그녀는 비현실적이야.

She is unrealistic.
*unrealistic = impractical

□ 그녀는 즉흥적이야.

She is whimsical.

05 지적인 타입

Investigator(조사자)란 별명답게 지적 탐구심이 강합니다. 이들은 logical (논리적인)하고 rational(이성적인)하여 객관적으로 판단하기를 좋아하고 스스로를 공명정대한 사람이라고 인식할 때 만족감을 느낀다고 하죠. 또한 새로운 것에 대한 호기심이 강하고 두뇌 활동을 좋아하기 때문에 배움에 대한 열정이 강하다고 합니다.

원어민 발음 듣기 ☑□   회화 훈련 □□   듣기 훈련 □□

☐ 그는 지적이야.	He is intellectual.
☐ 그는 논리적이야.	He is logical.
	He is a logical thinker.
☐ 그는 이성적이야.	He is rational.
☐ 그는 객관적이야.	He is objective.
☐ 그녀는 공명정대해.	She is fair.
	*fair = impartial
	She doesn't take any sides.
☐ 그녀는 머리 쓰기를 좋아해.	She likes to use her head.
	*head = brain
	She likes to challenge her brain.
☐ 그는 배우는 것을 좋아해.	He likes learning.
	He likes to learn new things.
☐ 그는 책임감이 강해.	He is responsible.
☐ 그는 자기반성에 진지해.	He is introspective.
	*introspective = self-reflective
☐ 그는 신중해.	He is careful.
	*careful = cautious, prudent
☐ 그녀는 (항상) 침착해.	She is calm and composed.
	She (always) stays cool and collected.
	She is cool-headed.
☐ 그녀는 좀처럼 화를 내지 않아.	She doesn't usually lose her temper.
	She doesn't get angry easily.

06 성실, 안정적인 성격

Loyalist(충성가)인 6번 유형은 devoted(헌신적인)하며 성실한 타입입니다. 사회 전체가 원활하게 제 기능을 하게끔 만드는 주역이라고 볼 수 있겠죠. 이 유형의 사람들은 안정 지향적 성향이 강해서 변화보다는 기존의 것을 고수하려고 하며, 불안한 것을 싫어하여 법과 질서를 맹신하는 경향이 있습니다.

원어민 발음 듣기 ☑☐　회화 훈련 ☐☐　듣기 훈련 ☐☐

□ 그녀는 성실해.

She is sincere.
*sincere = faithful, honest

□ 그녀는 헌신적이야.

She is devoted.
*devoted = dedicated

She feels comfortable with following orders.

□ 그는 안정 지향적이야.

He tries to keep the balance.

He tries to keep things in order.

Safety is important to him.

He tries everything stable.
*stable = settled, steady, balanced

□ 그녀는 얌전해.

She is well-behaved.
*well-behaved = well-mannered

□ 그녀는 순종적이야.

She is docile.
*docile = obedient

□ 그녀는 누구하고나 잘 어울려.

She gets along with anyone.

She makes friends easily.

□ 그는 현실적이야.

He is down-to-earth.
*down-to-earth = realistic, practical

□ 그는 경계심이 많아.

He is precautious.
*precautious = wary

□ 그녀는 의심이 많아.

She is skeptical.

She is doubting about ~.
*doubting = doubtful
*about 뒤에는 무엇에 대해 의심이 많은지 대상이 나온다.

□ 그녀는 엄격해.

She is strict.
*strict = stern, severe

07 열정적인 성격

7번 유형은 Enthusiast(열정가)로 매사에 낙관적이고 긍정적인 삶의 태도를 지닌 사람들입니다. 호기심이 대단히 많아 항상 분주히 돌아다니기 때문에 때때로 어린아이처럼 distracted(산만한)하다는 말을 듣기도 합니다. 유머 감각이 풍부하고 짜릿한 흥분과 자극을 즐깁니다.

원어민 발음 듣기 ☑□　회화 훈련 □□　듣기 훈련 □□

☐ 그는 긍정적이야.

He is positive.
*positive = half-full, optimistic, affirmative

☐ 그는 말보다 행동이 앞서.

He is hasty.
*hasty = rash, brash

He acts rashly.

☐ 그는 앞에 나서기를 좋아해.

He likes people's attention.

He likes to be spotlighted.
*spotlighted = limelighted

☐ 그녀는 호기심이 많아.

She is full of curiosity.

She wants to satisfy her curiosity.

☐ 그녀는 (매우) 열정적이야.

She is (tremendously) passionate.

She is enthusiastic.

☐ 그녀는 짜릿한 흥분과 자극을 즐겨.

She enjoys being thrilled.

She needs a constant stimulus.

☐ 그는 유머 감각이 있어.

He has a sense of humor.

☐ 그는 어린아이 같아.

He acts like a kid.

☐ 그는 항상 분주해.

He is always busy.

He keeps himself busy.

☐ 그녀는 산만해.

She is always distracted.
*distracted = unfocused, inattentive

☐ 그녀는 무모해.

She can be reckless.
*reckless = thoughtless, heady

She does reckless things.

📝 **Notes**

half-full (술잔의 술이 반이나 남았다고) 긍정적으로 생각하는　brash 성급한, 경솔한　tremendously 엄청나게
stimulus 자극, 자극적인 것　distracted 주의가 산만한, 심란한　heady 성급한　reckless 앞뒤를 가리지 않는

08 솔직하고 과감한 성격

Challenger(도전가)인 8번 유형은 self-confident(자신만만한)하고 의지가 강해서 남으로부터 간섭받는 것을 매우 싫어하고 자기 생각대로 판단하는 스타일입니다. open-hearted(솔직하고)하고 결단력 있으며 타고난 리더십이 있어 사람들을 쉽게 끌어모을 수 있습니다.

원어민 발음 듣기 ☑□   회화 훈련 □□   듣기 훈련 □□

□ 그는 의지가 강해.
He is strong.
He has a strong will.

□ 그녀는 남의 간섭을 매우 싫어해.
She hates interruption.
*interruption = interference

□ 그는 독자적으로 판단해.
He is independent.
He is opinionated.
He has his own idea.

□ 그녀는 자기주장대로 행동해.
She acts independently.
She doesn't listen to anyone.

□ 그녀는 자신만만해.
She is self-confident.
She is full of self-confidence.
She has great faith in herself.

□ 그는 솔직해.
He is honest.
*honest = straight-forward

□ 그는 숨김이 없어.
He is open-hearted.

□ 그녀는 결단력이 있어.
She is decisive.
*decisive = determined

□ 그녀는 리더십이 있어.
She has leadership.

□ 그녀는 (틈만 나면) 남과 잘 다퉈.
She picks a fight at the slightest.
She likes to argue.
She looks for friction.

📋 Notes

strong will 강한 의지   opinionated 자기주장을 굽히지 않는, 독선적인   self-confident 자신감 넘치는   have faith in ~에 믿음이 있다   open-hearted 속을 터놓는, 숨김없는   pick a fight 싸움(시비)를 걸다   at the slightest 틈만 나면, 걸핏하면   friction (사람, 물건 간의) 마찰, 분쟁

09 외유내강인 성격

Peacemaker(조정자, 중재자)라는 별칭답게 9번 유형은 성격이 온화해서 긍정적으로 생각하며 항상 모든 것에서 장점을 찾으려는 노력을 게을리하지 않습니다. 자신의 노력으로 화합을 이끌어 냈을 때 가장 큰 기쁨을 느끼지만, 자기주장이 없어 '태평하다', '걱정이 없다', '소극적이다'라는 평가를 받기도 합니다.

원어민 발음 듣기 ☑□   회화 훈련 □□   듣기 훈련 □□

☐ 그는 좋은 쪽으로만 생각해.	He tries to be positive. He looks on the bright side.
☐ 그녀는 장점을 찾으려고 노력해.	She tries to find strong points of everything.
☐ 그는 온화한 성격이야.	He is gentle. *gentle=quiet, mild
☐ 그는 화합을 도모하는 역할을 좋아해.	He wants to be the one who brings harmony to people.
☐ 그는 평화를 갈구해.	He longs for peace.
☐ 그녀는 외유내강해.	She looks gentle but tough in spirit. She is an iron hand in a velvet glove.
☐ 그는 자기주장을 하지 않아.	He doesn't usually express his opinion.
☐ 그는 남의 의견에 쉽게 동의해.	He easily agrees with others.
☐ 그는 걱정이 별로 없어.	He doesn't worry much. He doesn't have many worries.
☐ 그녀는 태평해.	She is easy-going. She has a happy-go-lucky attitude.
☐ 그는 소극적이야.	He is passive (in everything). He is faint-hearted.
☐ 그는 현실 도피적이야.	He buries his head in the sand. *buries=hides He can't confront reality.

📑 **Notes**

long for 갈구하다, 염원하다 iron hand 내면의 강인함 velvet glove 벨벳 장갑, 외면적인 상냥함 happy-go-lucky 태평스러운, 되는 대로 맡겨두는 bury one's head in the sand 겁 많은, 현실 도피적인

10 기타

이번에는 성격을 묻는 표현부터 다소 부정적인 성격을 묘사하는 표현들을 살펴보겠습니다. '이기적인', '매사에 부정적인', '교활한', '폭력적인', '덜렁대는', '우유부단한', '고집불통인', '미성숙한' 등은 영어로 뭐라고 할까요?

원어민 발음 듣기 ☑□   회화 훈련 □□   듣기 훈련 □□

□ 그녀의 성격은 어떠니?
What is she like?
What's her personality?

□ 그의 성격을 묘사해 봐.
Describe what he's like.
Can you describe what he's like?

□ 그녀는 이기적이야.
She is selfish.

□ 그녀는 영리해.
She is smart.
*smart = bright, clever
She has the brains.

□ 그는 아주 명석해.
He is quite brilliant.

□ 그녀는 현명한 여자야.
She is a wise woman.

□ 그녀는 부정적이야.
She is pessimistic.
*pessimistic = half-empty, gloomy

□ 그녀는 성숙하지 못해.
She is immature.

□ 그녀는 고집불통이야.
She is stubborn.

□ 그는 쌀쌀맞아.
He is cold.

□ 그는 교활해.
He is cunning.
*cunning = manipulative

□ 그는 성질이 급해.
He is hot-tempered.
*hot-tempered = short-tempered
He has a hot temper.
*hot temper = short temper

□ 그는 폭력적이야.
He is violent.

□ 그녀는 덜렁대.
She is clumsy.

□ 그녀는 꼼꼼해.
She is meticulous.

Chapter 07

성격

127

☐ 그녀는 정리 정돈을 잘하는 사람이야.	She is organized.	

☐ 그녀는 정리 정돈을 잘하는 사람이야.　She is organized.

☐ 그녀는 외향적이야.　She is very outgoing.
*outgoing = extrovert

☐ 그녀는 내성적이야.　She is an introvert.

☐ 그는 개인적인 일은 이야기하지 않아.　He is private.

☐ 그는 비밀이 많아.　He has many secrets.

☐ 그는 사치스러워.　He is extravagant.

☐ 그는 보수적이야.　He's conventional.
*conventional = traditional, orthodox

☐ 그녀는 충동적이야.　She is impulsive.
*impulsive = impetuous

☐ 그녀는 엉뚱해.　She is eccentric.

☐ 그녀는 미쳤어.　She is a psycho.

☐ 그는 수다스러워.　He talks a lot.
　He is talkative.

☐ 그는 말없이 조용해.　He is quiet.

☐ 그는 거만해.　He is arrogant.
*arrogant = haughty
　He acts big.
　He is too proud of himself.

☐ 그녀는 겸손해.　She is moderate.
*moderate = humble

☐ 그는 우유부단해.　He is indecisive.
*indecisive = wishy-washy
　He can't make up his mind easily.

☐ 그는 밝고 명랑해.　He is bright and cheerful.

☐ 그는 여성적이야.　He is sissy.
*sissy = womanish
　He is a pussy (cat).

☐ 그녀는 남성적이야.　She is manlike.
*manlike = mannish

Chapter 08

사랑
Love

01 소개팅에서

지인의 소개로 만나는 blind date(소개팅)와 관련해서 '~와 소개팅을 시켜 주다'는 set ~ up이라고 표현합니다. 모르는 사람들끼리 만날 수 있도록 setting(주선)을 해 준다는 의미이죠. 소개팅과 관련된 다양한 표현들을 영어로 어떻게 말하는지 알아볼까요?

원어민 발음 듣기 ☑️☐   회화 훈련 ☐☐   듣기 훈련 ☐☐

☐ 소개팅 시켜 줄게.
I'll set you up with someone.
*set = fix
Let me introduce you to someone.

☐ 그녀는 내 친구야.
She is my friend.
*friend → colleague from work (직장 동료)

☐ (좋은 사람) 소개시켜 줘.
Set me up with someone (nice).
Fix me up.
Would you introduce me to someone?
Can you set me up on a blind date?

☐ 어떤 남자 스타일을 좋아해?
What is your type?
What kind of guys do you like?
*like = prefer
What are you looking for in a guy?

☐ 성격 좋은 사람이 좋아.
I like a good-hearted person.
I like someone who has good personality.

☐ 잘생긴 사람이 좋아.
I like a good-looking guy.

☐ 돈 잘 쓰는 사람이 좋아.
I like a big spender.
I like a guy who's generous with his money.

☐ 같이 나가 줄까?
Do you need a chaperon(e)?
Do you need some help?

☐ 소개팅 어땠어?
How was your blind date?

☐ 그 여자(소개팅 상대) 어땠어?
What's she like?

☐ 그녀가 너무 마음에 들어.
I really like her.
She is so my type.
She is the person that I've dreamed about.
She is such a turn-on.

□ 그녀는 내게 너무나 과분해.	She is out of my league.	
□ 그 사람 괜찮았어.	He is fine.	
	He is not so bad.	
□ 또 만나기로 했어?	Are you guys going to meet again?	
	Are you going to ask her out again?	
	Do you have a second date with him?	
□ (그다지) 내 타입은 아니야.	She is (so) not my type.	
	*so → exactly (not 뒤에 붙는다.)	
	She is not my kind of girl.	
	She is such a turn-off.	
□ (그녀와) 서로 잘 안 맞아.	We don't have chemistry together.	
	The chemistry with her isn't right.	
□ 그와 더 만나 봐.	Why don't you have another date with him?	
	Give him another chance.	
□ 그는 너를 맘에 들어 하던데.	I hear he likes you.	

DIALOGUE

A How was your first date?
B Well, she's not exactly my type.
A So, you're not going to ask her out again?
B Of course I am. Actually, I already did. We have a second date tonight.

A 소개팅 어땠어?
B 뭐, 글쎄. 그녀가 내 스타일은 아니어서.
A 그러면 데이트 신청 안 하겠네?
A 물론 하지. 사실 이미 했는걸. 오늘 밤에 다시 만나기로 했어.

Chapter 08 사랑

📑 Notes

set A up with B A를 B에게 소개시켜 주다(= fix A up with B) big spender 돈 씀씀이가 큰 사람
chaperon(e) 샤프롱(젊은 여성이 사교계에 나갈 때 도와주는 중년 여성), 남녀가 처음 만날 때 중간에서 도와주는 사람
turn-on 흥분시키는 것(사람) be out of one's league 과분하다, 상대가 안 되다 ask out 데이트 신청하다
turn-off 지루하게 만드는 것(사람) chemistry 서로 친해지는 친근감 give ~ a chance ~에게 기회를 주다

02 신상 파악하기

MP3를 들어보세요 08-U02

소개팅 자리에서 만난 사람들이 서로에 대한 본격적인 신상 파악에 들어갈 때 age(나이)와 occupation (직업)은 물론 family(가족), hobby(취미), school(학교), major(전공) 등에 대한 다양한 이야기를 나누죠. 하지만 초면에 너무 무례하거나 실례가 되는 질문은 자제하는 것이 좋습니다.

원어민 발음 듣기 ☑□ 회화 훈련 □□ 듣기 훈련 □□

□ 궁금한 거 물어보세요.
Ask anything about me.
What do you want to know about me?

□ 저한테 궁금한 거 없으세요?
Aren't you curious about me?

□ 나이는 몇 살이에요?
How old are you?
May I ask how old you are?
What is your age?

□ 저와 동갑이네요.
We're both of same age.

□ 저보다 세 살 위네요.
You're three years older than me.

□ 저보다 세 살 아래네요.
You're three years younger than me.

□ 몇 살 같아 보여요?
How old do I look?
Can you guess my age?

□ 직업은 뭐예요?
What do you do (for a living)?
What's your profession?
What's your occupation?
What line of business are you in?

□ 일은 마음에 들어요?
Do you like your job?
*job = work
Are you satisfied with your work?

□ 가족은 어떻게 되나요?
How big is your family?

□ 형제는 어떻게 되나요?
Do you have any siblings?

□ 취미는 무엇인가요?
What's your hobby?
What do you usually do when you are free?

□ 소개팅 자주 하나요?
Are you on a blind date a lot?

□ 주말엔 주로 뭐하나요?	What do you do on the weekend?
□ 어떤 공부했어요?	What did you study?
	What was your major?
□ 종교는 뭐예요?	What's your religion?
	What religion do you believe in?
□ 무슨 띠예요?	What's your zodiac sign?
□ 전 쥐띠예요.	(I was born in the Year of) The Rat.
□ 별자리는 무엇인가요?	What's your star sign?
	What's your constellation?
□ 탄생석은 뭐예요?	What's your birth stone?
□ 물고기자리예요.	It's the Fishes.
□ 요즘은 어떤 것에 관심 있나요?	What interests you these days?
	What are you interested in these days?

📋 **별자리**(star sign, constellation)

Aries/the Ram 양자리	Libra/the Scales 천칭자리
Taurus/the Bull 황소자리	Scorpio/the Scorpion 전갈자리
Gemini/the Twins 쌍둥이자리	Sagittarius/the Archer 사수자리
Cancer/the Crab 게자리	Capricorn/the Goat 염소자리
Leo/the Lion 사자자리	Aquarius/the Water Bearer 물병자리
Virgo/the Virgin 처녀자리	Pisces/the Fishes 물고기자리

DIALOGUE

A Ask anything about me.
B Okay, I don't even know your age. How old are you?
A How old do I look?
B I'm not good at guessing people's age, but maybe around 30?

A 저에 대해 뭐든지 물어보세요.
B 좋아요. 아직 당신 나이도 모르는데요. 몇 살이세요?
A 몇 살처럼 보여요?
B 사람들 나이 맞추는 거 소질 없기는 하지만 한 서른 살쯤인가요?

03 데이트 신청하기

상대방이 마음에 들어 데이트 신청을 할 때 가장 흔하게 쓰는 표현은 Would you like a coffee with me?(커피 한잔 할래요?)나 Would you like to have dinner with me?(저녁 같이 할래요?)입니다. 꼭 커피나 식사에 관심이 있다기보다는 그 시간 동안 서로에 대해 알아가고 좀 더 발전된 관계를 원한다는 의미입니다.

원어민 발음 듣기 ☑□   회화 훈련 □□   듣기 훈련 □□

☐ 데이트 신청할게요.	I'd like to ask you out.
☐ 저랑 데이트할래요?	Do you want to go out with me? Would you go on a date with me?
☐ 오늘 저녁 데이트해 줄래요?	Would you be my date this evening?
☐ 이번 주말에 시간 있어요?	What are you doing this weekend? Are you free this weekend?
☐ 사귀는 사람 있어요?	Are you seeing someone? Do you have a boyfriend?
☐ 나 어떻게 생각해요?	What do you think about me? What do you think of me as your girlfriend?
☐ 커피 한잔 할래요?	Would you like a (cup of) coffee with me?
☐ 저녁 같이 할래요?	Would you like to have dinner with me? Do you want to have dinner with me?
☐ 술 한잔 할래요?	Can I buy you a drink?
☐ 영화 보러 갈래요?	Do you want to see a movie with me?
☐ 드라이브 갈래요?	Do you want to go for a ride?
☐ 좋아요.	That sounds great. I'd love to.
☐ 안 되겠어요.	Sorry, I can't.
☐ 먼저 데이트 신청한 적 있어?	Have you (ever) asked a guy out? Have you made the first move?

04 사랑 고백

사랑을 고백하는 표현은 매우 다양합니다. 흔하게는 I love you.(사랑해.)에서부터 I'm in love with you.(사랑에 빠졌어.), I'm crazy about you.(너에게 미쳐 있어.), I can't live without you.(너 없이 못살아.), I've never felt this way before.(이런 느낌 처음이야.)와 같이 강한 표현들도 있습니다.

원어민 발음 듣기 ☑□　회화 훈련 □□　듣기 훈련 □□

☐ 사랑해. / 사랑에 빠졌어.	I love you. I'm in love with you. I'm falling in love with you.
☐ 넌 내 마음을 훔쳐 갔어.	You stole my heart.
☐ 내 마음 전부를 주고 싶어.	I want to give you my whole heart.
☐ 홀딱 반했어.	I have a huge crush on him. *huge=major I have the biggest crush on her.
☐ 첫눈에 반했어.	It was love at first sight. We clicked right away. I just knew she was the one.
☐ 널 사랑하는 것 같아.	I think I'm in love with you.
☐ 그를 좋아하는 것 같아.	I have feelings for him. I think I like him.
☐ 그녀에게 끌려.	I'm attracted to her.
☐ 이런 느낌 처음이야.	I've never felt this (way) before. It's the first time to feel this way.
☐ 네가 염려돼.	I care about you.
☐ 너한테 미쳐 있어.	I'm crazy about you.
☐ 난 너 없이 못 살아.	I can't live without you. *live=survive, breathe
☐ 너는 내게 전부야.	You're everything to me. You're the world to me.

Chapter 08

사랑

135

네가 늘 보고 싶어.	I miss you all the time.
요즘 네 생각만 해.	You're all I think about lately.
	I think about you all the time.
너에 대해 모든 것을 알고 싶어.	I want to get to know all about you.
우린 잘 어울리는 한 쌍이야.	We belong together.
혼자인 건 정말 싫어.	I hate being single.
네 남자 친구가 되고 싶어.	I want to be your boyfriend.
내 인생에 여자는 너뿐이야.	You're the woman of my life.
너처럼 아름다운 여자는 처음 봤어.	You're the most beautiful girl I've ever seen.

 Notes

be in love with ~와 사랑에 빠지다(= fall in love with) have a crush on ~에게 반하다 click 서로 잘 통하다
right away 바로, 단번에 feelings 감정, 느낌 be attracted to ~에게 끌리다, 매력을 느끼다 get to know
알게 되다, 친해지다 belong ~에게 속하다

05 수락과 거절

상대방의 사랑 고백을 받아들일 때 I love you, too.(나도 널 사랑해.) 혹은 Let's date.(우리 사귀자.)와 같은 표현을 쓸 수 있습니다. 거절할 때는 I like you, but I don't love you.(널 좋아하지만 사랑하지는 않아.), You're a great person, but….(넌 좋은 사람이지만…….)과 같은 말로 얼버무리기도 합니다.

원어민 발음 듣기 ☑□   회화 훈련 □□   듣기 훈련 □□

☐ 나도 널 사랑해.	I love you, too.
	I'm in love with you, too.
	Ditto.
☐ 그래, 우리 사귀자.	Okay, let's date.
	We're boyfriend and girlfriend now.
☐ 언제 고백하나 기다렸어.	I thought you never ask me out.
☐ 생각해 볼게.	It's sweet, but I'll think about it.
	Give me some time to think about it.
☐ 너한테 관심 없어.	I'm not interested in you.
	I don't feel anything for you.
☐ 널 좋아하지 않아.	I don't like you.
☐ 널 이성으로 여기지 않아.	You're just my friend, nothing more.
	I don't have any romantic feelings for you.
	I don't feel the same way you feel about me.
☐ 몇 번 잔 것뿐이잖아.	We slept together a few times.
	We just hooked up a couple of times.
☐ 서로 즐겼을 뿐이잖아.	We were (just) having fun.
☐ 친구로 지내자.	Let's be friends.
☐ 우린 너무 달라.	We're completely different.
	We're total opposite.
☐ 다른 사람과 헤어진 지 얼마 안 됐어.	I've just got out of long relationship.
	I just broke up with someone.

Chapter 08
사랑

06 연애 초기

연애할 때 What shall we do today?(뭐 할까?), Is there a place you want to go?(가고 싶은 데 있어?)라는 말은 일상적으로 쓰고, 집에 데려다 주면서 Don't go.(가지 마.), When can I see you again?(또 언제 만나?)와 같은 말도 자주 하죠. 이러한 표현들을 영어로는 어떻게 하면 되는지 살펴보겠습니다.

원어민 발음 듣기 ☑□   회화 훈련 □□   듣기 훈련 □□

□ 오늘 뭐 할까요?
What do you want to do today?
What shall we do today?

□ 어디 가고 싶어요?
Is there a place you want to go?
Do you want to go somewhere?

□ 집에 일찍 가야 돼요.
I have to go home early.

□ 좀 더 같이 있어요.
Stay a little longer.
Can't you stay a little longer?
I'd like to be with you a little longer.

□ 가지 마세요.
Don't go.
*go = leave

□ 집에 바래다줄게요.
I'll walk you home.
I'll drive you home.
I'll escort you home.

□ (집에) 다 왔네요.
We're already here.
This is me.
It's my place.

□ 오늘 즐거웠어요.
I had a great time today.
*great = wonderful, nice
It was fun today.
Thank you for taking me out today.

□ 언제 또 만날 수 있어요?
When can I see you again?
I want to see you again.

□ 전화해요.
Call me.

□ 밤에 전화해도 돼요?
Can I call you at night?

□	손잡고 싶어요.	I want to hold your hand.
□	키스해도 돼요?	Can I kiss you? I want to kiss you.
□	꽃을 사 주고 싶어요.	I want to buy you a flower.
□	내 친구들 소개시켜 줄게요.	I want to introduce my friends to you. I'd like you to meet my friends.
□	당신을 좋아할 거예요.	They're going to love you.
□	만난 지 세 달 정도 됐어요.	We've been going out for about three months. We've been seeing each other for over three months.

DIALOGUE

A I had a great time today.
   Thank you for taking me out.
B My pleasure. When can I see you again?
A Soon. Call me.

A 오늘 정말 즐거웠어요. 데이트 신청해 줘서 고마워요.
B 천만에요. 언제 또 만날 수 있어요?
A 조만간이요. 전화 줘요.

Notes

walk ~ home ~를 걸어서 집까지 데려다 주다 drive ~ home ~를 차를 태워서 집까지 데려다 주다 escort 에스
코트하다, 바래다주다 take ~ out ~를 데리고 나가다 go out 데이트하다, 교제하다

07 연애 중

정식으로 사귀게 되었다면 We're a couple now.(우리 이제 커플이야.) 혹은 We're together now.(우리 이제 사귀어.)라고 말할 수 있습니다. 이때 You look cute together. 하면 "둘이 잘 어울려요."라는 뜻이 됩니다.

원어민 발음 듣기 ☑☐   회화 훈련 ☐☐   듣기 훈련 ☐☐

□ 너희 둘 잘 어울려.

You look cute together.
You are a lovely couple.
*lovely = adorable
You are perfect for each other.

□ 너희는 천생연분이야.

You guys are a match made in heaven.
You are meant for each other.
You're made for each other.

□ 둘이 사귀면 잘 어울릴 텐데.

You can make a cute couple.

□ 너희 사귀니?

Are you two dating?
Are you a couple?
Are you seeing each other?

□ 우리 (이제) 사귀어.

We're a couple (now).
We're together (now).
We're dating.

□ 둘이 어떻게 만났어?

How did you (two) meet?

□ 데이트한 지 얼마나 됐어?

How long have you been going out?
How long have you been seeing her?

□ 1년 됐어.

It's been a year.

□ 만났다 헤어졌다 한 지 2년 됐어.

On and off for two years.

□ 사귄 지 오래됐어.

We've been seeing each other for a long time.

□ 우린 결혼한 노부부 같아.

I feel like we're an old married couple.

□ 우리 처음으로 싸웠어.

We had our first fight.

□ 무엇 때문에 싸웠는데?

What did you fight about?

□ 우린 늘 싸워.	We constantly argue. *argue=fight	
□ 그가 요즘 이상하게 굴어.	He has been acting weird.	
□ 양다리 걸치고 있는 것 같아.	I think he is sitting on the fence.	
□ 바람피우는 것 같아.	I think he is cheating on me.	
□ 우리 구속하는 사이 아니잖아, 그렇지?	We're not exclusive, aren't we?	
□ 그가 진지한 관계를 회피해.	He has a commitment issue. He's terrified by commitment.	
□ 그는 남자 친구 감이 아니야.	He is not boyfriend material. He doesn't know how to be a boyfriend.	

DIALOGUE

A How long have you two been going out?

B Well, let's see. On and off for four years.
   I feel like we're already an old married couple.

A 너희 두 사람 데이트한 지 얼마나 됐니?

B 글쎄, 어디 보자. 만났다 헤어졌다 하면서 4년 됐지.
   이미 결혼한 노부부 같은 느낌이야.

 Notes

adorable 귀여운, 사랑스러운 match made in heaven 천생연분(=meant for each other) on and off
했다 안 했다 하는 constantly 지속적으로, 늘 act weird 이상하게 행동하다 sit on the fence 양다리 걸치
다 cheat on ~를 속이다, ~에게 사기 치다, 바람피우다 exclusive 서로에게 독점적인 존재인, 한 사람만 만나는
commitment 진지한 약속, 언약 be terrified by ~에 질겁하다, 공포에 질리다 boyfriend material 남자 친구
가 될 만한 자질

08 프러포즈

청혼의 표현 역시 매우 다양합니다. 간단하게는 Will you marry me?(결혼해 줄래?)부터 조금 더 로맨틱하게 I want to grow old with you.(너와 함께 나이 들고 싶어.), I want to spend the rest of my life with you.(너와 평생 함께 있고 싶어.)와 같은 표현도 있습니다.

원어민 발음 듣기 ✔☐　　회화 훈련 ☐☐　　듣기 훈련 ☐☐

☐ 그녀에게 언제 프러포즈할 거야?	When are you going to propose to her? *When 대신 How를 쓰면 '어떻게' 청혼할지 방법을 묻는 표현.
☐ 반지 샀어?	Did you pick a ring? *pick=buy
☐ 오늘 프러포즈할 거야.	I'm going to propose to her today. I'm going to pop the question today.
☐ 거절하면 어쩌지?	What if she says "No"?
☐ 결혼해 줘.	Marry me. Will you marry me? *will 대신 would를 쓰면 좀 더 정중한 표현이 된다.
☐ 내 아내가 되어 줘.	Would you be my wife?
☐ 내 아이의 엄마가 되어 줘.	Would you be mother of my children?
☐ 함께 나이 들고 싶어.	I want to grow old with you.
☐ 아침에 함께 눈뜨고 싶어.	I want to wake up in the morning together.
☐ 너와 늘 함께 있고 싶어.	I want to be with you all the time. I want to spend the rest of my life with you.
☐ 너는 바로 내가 찾던 그 사람이야.	You're the one.
☐ 넌 내 거야.	You're mine.
☐ 넌 나를 채워 주는 사람이야.	You complete me.
☐ 따님과의 결혼을 허락해 주세요.	May I have your blessing to marry your daughter?
☐ 그래, 결혼하자.	Yes, let's get married.

09 결혼 생활

"결혼 생활이 행복해."는 I'm happily married.라고 말합니다. 아이를 가지려고 준비 중일 때는 I want to be a mom.(아이를 가질까 해.)이라고 하죠. 임산부에게 출산일이 언제인지를 물을 때는 When is your due date?라고 합니다.

원어민 발음 듣기 ☑□　회화 훈련 □□　듣기 훈련 □□

□ 우리 막 약혼했어.	We just got engaged.
□ 우리 곧 결혼해.	We're getting married.
□ 날짜는 정했어?	Did you set the wedding date?
□ 결혼식은 언제야?	When is your wedding?
□ 내년 가을이야.	It's next autumn.
□ 결혼 준비는 잘 되어 가?	How's your wedding preparation (going)?
□ 준비할 게 너무 많아.	There are too many things to prepare for the wedding.
□ 우리 막 결혼했어.	We just got married. We're newlyweds.
□ 중매 결혼 했어.	We had an arranged marriage.
□ 연애 결혼 했어.	We had a love marriage.
□ 아직 신혼이야.	We are in our honeymoon.
□ 7년 연애 끝에 결혼했어.	We got married after 7 years dating.
□ 결혼 생활이 행복해.	I'm happily married.
□ 우리 집 샀어.	We've bought a new house.
□ 가족 모임이 있어.	We have a family gathering. We have the family reunion.
□ 아이를 가질까 해.	We're thinking of having a baby. I want to be a mom.
□ 나 임신했어.	I'm pregnant. I'm going to have a baby.

143

I'm going to be a mother.

I have a bun in the oven.

□ 임신 축하해!   Congratulations on becoming a mom!

□ 출산 예정일이 언제야?   When is your due date?

When are you expecting?

□ 두 달 남았어.   Two more months to go.

Two months are left.

□ 그녀는 쌍둥이 아들을 낳았어.   She gave birth to twin boys.

□ 아이가 너를 꼭 닮았어.   Your baby looks just like you.

□ 아이가 네 코를 빼닮았어.   Your baby has got your nose.

□ 잘 키워야지.   We'll take good care of our baby.

We'll do our best to raise our baby well.

□ 육아 도우미가 와.   I have a helper for baby-caring.
*helper for baby-caring
→ helper for housekeeping (가사 도우미)

□ 항상 돈이 궁해.   I'm always short of money.

Money is always tight.

□ 우리 결혼 10주년이야.   It's our 10th wedding anniversary.

We've been married for 10 years.

□ 우리 별거 중이야.   We're separated.

□ 우리(나) 이혼할 거야.   We're getting divorced.

We're falling apart.

I'm leaving him.

DIALOGUE

A   I have big news for you. I'm two months pregnant.
B   Congratulations. You're going to be a great mom.

A   빅 뉴스가 있어. 나 임신 2개월이야.
B   축하해. 넌 훌륭한 엄마가 될 거야.

10 이별할 때

"우리 헤어져."라고 말할 때는 '헤어지다', '결별하다'의 의미인 break up을 써서 Let's break up.이라고 합니다. 이별의 이유로는 We're completely different.(우린 너무 달라.), I've met someone else.(다른 사람이 생겼어.), I don't love you.(너를 사랑하지 않아.) 등이 있겠죠.

원어민 발음 듣기 ☑☐　회화 훈련 ☐☐　듣기 훈련 ☐☐

☐ 우리 헤어져.	Let's break up.
	I have to break up with you.
☐ 다시는 만나지 말자.	I don't (ever) want to see you again.
☐ 전화도 하지 마.	Don't even call me.
☐ 너를 (더 이상) 사랑하지 않아.	I don't love you (any more).
☐ 우린 너무 달라.	We're completely different.
	We want completely different things.
☐ 나 다른 사람이 생겼어.	I've met someone else.
	I love someone else.
☐ (나에게) 이러지 마.	Please don't do this (to me).
☐ 가지 마.	Don't leave me.
☐ 내가 뭘 잘못했어?	What did I do wrong?
	Tell me what I've done.
	It's because of me?
☐ 다 내 탓이야.	It's because of me.
	It's all my fault.
☐ 기회를 줘.	Give me another chance.
☐ 앞으로 잘 할게.	I'll do better. *better → different (다른)
	I'll make it up to you.
☐ 우린 끝났어.	We're done.
	I'm done with you.
☐ 더 이상 참을 수 없어.	I can't take him anymore.
	I'm sick and tired of him.

나 그녀에게 차였어.	I got dumped by my girlfriend.
	She dumped me.
내가 찼어.	I dumped him.
마음이 (갈가리) 찢어져.	He broke my heart (piece by piece).
	I'm heart-broken.
	Something broke inside of me.
그녀를 못 잊겠어.	I can't forget her.
	I can't get over her.
	I miss her.
그녀에 대한 내 사랑을 멈출 수 없어.	I can't stop loving her.
그가 그리울 거야.	I'll miss him.
세상에 남자(여자)는 많아.	There are many other fish in the sea.
그만 정리해.	(It's time to) Move on.

📝 Notes

make it up to ~에게 보상하다 be done with ~과 끝나다, 끝장나다 be sick and tired of ~에 넌더리가 나다 get dumped 차이다 dump ~를 차다 heart-broken 가슴이 찢어지는, 슬픔에 잠긴 get over 어려움을 극복하다, 잊다 other fish in the sea 바다의 다른 물고기(교제할 상대가 많다는 의미) move on 지난 것을 정리하고 새것으로 옮겨가다, 새 출발하다

146

11 재회

헤어졌다가 다시 만난 연인들은 I missed you.(보고 싶었어.), I thought about you a lot.(네 생각 많이 했어.)과 같은 말을 할 수 있겠죠. 관계를 다시 시작할 생각이라면 Are you seeing anyone?(만나는 사람 있어?)이라고 물어보겠지만, 다시 시작하지 않을 거라면 I wish you happiness.(너의 행복을 빌게.)라고 하죠.

원어민 발음 듣기 ☑️□   회화 훈련 □□   듣기 훈련 □□

□ 네가 보고 싶었어.	I missed you.
□ 내 생각한 적 있어?	Have you ever thought about me?
□ 네 생각 많이 나더라.	I thought about you a lot.
□ (조금) 어색하다.	It's (a little) awkward. I feel awkward.
□ 하나도 안 변했네.	You haven't changed a bit.
□ 너 (많이) 변했구나.	You've changed (a lot).
□ 요즘 사귀는 사람 있어?	Are you seeing anyone special? Are you seeing someone romantically? Are you in a relationship? Do you have anyone in particular now?
□ 만나는 사람 있어.	I have someone special.
□ 너의 행복을 빌게.	I wish you a happy life. I wish you happiness. Have a great life.
□ 나 아직 혼자야.	I'm still single. I'm not involved with anyone. I have no one in particular now.
□ 우리 다시 시작하자.	Let's start (all) over.
□ 이번엔 다를 거야.	It'll be different this time.
□ 그땐 내가 너무 어렸어(어리석었어).	I was too young and foolish.

Chapter 08 사랑

147

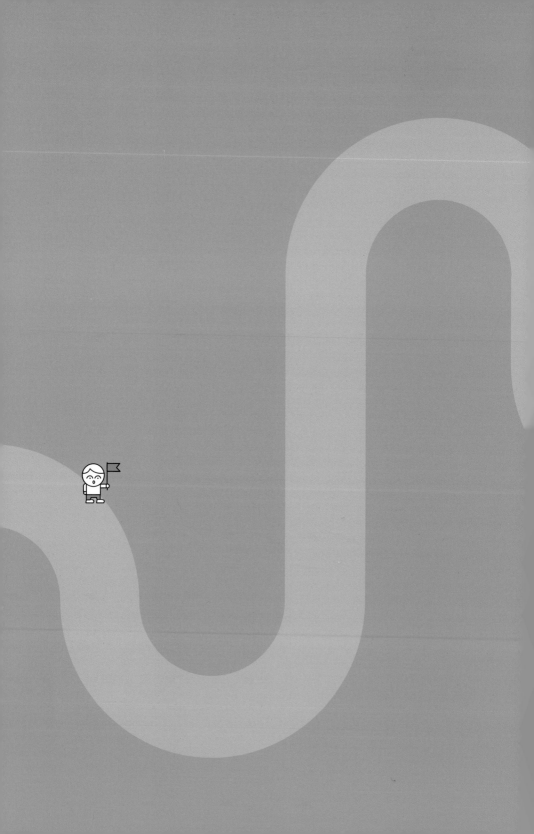

하루 일과
Daily routine

01 평일 오전

weekdays(평일) 오전은 대부분 출근이나 등교 준비로 바쁩니다. 씻고, 식사를 하고, 옷을 챙겨 입는 등의 준비를 하죠. 아이가 있다면 책가방 싸기나 과제물 챙기는 것을 도와주고 학교에 바래다주어야 합니다. 집을 나서기 전 문단속하는 것도 빼먹으면 안 되겠죠. 이런 평일 오전에 하는 일에 대한 표현들을 살펴보겠습니다.

원어민 발음 듣기 ☑□   회화 훈련 □□   듣기 훈련 □□

☐ 아침에 일어납니다.	I get up in the morning. *get up = wake up
☐ 하품을 합니다.	I yawn.
☐ 기지개를 켭니다.	I stretch myself.
☐ 침대를 정돈합니다.	I make my bed.
☐ 조깅을 합니다.	I jog.
☐ 양치질을 합니다.	I brush my teeth.
☐ 세수를 합니다.	I wash my face.
☐ 샤워를 합니다.	I take a shower.
☐ 머리를 감습니다.	I wash my hair. I shampoo my hair.
☐ 머리를 빗습니다(손질합니다).	I comb my hair. *comb = brush
☐ 화장을 합니다.	I put on some make-up.
☐ 모닝커피를 마십니다.	I have morning coffee.
☐ 아침 식사를 합니다.	I have breakfast. *have 대신 skip을 쓰면 "아침 식사를 거르다"의 의미이다.
☐ 신문을 봅니다.	I read the newspaper.
☐ 라디오를 듣습니다.	I listen to the radio.
☐ 용변을 봅니다.	I go to the bathroom. I use the toilet.
☐ 옷을 갈아입습니다.	I get dressed. I change my clothes.

☐	교복을 입습니다.	I put on my school uniform.
☐	넥타이를 맵니다.	I wear a tie.
☐	신발을 신습니다.	I put on shoes.
☐	아이들을 깨웁니다.	I wake my kids up.
☐	아이의 옷을 입힙니다.	I get my kids dressed.
☐	아이가 가방 싸는 것을 챙겨 줍니다.	I help my kids pack the school bag.
☐	가스를 점검합니다.	I check the gas stove turned-off. *gas stove → room light(전등)
☐	문단속을 합니다.	I check the door locked.
☐	아이를 학교에 바래다줍니다.	I take my kids to school.
☐	출근을 합니다.	I go to work. *go to work = go to the office I leave for work.
☐	학교에 갑니다.	I go to school.
☐	도서관에 갑니다.	I go to the library.

📑 **Notes**

put on 입다, 쓰다, 걸치다 skip 건너뛰다, 뛰어넘다 get dressed 옷을 입다 pack the bag 가방을 싸다 gas stove 가스레인지 lock 잠그다, 닫아걸다 leave for ~하러 떠나다

02 평일 오후, 저녁

평일 오후와 저녁에는 학교 수업이나 업무를 마치고 귀가하기, 저녁 식사 등의 활동이
이루어집니다. 잠자리에 들기까지 TV를 시청하거나 가족들과 담소를 나누기도 하죠.
자기 전에 알람 시계를 맞춰 놓는 일도 잊지 마세요.

원어민 발음 듣기 ☑□ 회화 훈련 □□ 듣기 훈련 □□

☐ 아이를 학교에서 데려옵니다.	I pick my kids up from school.
☐ 식료품을 사러 갑니다.	I go to the grocery store.
☐ 간식거리를 삽니다.	I get some snacks.
☐ 귀가합니다.	I come (back) home.
☐ 불을 켭니다.	I turn on the light.
☐ 저녁을 차립니다.	I cook dinner.
	I fix a meal.
☐ 저녁 식사를 합니다.	I have dinner.
☐ 식탁을 치웁니다.	I clean up the kitchen table.
☐ 설거지를 합니다.	I wash the dishes. *wash = clean
☐ TV를 시청합니다.	I watch TV.
☐ 가족들과 담소를 나눕니다.	I chat with my family.
☐ 아이 잠자리를 봐 줍니다.	I make a bed for my kids.
☐ 아이를 재웁니다.	I put my kids to bed.
☐ 잠자리에 듭니다.	I go to bed.
	I crawl into bed. *crawl into = get into
☐ 알람 시계를 맞춥니다.	I set the alarm clock.
☐ 잠이 듭니다.	I fall asleep.

📑 Notes

grocery (store) 식료품점, 식료잡화점 fix a meal 식사 준비를 하다 make a bed 잠자리를 펴다 put ~ to
bed ~를 재우다

03 주말

꼼짝하기 싫은 weekends(주말)이지만 해야 할 밀린 일들이 많습니다. 집 안 구석구석 청소하기, 빨래하기, 화초에 물 주기, 세탁물 찾기 등이 끝나면 느긋하게 책을 읽거나 음악을 듣기도 하죠. 또한 한 주간 쌓인 스트레스를 풀기 위해 가벼운 운동을 하거나 산책을 즐기는 것도 좋습니다.

원어민 발음 듣기 ☑□   회화 훈련 □□   듣기 훈련 □□

□ 늦잠을 잡니다.	I get up late.
	I sleep in.
	I oversleep.
□ 아침 겸 점심(브런치)을 먹습니다.	I have brunch.
□ 집 안 청소를 합니다.	I clean the house.
□ 바닥을 비질합니다.	I sweep the floor.
□ 가구의 먼지를 텁니다.	I dust the furniture.
□ 욕조를 문질러 닦습니다.	I scrub the bathtub.
	*bathtub → washstand(세면대)
□ 화초에 물을 줍니다.	I water the plants.
□ 빨래를 합니다.	I do laundry.
□ 빨래를 건조대에 넙니다.	I hang wet clothes.
□ 빨래를 갭니다.	I fold clothes.
□ 재활용 쓰레기를 분리합니다.	I recycle garbage waste.
□ 세탁물 찾습니다.	I pick up my clothes from a (dry) cleaner's.
□ 다림질을 합니다.	I iron.
□ 환기를 시킵니다.	I open the windows to get some fresh air.
	I open the windows to let some fresh air in.
□ 영화를 보러 갑니다.	I go to the movies.
□ 음악을 듣습니다.	I listen to the music.
□ 독서를 합니다.	I read a book.
□ 잡지를 뒤적거립니다.	I look through the magazines.
	*magazines → newspapers(신문)

Chapter 09

하루 일과

153

☐ 쇼핑을 갑니다.	I go shopping.
☐ 외식을 합니다.	I eat out.
☐ 미용실에 갑니다.	I go to the beauty salon. *beauty salon = beauty shop
☐ 머리를 자릅니다.	I get my hair cut. *cut = trimmed
☐ 손톱을 깎습니다.	I clip my nails. *clip = cut, trim
☐ 손톱을 다듬습니다.	I do my fingernails. *do = polish, manicure
☐ 집에서 쉽니다.	I relax at home.
☐ 먹는 것으로 스트레스를 풉니다.	I release stress by eating. *release = ease, get rid of
☐ 컴퓨터 게임을 합니다.	I play computer games.
☐ 낮잠을 잡니다.	I take a nap. I nap. *nap = doze off
☐ 빈둥거립니다.	I loaf around all day long.
☐ DVD를 빌립니다.	I borrow a DVD.
☐ 산책을 합니다.	I take a walk. I go for a walk.
☐ 피크닉을 갑니다.	I go for a picnic.
☐ 운동을 합니다.	I exercise. I work out.
☐ 자전거를 탑니다.	I ride a bike. *bike = bicycle
☐ 인라인 스케이트를 타러 갑니다.	I go inline-skating.
☐ 교외로 드라이브를 갑니다.	I go for a drive to the suburbs.
☐ 교회(성당)에 갑니다.	I go to church.
☐ 야식을 먹습니다.	I eat late night comfort food. I enjoy late night snacks.

04 명절, 국경일, 기념일

holidays(명절)에는 가족들이 모두 모여 제사를 지내거나 성묘를 갑니다. 또 전통 음식을 함께 먹고 전통 놀이를 하며 즐거운 시간을 보내기도 하죠. national holidays (국경일)에는 국기를 달고 anniversaries(기념일)에는 축하 파티와 함께 선물을 주고받습니다. 이런 다양한 상황을 영어로는 어떻게 표현할까요?

원어민 발음 듣기 ☑□   회화 훈련 □□   듣기 훈련 □□

☐ 고향 부모님 댁에 갑니다.	I visit my parents at home. I come home. *come = return
☐ 가족과 친척들이 한 자리에 모입니다.	Family and relatives are gathered all together.
☐ 근간의 소식을 교환합니다.	We catch up. We share the news.
☐ 차례(제사)를 지냅니다.	We have memorial services for our ancestors. *memorial services = rites
☐ 제사상을 준비합니다.	We set the memorial table.
☐ 조상님께 절을 합니다.	We show our respect to our ancestors. We bow to our ancestors.
☐ 전통 음식을 먹습니다.	We have our traditional food.
☐ 전통 놀이를 합니다.	We play our traditional games. *games = activities
☐ 성묘를 갑니다.	We go to our family grave. *go to = visit
☐ 벌초를 합니다.	We pull out the weeds around the grave. *grave = site
☐ 국경일에 국기를 답니다.	I fly a flag on a national holiday.
☐ 크리스마스트리를 세웁니다.	I set up a Christmas tree.
☐ 제야의 종소리를 듣습니다.	We listen to the New Year's bell stroke.
☐ 기념일을 축하합니다.	We celebrate our anniversaries.

Chapter 09

하루 일과

155

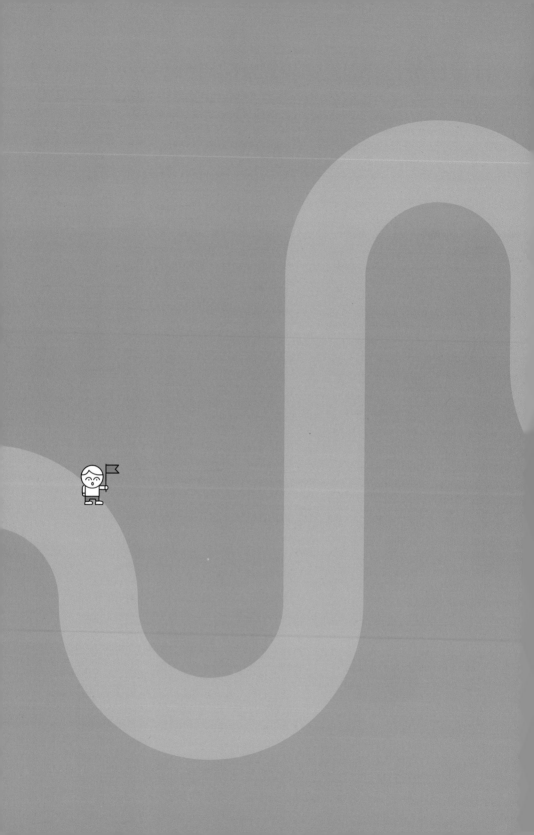

Chapter 10

일상생활
Daily life

01 은행에서

은행에 돈을 '예금하다'는 deposit, '인출하다'는 withdraw입니다. 미국 은행은 통장이 없고, 돈을 입금하거나 출금할 때는 주로 은행에서 발급받은 debit card(현금 지급 카드)를 가지고 ATM에서 처리합니다.

원어민 발음 듣기 ☑☐　회화 훈련 ☐☐　듣기 훈련 ☐☐

☐ 무엇을 도와드릴까요?	What can I help you?
☐ 번호표 뽑고 잠시 기다리세요.	Get your ticket number and wait for a moment.
☐ 계좌를 개설하려고요.	I'd like to open a bank account.
☐ 계좌를 해지하려고요.	I'd like to close my bank account.
☐ 신분증 보여 주세요.	May I see your ID?
☐ 양식을 작성해 주세요.	Fill out this form, please. Would you please fill out this form?
☐ 돈을 예금하고 싶어요.	I'd like to deposit money. I want to make a deposit.
☐ 돈을 인출하고 싶어요.	I'd like to withdraw money. I want to make withdraw.
☐ 돈은 어떻게 드릴까요?	How do you want your money? How would you like your money?
☐ 현금으로, 아니면 수표로 드릴까요?	Cash or check?
☐ 큰 금액, 아니면 소액으로 드릴까요?	Large or small bills?
☐ 금액을 확인하세요.	Check your amount, please. Make sure you have the correct amount.
☐ 신용 카드를 신청하려고요.	I'd like to apply for a credit card.
☐ 현금 서비스를 받고 싶어요.	I'd like to get a cash advance.
☐ 현금 인출 최대 한도액은 얼마죠?	What's the limit on the cash advance? How much money can I withdraw from it?

□ 한도액 초과입니다.	You're overdrawn. You're over your credit limit. Your credit card maxed out.
□ 신용 카드 만기입니다.	Your credit card is expired. Your credit card has been expired. You can't use this credit card.
□ 대출 받으려고요.	I'd like to apply for a loan.
□ 대출 이자는 어떻게 되나요?	What's the interest rate on the loan?
□ 집을 담보로 하려고요.	I'd like to mortgage my house.
□ 금융 상품 상담을 받으려고요.	I'd like to get a counsel about your financial products. Can I get an advice about your financial products?
□ 신규 저축 예금을 들려고요.	I'd like to open a new savings account.
□ 이자율은 어떻게 되나요?	What's the interest rate on deposits?
□ 새 통장을 받으려고요.	I'd like to get a new bankbook. *bankbook = passbook
□ 통장 정리를 해 주세요.	I'd like to update my bankbook.
□ 지폐를 잔돈으로 바꿔 주세요.	Can I get some changes for these bills?
□ 수표를 현금으로 바꾸려고요.	I'd like to cash a check. Could you cash this check?
□ 모두 5만 원짜리로 주세요.	I'd like to have my money in 50,000 won bills. Can I have my money in 50,000 won bills?
□ 인터넷 뱅킹을 신청하려고요.	I'd like to apply for an internet banking service.
□ 자동 이체 신청할게요.	I'd like to set up automatic billing payments.
□ ATM 기계는 어디 있죠?	Where are ATM machines? Where can I find ATM machines?
□ 공과금 전용기는 어디 있죠?	Where is the ATM machine for utility bills?

의사생활
일상생활

◻ ATM에서 통장이 안 나와요.	My bankbook doesn't come out from the ATM machine.
	My bankbook is stuck inside the ATM machine.
◻ (카드) 비밀번호를 잊어버렸어요.	I forgot my (credit card) PIN number.
	I can't remember my PIN number.
◻ 돈이 무단으로 출금됐어요.	Money has been withdrawn without my permission.
	Somebody has withdrawn my money.
◻ 해외 송금은 어떻게 하죠?	How can I send money to overseas?
◻ 요즘 환율이 어떻죠?	What's the current exchange rate?
◻ 달러를 매입하려고요.	I'd like to buy some dollars.
◻ 환전 수수료는 얼마인가요?	How much do you charge for the foreign exchange?
	What's the charge for the foreign exchange?

*charge = fee

📋 각종 공과금(utility bills)

도시가스 gas bill
수도세 water bill
전기세 electricity bill
전화 요금 phone bill
재산세 property tax

주민세 resident tax
국민연금 national pension
의료 보험 medical insurance
자동차세 automobile tax

📝 Notes

bank account 은행 계좌 fill out (서류 등을) 작성하다, 채우다 deposit 예금, 예금하다 withdraw 인출하다, 취소하다 apply for 신청하다 cash advance 현금 서비스 overdraw 초과 인출하다 max out 최고점에 달하다 be expired 만기되다 loan 대출 interest rate 이자율 mortgage 저당, 저당 융자금, 저당잡히다 get a counsel 상담 받다 financial product 금융 상품 bankbook 통장 update one's bankbook 통장 정리하다 automatic billing 자동 이체 utility bills 공과금 be stuck ~에 끼이다 PIN 개인 식별 번호(= personal identification number) permission 허가, 허락 exchange rate 환율 foreign exchange 외국환 거래

160

02 약국에서

미국이나 영국의 약국에서는 약뿐만 아니라 화장품, 잡화류 등도 판매합니다. '약국'을 미국에서는 pharmacy 또는 drugstore라고 하지만, 영국에서는 chemist('s)라고 하니 주의합시다.

원어민 발음 듣기 ☑☐ 회화 훈련 ☐☐ 듣기 훈련 ☐☐

☐ 두통약 주세요.

Can I have some headache pills?

Do you have anything to relieve a headache?

☐ 하루에 몇 번 먹죠?

How many times a day should I take this medication?

☐ 이 약을 식후에 하루 세 번 드세요.

Take this three times a day after meals.

☐ 부작용에 대해 설명해 주세요.

What are some side effects?

Are there any side effects?

☐ 처방전 주세요.

Can I have the prescription?

☐ 끝까지 다 드세요.

Don't skip your medication.

Don't stop taking your medication in the middle.

☐ 시간 맞춰 드세요.

Take the medicine right on time.

Take the medicine regularly.

☐ 한 번에 한 알씩 드세요.

Take a pill at a time.
*pill = tablet, capsule

☐ 한 번에 한 봉씩 드세요.

Take a packet of medicine at a time.

☐ 몸을 따뜻하게 하세요.

Keep your body warm.

☐ 건조한 공기는 안 좋아요.

Keep your nose wet.

☐ 가습기를 쓰세요.

Use a humidifier.

☐ 연고는 상처 부위에 얇게 펴 바르세요.

Apply this ointment thinly on the cut.
*apply = rub

☐ 부작용이 나타나면 복용을 중단하세요.

If you have any side effects, stop taking pills.

☐ 평소에 먹는 약이 있나요?

Are you taking any other medicine?

03 세탁소에서

'세탁소'는 laundry 혹은 dry cleaner's라고 합니다. 미국 등에서는 기계에 코인을 넣고 직접 세탁하는 coin laundry가 많이 보급되어 있어 한국과는 조금 다르죠.

원어민 발음 듣기 ☑☐ 회화 훈련 ☐☐ 듣기 훈련 ☐☐

□ 이 옷들 드라이클리닝해 주세요.
I'd like to get these clothes dry-cleaned.
I want these clothes dry-cleaned.

□ 이 셔츠 다림질해 주세요.
Iron this shirt, please.
Can you iron this shirt?
*iron=press

□ 얼룩 제거해 주세요.
Can you remove these stains?
Do you think you can remove these stains?
*remove=get rid of
*stains=marks, spots

□ 지퍼를 달아 주세요.
Can you get a new zipper on the pants?

□ 바지 길이를 늘려 주세요.
Can you extend the length of the pants?

□ 바지 길이를 줄여 주세요.
Can you shorten the length of the pants?

□ 허리(라인)를 늘려 주세요.
Can you enlarge the waistline?

□ 허리(라인)를 줄여 주세요.
Can you reduce the waistline?

□ 커프스는 잡아 주세요.
Can you make the cuffs?
*make=fold

□ 터진 곳을 기워 주세요.
Can you patch this part?
*patch=stitch

□ 다 되면 문자 드릴게요.
When it's done, I'll text you.
When it's done, I'll let you know by a text.

□ 세탁물 찾으려고요.
I'm here to pick up my laundry.
Can I get my laundry?

□ 다 됐습니다.
Your laundry is all done.
Here they are.

162

□ 아직 덜 됐는데요.	Your laundry is not done yet.
	Your laundry is not ready.
□ 다음에 다시 올까요?	Should I come back later?
	Do you want me to come back later?
□ 내일 저녁에 오세요.	Stop by tomorrow evening.
	*stop by = come by
□ 세탁물 수거(배달)왔습니다.	I'm here to pick up your laundry.
	I'm here to deliver your laundry.
	I'm from a laundry.
	*laundry = cleaner's
□ 다림질이 제대로 안 됐어요.	This isn't pressed properly.
	This part is still wrinkled.
□ 얼룩이 그대로네요.	The stains are still there.
	The stains don't come out at all.
□ 손님의 세탁물을 분실했습니다.	We lost your laundry.
□ 돈은 안 받겠습니다.	I won't charge for this.

A I'd like to get these clothes dry-cleaned.
And please remove these stains.
B Where did you get these stains?
I'm not sure if they will come out.

A 이 옷들 드라이클리닝해 주세요. 그리고 이 얼룩들도 제거해 주시고요.
B 얼룩은 어디서 묻은 겁니까? 빠질지 모르겠네요.

Chapter 10
일상생활

📝 **Notes**

remove 없애다, 제거하다 stain 얼룩, 때 mark 얼룩, 자국, 더러움(= spot) extend 늘리다, 확장시키다
shorten 길이를 줄이다, 짧게 하다 enlarge 크게 하다 reduce 축소하다, 감소시키다 patch 헝겊 조각 등으로 때
우다 pick up (사람, 물건 등을) 데려오다, 찾다 stop by 잠깐 들르다 properly 제대로, 적합하게 wrinkled 주름
진, 구겨진 come out 나오다, 지워지다 charge 부과하다, 값을 매기다

04 미용실에서

'미용실'은 beauty salon이나 hairdresser's shop이라고 합니다. '머리를 자르다'라고 할 때 I cut my hair.라고 하기 쉬운데, 이는 자신의 머리를 직접 잘랐다는 뜻이 됩니다. 미용실 등에서 제삼자가 머리를 잘라 준 것이라면 I got my hair cut. 또는 I had my hair cut.이라고 해야 합니다.

원어민 발음 듣기 ☑☐   회화 훈련 ☐☐   듣기 훈련 ☐☐

□ 어떤 헤어스타일을 원하세요?

What kind of (hair)style would you like?
Do you have any particular style in mind?

□ 어떤 헤어스타일이 유행인가요?

What style is popular these days?

□ 추천해 주세요.

Would you recommend for me?
Any recommendations?

□ 헤어스타일을 바꾸고 싶어요.

I'd like to change my hairstyle.
I want to try something new.

□ 이 사진대로 해 주세요.

I want the hairstyle in this photo.

□ 커트해 주세요.

I'd like to cut my hair.
I want to get a cut.

□ 약간만 다듬어 주세요.

Can you trim my hair?
I just want a trim.

□ 단발머리로 해 주세요.

I want bobbed hair.

□ 뒷머리는 짧게 해 주세요.

Could you cut my back hair shorter?

□ 그냥 길게 기를 거예요.

I'm going to grow my hair long.

□ 파마하려고요.

I'd like to perm my hair.
I want to get a perm.

□ 웨이브는 작게 해 주세요.

Small waves perm, please.

□ 염색할게요.

I'd like to dye my hair.

□ 머리 스타일링(세팅) 해 주세요.

Could you style my hair with a blow-drier?

□ 영양제를 넣어 주세요.

I'd like some extra treatment.

□ 가르마는 어디로 할까요?

How do you part your hair?

□ 가운데로 해 주세요.	In the middle, please.
□ 왼쪽으로 해 주세요.	On the left, please.
□ 앞머리는 어떻게 할까요?	How would you like your bangs?
□ 머리숱이 많네요.	You have (very) thick hair.
	Your hair is (very) thick.
□ 곱슬머리예요.	You have (naturally) curly hair.
	You have wavy hair.
	Your hair is curly.
	*curly = wavy
□ 탈모가 있네요.	I think you're losing your hair.
	Your hair is falling out.
□ 마음에 드세요?	Do you like it?
□ 아주 마음에 들어요.	I love it.
	This is exactly what I wanted.
□ 머리 길이가 안 맞네요.	I think the length of my hair is uneven.
□ 웨이브가 잘 안 나왔네요.	I wanted more (natural) wavy hair.
□ 염색이 너무 진하네요.	I wanted lighter color.
□ 다시 해 주세요.	Can you do it over?
	Do it over, please.

📝 **Notes**

have in mind 생각하다, 마음에 두다 get a cut 커트하다 bobbed 단발머리의 grow long 기르다 get a perm 파마를 하다 blow-drier 헤어드라이어 part one's hair 머리 가르마를 타다 bangs 가지런히 잘라 내린 앞머리 lose one's hair 탈모가 되다 fall out 빠지다, 떨어져 나가다 uneven 고르지 않은, 양쪽이 균형이 안 맞는 do over 다시 하다

우체국에서

외국에서 생활할 때 (국내에 있을 때보다) 자주 방문하게 되는 곳이 post office(우체국)일 것입니다. 외국에 따라 우편물을 보낼 때 zip code(우편번호)를 꼭 써 줘야 하는 곳이 있습니다. 국제 우편은 international mail, 빠른우편은 express mail이라고 합니다.

원어민 발음 듣기 ☑☐   회화 훈련 ☐☐   듣기 훈련 ☐☐

☐ 이 편지를 부치고 싶습니다.
I'd like to send this letter.
I need to send this letter.

☐ 국내 우편인가요, 해외 우편인가요?
Is this domestic or international?

☐ 서울로 보내려고 합니다.
I'm sending this to Seoul.

☐ 일반으로 할게요.
Regular mail, please.
*regular mail → express mail(특송), registered mail(등기)

☐ 소포를 부치려고요.
I'd like to send this package.

☐ 소포 내용물이 뭐죠?
What's inside the package?

☐ 항공편으로 보낼게요.
I'd like to send this package by airmail.
By air, please.

☐ 저울에 올려 주세요.
Could you please put the package on the scale?

☐ 요금이 얼마죠?
How much does it cost?

☐ 요금은 무게에 따라 다릅니다.
The cost depends on the weight.

☐ 가장 저렴한 방법이 뭐죠?
What is the cheapest way to send this?

☐ 언제 도착하죠?
When will it arrive?
How long will it take to reach the destination?

☐ 3~5일 걸립니다.
It will take 3~5 days.

☐ 봉투 살게요.
I'd like to buy an envelope.

☐ 주소 재확인하세요.
Please recheck the receiver's mail address.

06 주민 센터에서

미국은 행정 구역이 우리와 다르기 때문에 '동사무소' 같은 것은 없지만, '주(state)>
카운티(county)> 시(city)'로 구분되어 각 주, 카운티, 시에 소속된 행정 사무실에서
행정 업무를 처리할 수 있습니다.

원어민 발음 듣기 ☑□   회화 훈련 □□   듣기 훈련 □□

☐ 주민 등록 등본(초본) 한 통 떼려고요.   I'd like to get a copy of my (extract) resident registration.

☐ 3번 창구로 가세요.   Go to window 3.

☐ 신청서 작성해 주세요.   Could you please fill out the application?

☐ (주민) 등록증이나 면허증 주세요.   Can I see your registration card or driver's license?

☐ 여기 서명해 주세요.   Please sign here.

☐ 여기 등본 한 통이고요. 600원입니다.   Here's your copy. It's 600 won.

☐ 전입 신고를 하러 왔습니다.   I'm here to notify my moving into this town.

☐ 쓰레기 배출 스티커를 사려고요.   I'm here to buy a disposal sticker.

☐ 버리시는 물건이 뭐죠?   What's the disposal item?

☐ 스티커가 얼마죠?   How much is a disposal sticker?

☐ 물건에 따라 다릅니다.   The cost will vary on the item.
The cost will depend on the item.

☐ 정해진 날에 집 앞에 배출하세요.   Please dispose your item on a given date.

☐ 도서관을 이용하고 싶습니다.   I'd like to use the library.

☐ 회원 등록증을 발급해 드릴까요?   If you register, we can give you a membership card.

☐ 문화센터 프로그램은 어떤 게 있나요?   What culture programs do you have in the community center?

📝 **Notes**

extract 발췌한 부분 registration card (주민)등록증, 신분증 move into ~로 이사 오다, 옮기다 disposal 처
리, 제거 vary 다양하다, 제각기 다르다 dispose 처리하다

Chapter 10
일상생활

07 헬스장에서

한국에서 흔히 '헬스장'이라고 부르는 곳을 영어로는 gym 혹은 fitness center라고 합니다. 보통 월 단위, 또는 할인을 받는 조건으로 몇 달 치를 한꺼번에 지불하는 경우도 많습니다. 개인 트레이너로부터 cardio exercise(유산소 운동), weight lifting (근력 운동) 등 다양한 운동의 효과적인 방법도 배울 수 있습니다.

원어민 발음 듣기 ✔☐   회화 훈련 ☐☐   듣기 훈련 ☐☐

☐ 한 달에 얼마인가요?

How much does it cost for a month?
How much for a month?

☐ 한 달에 5만 원입니다.

50,000 won for a month.

☐ 석 달을 미리 등록하면 할인됩니다.

If you register for three month in advance, you can get a discount.

☐ (개인) 트레이너 지도를 받을 수 있나요?

Can I get a (personal) trainer?
I need a trainer.

☐ 트레이너 지도 시 추가 요금이 있습니다.

You have to pay extra for a trainer.

☐ 운동 프로그램이 있나요?

Do you have an exercise program?

☐ 개인 맞춤 프로그램을 해 드립니다.

We'll set up an individual exercise program.

☐ 여성 전용인가요?

Is this gym for women only?

☐ 남녀 공용입니다.

This gym is for both men and women.

☐ 유산소 운동은 어떻게 하나요?

How do I do cardio exercise?

☐ 러닝 머신에서 30분간 걸으세요.

Walk on a treadmill for thirty minutes.

☐ 근력 운동은 어떻게 하나요?

How do I do weight lifting?

☐ 아령이나 역기를 이용하세요.

Use dumbbells or barbells.

☐ 매일 몇 시간씩 운동해야 하나요?

How long should I work out every day?

☐ 하루에 30분~1시간이 적당합니다.

Thirty minutes to an hour should be proper.

☐ 영업시간은 어떻게 되나요?

What are your business hours?

☐ 매일 아침 9시부터 자정까지입니다.

It's 9 a.m. to midnight, everyday.

Chapter 11

이사
Move

부동산에서

house hunting을 할 때에는 가격, 교통, 주변 환경 등 여러 가지를 고려해야겠죠. 우리나라의 경우는 key money(전세금)라는 제도가 있는데, 미국은 monthly rent (월세)의 경우 첫 달에 한 달 치 security deposit money(보증금)를 포함, 석 달치 월세를 선불하는 제도가 있습니다.

원어민 발음 듣기 ☑□   회화 훈련 □□   듣기 훈련 □□

☐ 어떤 집을 구하세요?	What type of house are you looking for?
☐ 원룸 오피스텔을 찾아요.	I'm looking for a studio.
	*원룸: studio / 빌라: multi-family / 아파트: apartment
☐ 가격대는 어느 정도 생각하세요?	How much are you looking to spend?
	What's your budget?
☐ 전셋집을 찾고 있어요.	I'm looking for a house leased for key money.
☐ 특별히 원하는 조건이 있으신가요?	Are you looking for anything in particular?
	Anything in particular in mind?
☐ 지하철역과 가까운 곳을 원합니다.	I want the place close to the subway station.
☐ 제 회사와 가까웠으면 해요.	I want the place close to my office.
☐ 방 두 개짜리 집을 찾습니다.	I'm looking for two bedrooms.
☐ 룸메이트와 함께 살 거예요.	I'm going to live with my roommate.
	I'm going to share the house with my roommate.
☐ 상점(시장)과 가까웠으면 해요.	I'd like the place close to the stores.
☐ 조용한 주택가가 좋아요.	I want the place in a quiet neighborhood.
☐ 대로변은 피하고 싶어요.	I want to avoid the roadside.
☐ 고층을 선호합니다.	I prefer the place on the upper floors.
☐ 주차 공간이 있었으면 해요.	I'd like a parking space.
☐ 제겐 무리한 금액이네요.	It's out of my price range.
	It's out of my budget.
☐ 집주인과 이야기해 볼게요.	I'll talk to the landlord.
	Let me talk to the landlord.

170

02 집 구하기

집을 계약하기 전 확인해야 할 것들이 많이 있습니다. 특히 요즘 들어 자주 문제가 되는 noises from upstairs(층간 소음)나 parking lot(주차장 시설)도 꼼꼼하게 따져 볼 필요가 있습니다.

원어민 발음 듣기 ☑□ 　회화 훈련 □□ 　듣기 훈련 □□

☐ 지금 집을 볼 수 있을까요?　　　　Can I see the house now?
　　　　　　　　　　　　　　　　I'd like to see the house now.

☐ 한번 알아볼게요.　　　　　　　　Let me check first.

☐ 오늘은 세 군데 보여 드릴 수 있습니다.　I can show you three houses today.

☐ 임대료가 얼마죠?　　　　　　　　How much is the rent?
　　　　　　　　　　　　　　　　What's the monthly rent?

☐ 교통은 편리한가요?　　　　　　　Is public transportation convenient?

☐ 괜찮아 보이기는 한데…….　　　　It looks okay, but….
　　　　　　　　　　　　　　　　It's not too bad, but….

☐ 집이 너무 낡았어요.　　　　　　　This house looks very old.

☐ 방이 너무 작아요.　　　　　　　　The rooms are too small.
　　　　　　　　　　　　　　　　I need bigger rooms.

☐ 햇볕이 부족해요.　　　　　　　　I want more sunshine.

☐ 하수구에서 냄새 나요.　　　　　　The drain smells (bad).
　　　　　　　　　　　　　　　　*drain = sewage

☐ 수압이 낮아요.　　　　　　　　　The water pressure isn't high enough.

☐ 층간 소음이 심하네요.　　　　　　I can hear noises from upstairs.
　　　　　　　　　　　　　　　　Noises from upstairs are too loud.

☐ 지하철역에서 너무 머네요.　　　　The house is too far from the subway station.
　　　　　　　　　　　　　　　　*subway station → bus stop (버스 정류장)

☐ 주차 공간이 없네요.　　　　　　　The house doesn't have a parking space.

03 집 계약하기

집 계약은 우리나라나 미국이나 별반 다를 것이 없습니다. landlord 혹은 landlady (집주인)와 resident (세입자)의 신분증명서, 계약서, 돈만 있으면 계약은 순조롭게 진행되죠. 계약서에는 금액과 지불 날짜 등이 명기됩니다. 각종 utility fees(공과금)는 세입자가 내는 것이 보통입니다.

원어민 발음 듣기 ☑☐   회화 훈련 ☐☐   듣기 훈련 ☐☐

☐ 이 집이 마음에 들어요.	I like this house.
☐ 좀 더 싸게는 안 될까요?	Can I get the house cheaper?
	Could you go any lower?
☐ 관리비는 얼마인가요?	How much is the maintenance fee?
☐ 공과금이 월세에 포함되나요?	Are the utility fees included in the rent?
☐ 공과금은 세입자가 냅니다.	Residents have to pay the utility fees.
☐ 계약할게요.	I'll sign the contract.
	I'm ready to sign the contract.
☐ 계약에 필요한 것은 뭐죠?	What do I need for the contract?
☐ 신분증, 계약금, 중개수수료 준비하세요.	Just bring your ID card, down payment for the landlord, and a commission for us.
☐ 등기부 등본을 떼어 주세요.	I'm going to need a certified copy of the real estate register.
	Can I get a certified copy of the register?
☐ 계약서를 읽어 보세요.	Read the contract, please.
☐ 계약서에 서명하세요.	Sign the contract, please.
☐ 계약은 1년간 지속됩니다.	The contract will be valid for a year.
☐ 월세는 매달 15일입니다.	Your rent is due on the 15th of every month.
☐ 보증금은 이사 나가는 날 돌려받습니다.	The rental deposit will be returned when you move out.
	You'll get back your deposit once you move out.

04 이사하기

계약을 마치면 moving out(이사 나오기)과 moving in(새 집으로 이사 들어오기)을 위한 작업이 이뤄집니다. 요즘은 movers(이삿짐센터)를 부르는 것이 보통인데, 따로 packing(짐을 싸기)하고 unpacking(짐을 풀기)할 필요가 없어 편리하기 때문이죠.

원어민 발음 듣기 ☑□　회화 훈련 □□　듣기 훈련 □□

☐ 이사 언제 나가니?

When are you moving out?
*move out ↔ move in

☐ 짐은 어떻게 할 거야?

How are you going to pack?

☐ 짐은 혼자 쌀 거야.

Are you going to pack by yourself?

☐ 이삿짐센터 부를 거야.

I'll call a mover.
*mover = remover, moving company

☐ 지금 이삿짐센터가 짐을 싸고 있어.

Movers are packing now.

☐ 침대는 어디에 놓아 드릴까요?

Where should we put your bed?

☐ 침실은 어디입니까?

Where is going to be your bedroom?

☐ 큰 방에 놓아 주세요.

Just put it in the biggest room.

☐ 컴퓨터를 설치해 주세요.

Set up my computer, please.
*set up = install

Could you please set up my computer?

☐ 도시가스 설치하러 왔습니다.

I'm here to install gas.

Do you need to set up gas?

☐ 케이블 설치하러 왔습니다.

I'm here to install the cable TV line.

☐ 보조 자물쇠 달러 왔습니다.

I'm here to put a spare door lock on the door.

☐ 새 집 어때?

How is your new house?

Do you like your new house?

☐ 집들이 언제 할 거야?

When is your housewarming party?

📑 Notes

by oneself 혼자서, 혼자 힘으로　**set up** 세우다, 설치하다(= install)　**spare** 여분의, 예비의　**door lock** 출입문 자물쇠

173

Chapter 12

학교
School

01 대학 지원하기

외국 대학을 준비하는 경우 filled-out application form(입학 지원서) 외에도 recommendation letters(추천서) 등이 필요하죠. tuition(등록금)이 걱정이라면 각 학교의 scholarships (장학금) 제도도 꼭 챙겨 봐야겠습니다.

원어민 발음 듣기 ☑☐   회화 훈련 ☐☐   듣기 훈련 ☐☐

☐ 가고 싶은 대학이 어디야?

What university do you want to go?
What university do you want to enter?
Any school you want to go?

☐ 학교에 대해 알아봤어?

Have you looked into schools?
Have you searched any school information?

☐ 입학 요강이 인터넷에 공고됐어.

The admission requirements of the school have been posted on the Internet.
*admission = entrance

☐ 입학 설명회는 가 봤어?

Have you attended a university briefing session on its admission requirements?

☐ 등록금은 얼마야?

How much is the tuition?

☐ 장학금 혜택은 있어?

Are there any scholarships available?

☐ 어떤 공부를 하고 싶니?

What do you want to study?
What major will you be studying?

☐ 실용 학문을 하고 싶어.

I want to study something practical.

☐ 요즘 취업이 힘드니까.

The job market is quite tough these days.

☐ 입학에 필요한 서류가 뭐야?

What documents do I need for an admission?
What documents are required for an admission?

☐ 입학 요강은 학교마다 달라.

Each school has different admission requirements.

☐ 대학 홈페이지에서 알아보려고.

I'm going to check out the school homepage.

□ 해외 대학 입학에 필요한 서류는 뭐야?	What documents do I need to enter the foreign universities? What documents are required to apply for the foreign universities?
□ 지원서와 추천서, 토플 성적이 필요해.	You need a filled-out application form, recom-mendation letters, and TOEFL scores.
□ 언제까지 접수해야 해?	When is the deadline for the application? When is the last day for the application?
□ 서류 작성 요령은 알아?	Do you know how to fill out the application form?
□ 영문 에세이도 써야 해?	Do I need to write an essay in English, too?
□ 준비할 것이 정말 많구나.	There are tons of things to prepare for the application. A lot of preparations are needed for the application.
□ 그 학교는 경쟁률이 아주 높을 거래.	The admission rate of the school will be very high. *admission rate = competition rate
□ 합격했어.	I've been accepted. They let me in. I've made it.
□ 방금 합격 통지서 받았어.	I just received the acceptance letter from the school.
□ 전액 장학금 받았어.	I've got a four-year, full(-ride) scholarship.
□ 부분 장학금 받았어.	I've got a partial scholarship.

Notes

look into 자세히 조사하다, 주의 깊게 살피다 post 붙이다, 공고하다, 게시하다 admission 입학, 입학 허가 requirement 요구사항 practical 실용적인, 실질적인 deadline 마감, 최종 시한 tons of 수많은, 아주 많은 admission rate 입학 경쟁률(= competition rate) be accepted 받아들여지다, 합격하다 make it 해내다, 성공하다 full-ride 전액의, 전체의 partial 부분의

02 수강 신청 하기

class schedule(강의 시간표)을 짤 때 이번 semester(학기)에 몇 학점을 들을 것인지, 어떤 과목을 선택할 것인지를 결정하는 것은 아주 중요합니다. 과목별 성격에 따라 required course(필수 과목), elective course(교양 과목) 등으로 나뉘지요.

원어민 발음 듣기 ☑☐   회화 훈련 ☐☐   듣기 훈련 ☐☐

☐ 이번 학기 몇 학점 들을 거야?	How many credits are you taking?
	How many credits will you be taking?
	How many credits for this semester?
☐ 이번 학기 어떤 과목 들을 거야?	What courses are you taking?
	What courses will you be taking?
	What courses for this semester?

☐ 이번 학기에 학점 꽉 채워서 들을 거야.   I'm going to take the full credits for this semester.

I'm planning to take the maximum credits for this semester.

☐ 이번 학기에 최소 학점만 들을 거야.   I'm going to take the minimum credits for this semester.

☐ 필수 과목이야.
It's a required course.
*require = mandatory, compulsory

☐ 선택 과목이야.
It's an elective course.
*elective = optional

☐ 그 과목은 예비 과목이 있어.
It has preliminary courses.

☐ 강의 시간표 다 짰어?
Did you make out your class schedule?
*make out = lay out

Did you finish your class schedule?

☐ 그 수업 나랑 같이 들을래?
Do you want to take the class together?

Let's take the class together.

☐ 수강 신청 마감이 언제야?
When is the deadline for signing up for the classes?

When is the deadline for the class registration?

□ 이번 주까지야.	The deadline is this week.
	You have to register this week.
□ 신청 과목을 변경하고 싶은데요.	I'd like to change my courses.
	*change = switch
	Is it okay to change my courses now?
□ 이미 등록 마감 됐어요.	The class registration has been closed.
	It's too late for the class registration.
□ 그 과목은 개설되지 않아요.	The course has failed to open for this semester.
	The course is not going to open for this semester.

DIALOGUE

A I'd like to change my courses.
B I'm sorry. The class registration has been closed.
A I just want to change my courses.
B You can do that only during the registration period.

A 신청 과목을 변경하고 싶은데요.
B 죄송합니다. 이미 등록 마감됐어요.
A 저는 이미 등록한 과목을 변경하려는 건데요.
B 변경은 등록 기간에만 가능합니다.

 Notes

take credit(s) 학점을 듣다(이수하다) semester (1년 2학기제 대학의) 학기 be planning to ~할 계획이다
maximum 최대의, 극대의 minimum 최소의, 극소의 make out 짜다, 작성하다(= lay out) sign up for ~을
신청하다 closed 마감한, 닫은 late for ~에 늦은

03 강의실에서

강의실에서는 먼저 학생들의 attendance check(출석 체크)를 하고 수업을 시작하죠. 학기 초에는 the course schedule(강의 계획표)를 나눠 주기도 하고요. 그 밖에 교수님이 강의를 하면서 쓰는 표현, 수업을 듣고 난 후 학생들의 평가 등의 표현을 살펴보겠습니다.

원어민 발음 듣기 ☑☐　회화 훈련 ☐☐　듣기 훈련 ☐☐

☐ 출석 체크하겠습니다.	Let me check attendance. Attendance check!
☐ 여기요!	(I'm) Here! Yes! Present!
☐ 전원 출석이네요.	(It's) Perfect attendance. Everyone's here. Everyone's present.
☐ 두 명이 결석이네요.	Two students are absent. Two students are not here.
☐ 강의 안내서입니다.	This is the syllabus for the class. Here's the course schedule. *schedule = outline
☐ (안내서를) 돌려 주세요.	Please pass the syllabus around.
☐ 강의 시작합시다.	Let's get started. Shall we begin?
☐ 책 24페이지를 펴세요.	Turn to page 24. Open your book to page 24.
☐ 페이지 넘겨 주세요.	Turn the page, please. Turn to the next page.
☐ 저번 시간에 어디까지 했죠?	Where were we last time? Does anyone know where we stopped last time?
☐ 이것에 대해 아는 사람?	Who knows about this? Anyone who has a thought about this?

□ 알겠어요? / 이해했어요?	Do you understand me? Everyone understand?
□ 오늘은 여기까지.	That's all for today. We have to stop here. It's time to finish.
□ 나머지는 다음 시간에 끝내도록 하죠.	We'll finish the rest of this chapter next time. We'll do the rest of it next time.
□ 다음 시간은 이것에 대해 배우겠습니다.	Our next class is about this. We'll talk about this next time.
□ 아직 수업 안 끝났어요.	I'm not done yet. The class is not finished yet.
□ 질문 있어요?	Does anyone have questions? Any questions?
□ 수업이 재미있었어요.	The class was fun. I really enjoyed the class.
□ 시간이 금방 갔어.	Time flew. Time passed quickly.
□ 강의가 훌륭했어요.	The class was great.
□ 수업이 지루했어요.	The class was boring.
□ 그 교수님은 (아주) 열정적이셔.	The professor is very passionate. He is a very passionate lecturer. The professor teaches us with great enthusiasm.
□ 그 교수님은 아주 인기가 많으셔.	The professor is immensely popular.
□ 우리 교수님은 강의 방식이 특이해.	The way our professor teaches us is unique. Our professor has a very unique teaching technique.
□ 필기를 많이 해야 해.	I have to take notes a lot. *take notes = write down
□ 우리 교수님은 말이 너무 빨라.	Our professor talks too fast.

181

04 과제물, 시험 준비

미국에서의 school paper(과제물)와 mid/final term(시험)은 유형이 다양한데, 보통 학생들은 그룹을 지어 주제에 대해 함께 조사하고 공부합니다. 물론 때때로 cramming(벼락치기)을 하는 경우도 있습니다.

원어민 발음 듣기 ☑☐   회화 훈련 ☐☐   듣기 훈련 ☐☐

□ 수업 끝나고 제출하세요. **Hand in your paper after the class.**

□ 못한 사람은 제게 오세요. **If you don't have your paper today, come and see me.**

□ 이번 주 금요일까지 리포트 제출해요. **You have to hand in the paper by Friday.**
*hand in = turn in

  Don't forget to hand in your paper by Friday.

  The due date for the paper is this Friday.

□ 다음 과제는 에세이입니다. **Your next assignment will be writing an essay.**

□ 적어도 두 장 분량으로 쓰세요. **Your paper should be minimum two pages.**
*paper = essay
*minimum = at least

□ 인터넷상의 자료를 활용하지 마세요. **Don't even try to use the materials on the Internet.**
*use = copy, plagiarize

□ 독자적으로 해 보세요. **Do it your own way.**

  Use your own imaginations.

  Be creative.

□ 중간고사 범위는 ~에서 …까지입니다. **The mid-term covers from ~ to….**
*mid-term → final-term (기말고사)

□ 자세한 내용은 인터넷 게시판 참조. **Please check out the Internet notice for more details.**

□ 다음 주엔 총정리 시간을 가질 거예요. **We'll have review hours next week.**

  Next week, we'll review what we've studied so far.

□ 시험은 객관식입니다. **It's a multiple choice test.**

□ 시험은 주관식입니다. **It's an essay type test.**

▢ 2시간 동안 오픈북 테스트입니다.	It will be a two-hour open book test.
▢ 부정행위가 적발되면 F학점입니다.	If you cheat, you'll get an F.
▢ 시험 잘 보세요.	Good luck for your exam. Good luck to you all.
▢ 과제물이 너무 많아요.	We have too many assignments.
▢ 그룹 스터디 하자.	Let's study in groups. Why don't we make a study group?
▢ 중간고사가 언제야?	When is the mid-term?
▢ 시험 범위가 어디야?	What should we study? The test covers from where to where?
▢ 시험공부 하나도 못 했는데.	I haven't studied at all.
▢ 벼락치기 해야겠다.	I'm going to cram for the exam.
▢ 밤새 벼락치기 했어.	I crammed all night.
▢ 재시험 볼 수 있어요?	Can we get a chance to re-sit? Can we retake the test?
▢ 이번 시험은 특히 중요해.	This exam is especially important.
▢ 한번 훑어봤어.	I just lightly went over it. I just skimmed through.
▢ 시험 어땠어?	How was the exam?
▢ (아주) 어려웠어.	It was (unbelievably) hard. It was very tough.
▢ 어렵지 않았어.	It wasn't so hard. It was a piece of cake.
▢ (아주) 잘 본 것 같아.	I think I did (pretty) well.
▢ 시간이 없었어.	I needed more time. I lacked time.
▢ 망쳤어.	I screwed up (the exam). I messed up (the exam). I failed the exam.

성적

GPA는 grade point average를 줄인 말로 우리말로 '평점'이라는 뜻입니다. 이 GPA가 나쁠 경우 retaking(재수강)을 해야 하거나 취업 시 나쁜 영향을 끼칠 수 있으니 잘 관리하는 것이 중요합니다.

원어민 발음 듣기 ☑☐   회화 훈련 ☐☐   듣기 훈련 ☐☐

□ 성적이 좋아.

I got good grades.

I got a good GPA.

□ 성적이 안 좋아.

I got bad grades.

I got a bad GPA.

□ 성적 확인했어?

Did you check your grades?

What are your grades?
*grade(s) = GPA

□ ~ 과목 등급 뭐 받았어?

What is your grade on ~ course?

□ 성적이 이상해.

Something went wrong with my grades.

There must be some mistakes with my grades.

□ 교수님께 여쭤 봐야지.

I need to talk to my professor.

I'm going to ask him about my grades.

□ 낙제하면 어쩌지?

What if I am flunked?

What if I fail the course?

□ 재수강해야겠다.

I'm going to retake the course.

I need to repeat the course.

□ 이번 학기에 그녀가 수석이야.

She is the top of the class for this semester.

□ 그는 우등생이야.

He is on the dean's list.

He is an honor student.

He is on the honor roll.

□ 예습과 복습은 매우 중요해.

Preparations and reviews of your lessons are very important.

06 기숙사

학교까지 commuting to school(통학)이 어려울 경우 dormitory(기숙사)에서 생활하며 공부를 하기도 합니다. 여러 가지 dorm rules(기숙사 규칙)를 지켜야 하는 번거로움이 있지만 dorm cost(기숙사 비용)가 저렴하고 traffic expenses(교통비)도 절약할 수 있기 때문이죠.

원어민 발음 듣기 ☑□   회화 훈련 □□   듣기 훈련 □□

□ 기숙사에 들어가고 싶어요.	I'd like to live in the dorm. I'd like to sign up for the dorm.
□ 필요한 서류가 뭐죠?	Are there any documents for the application? What documents do I need to prepare?
□ 학기당 기숙사 비용은 얼마죠?	How much does the dorm cost per semester? How much is it per semester?
□ 80만 원입니다.	It costs 800,000 won per semester.
□ 비용은 언제, 어떻게 내나요?	When and how should I pay for the cost?
□ 기숙사 통금 시간이 있나요?	Is there a curfew in a dorm?
□ 자정 통금이 지나면 들어올 수 없어요.	You're not allowed to get into the dorm after midnight curfew. *get into=come in
□ 욕실과 주방은 공용입니다.	The bathrooms and the kitchens are shared. You have to share the bathrooms and the kitchens.
□ 인터넷은 24시간 사용 가능합니다.	You can access the Internet for 24 hours.
□ 방은 1인실에서 4인실까지 있어요.	We have a single, double, triple and quadruple room.
□ 기숙사에 있으면 어떤 점이 좋아?	What are the advantages of living in the dorm?
□ 통학 시간이 절약돼.	You can save time to commute to school.
□ 친구들을 많이 사귈 수 있어.	You can make many friends in the dorm.
□ 술자리가 많은 게 탈이야.	It's hard to avoid drinking parties.

185

07 학교 도서관

학교 도서관을 이용하려면 student ID(학생증)와 library card(도서관 카드)가 필요합니다. 편리한 도서 검색은 물론 book check-out(대출) 여부도 알 수 있죠. 하지만 due date(반납일)를 어기면 late fee(연체료)를 물어야 하니 미리 renew(기간 연장 신청)를 하거나 반납일을 꼭 지켜야 합니다.

원어민 발음 듣기 ☑□   회화 훈련 □□   듣기 훈련 □□

□ 책을 빌리려면 도서관 카드가 필요해요.	You need a library card to check out books.
□ 도서관 카드는 어디에서 발급받죠?	Where can I get a library card? Where should I go to get a library card?
□ 학생과로 가세요.	Go to the student affairs office.
□ 책을 대출하려고요.	I'd like to check out a book. I'd like to borrow a book.
□ 책은 어떻게 찾죠?	How can I search books? *search = look up
□ 컴퓨터로 검색하세요.	You can look up what you need on the computer.
□ 직접 서고에서 찾으세요.	You can go in the library and look up for yourself.
□ 학생증을 보여 주세요.	Can I see your student ID? Your student ID, please.
□ 도서 열람표를 작성해 주세요.	Please fill out the call slip card.
□ 대출 확인증에 서명하세요.	Please sign on the book check-out card.
□ 대출 기한은 언제까지죠?	How long can I check out this book? How long can I borrow this book?
□ 5권 이내 보름입니다.	You can check out less than five books for 15 days. You have to return your books in 15 days.
□ 반납일 전에 기간 연장 신청하세요.	You have to renew before the due date. If you want to renew, please do before the due date.

□ 기한이 지나면 연체료는 하루 50원입니다.	There's the 50 won late fee for overdue books per day.
	The delay fee for overdue books is 50 won per day.
□ 제가 찾고 있는 책이 없네요.	I can't find the book that I'm looking for.
□ 그 책은 대출 중입니다.	That book has been checked out.
	Someone already borrowed it.
□ 책을 반납하려고요.	I'd like to return these books.
	I'm returning these books.

 Notes

check out books 도서를 빌리다, 대출하다   look up 찾다, 조사하다   for oneself 자기 힘으로, 스스로   call
slip card 도서 열람표   return books 빌린 도서를 반납하다   renew 도서 대출 기한을 연장하다   overdue 반납
이 늦은, 마감 시한을 넘긴

08 카운슬링

각 대학에서는 학생 상담실을 두고 각종 상담을 받습니다. 학교 성적 상담에서 student loan(학자금 융자), career advice(취업 상담), part-time job(아르바이트 정보), international internship(해외 인턴십), exchange student(교환 학생) 등 그 내용도 다양합니다.

원어민 발음 듣기 ☑□   회화 훈련 □□   듣기 훈련 □□

☐ 이 수업을 따라가기 힘들어요.	This course is too difficult for me.
	I don't understand a thing.
	I can't keep up with this class.
	I'm totally lost.
☐ 학교 성적이 너무 안 좋아요.	My grades are too low.
	My GPA is seriously bad.
☐ 이번 학기에 휴학해야겠어요.	I'm going to take this semester off from school.
☐ 학자금 대출을 받고 싶어요.	I'd like to apply for a student loan.
☐ 대출 조건은 어떻게 되죠?	What are the loan conditions?
☐ 제가 학자금 대출을 받을 수 있나요?	Am I eligible to apply for a student loan?
☐ 취업 상담을 하고 싶어요.	I'd like to talk to a career adviser.
	Can I have an interview with a career adviser?
☐ 졸업 논문에 대해 상담하려고요.	I'd like to get advice for my graduation thesis.
	Can I have an interview with the professor about my graduation thesis?
☐ 대인 관계가 원만치 않아요.	I have problems to get along with other students.
	I have problems making friends.
☐ 항상 우울해요.	I'm depressed all the time.
☐ 정서적으로 불안해요.	I feel insecure and unstable.

☐ 교내 아르바이트 정보를 얻으려고요.	I'd like to get information about a part time job on campus. I'm looking for a part time job on campus.
☐ (해외) 인턴십을 신청하려고요.	I'd like to apply for an (international) internship.
☐ 교환 학생 자격 요건이 뭐죠?	What are the qualifications to be an exchange student?
☐ 사회봉사 프로그램에 참여하고 싶어요.	I'd like to participate in community service program.
☐ 단기 어학연수 프로그램 지원하려고요.	I'd like to apply for a short-term foreign language program.

DIALOGUE

A I'd like to apply for a student loan.
B Okay. You need to fill out this form.
  And I'm going to need your student ID.
A I'm just curious. What are the loan conditions?
B Here's the guidebook for a student loan.

A 학자금 대출을 받고 싶은데요.
B 예. 이 양식을 작성해 주세요. 그리고 학생증도 필요합니다.
A 궁금해서 그러는데요. 대출 조건은 어떻게 되죠?
B 여기 학자금 대출 관련 안내서가 있습니다.

📑 Notes

keep up with ~을 따라가다, ~에 뒤지지 않다 **lost** 길(방향)을 잃은, 어찌할 바를 모르는 **take off from school** 휴학하다 **eligible** 적격의, 자격이 있는 **career adviser** 취업 상담가(= counselor) **get advice** 조언을 얻다 **depressed** 우울한, 처진 **insecure** 불안한 **unstable** 안정되지 않은 **on campus** 교내의 **qualification(s)** 자격 요건 **participate in** ~에 참여하다

Chapter 13

직장
Workplace

01 구직 활동

job hunting(구직) 할 때 여러 job-search websites(구직 사이트)에서 실속 있는 job openings(일자리 정보)를 얻어야겠죠. résumé(이력서), cover letter(자기 소개서), certificate of graduation(졸업 증명서) 등 필요한 서류를 미리 준비해 두는 것이 좋습니다.

원어민 발음 듣기 ☑□   회화 훈련 □□   듣기 훈련 □□

☐ 일자리를 찾고 있어.

I'm looking for a job.
*job = position

I'm looking for employment.

I'm job-hunting now.

☐ 어떤 일자리를 원해?

What kind of work do you want?

What kind of job are you looking for?

☐ 구직 사이트를 확인해 봤어?

Have you checked the Internet job-search websites?

Did you search for job opportunities on the Internet?

☐ 좋은 일자리 정보를 얻었어.

I've found some great job openings.
*job openings = hiring information

☐ 마땅한 일자리 정보가 없어.

I can't find anything good for me.

☐ 입사 지원에 필요한 서류는 뭐야?

What do you need to prepare for the job appli-cation?

What documents do you need for the job appli-cation?

☐ 입사 지원서, 졸업 증명서, 자기 소개서, 추천서야.

I need a filed-out job application form, a certi-ficate of graduation, a letter of introduction, and reference letters.

☐ 이력서와 자기 소개서가 필요해.

I need a detailed résumé and cover letter.

I need to submit a résumé and letter.

☐ 합격자 발표는 언제야?

When do they announce successful candidates?

When will they let you know the result?

☐ 합격자에게 따로 전화한대.

They will call each successful candidate separately.

☐ 전화를 기다리고 있어.	I'm waiting for a call from the company.
☐ 전화가 안 와.	I haven't heard from them.
☐ 나 합격했어.	I got the job. I've made it.
☐ 다음 주부터 출근해.	I start from next week.
☐ 나 떨어졌어.	I didn't get the job.
☐ 자격 미달이래.	They said I was underqualified.
☐ 자격이 충분하대.	They said I was overqualified.
☐ 나이가 많대.	They said I'm too old for the job. They said I went over the age limit.
☐ 그 회사 아무도 안 뽑았대.	They said they didn't choose any of candidates.
☐ 다른 회사 알아봐야지.	I'll start looking (for a job) again.

Notes

employment 고용, 직업, 일 prepare for ~을 준비하다 certificate 졸업 증명서(= diploma) detailed 자세한, 상세한 submit (서류 등을) 제출하다 announce 공식적으로 발표하다 successful candidate 합격자 separately 따로 start from ~부터 시작하다 underqualified 자격이 안 되는, 자격 미달의 overqualified 자격이 되고도 남는, 자격이 넘치는 age limit 나이 제한

02 면접 보기

job interview(면접)에서 자주 등장하는 질문과 가능한 대답을 살펴보겠습니다. campus life(대학 생활)와 major(전공), 자신의 strengths(강점)와 weaknesses (약점), career(경력) 등을 말하는 다양한 표현도 같이 알아둡시다.

원어민 발음 듣기 ☑☐   회화 훈련 ☐☐   듣기 훈련 ☐☐

☐ 면접이 언제야?	When is your job interview?
☐ 단정한 옷차림을 해.	Dress neat and tidy.
☐ 면접에 늦지 마.	Don't be late for the interview. Be there on time.
☐ 면접 전에 리허설을 해 봐.	Why don't you have a rehearsal before the interview? Rehearse before the actual interview.
☐ 자신에 대해 소개해 보세요.	Why don't you introduce yourself to us? Tell us about yourself.
☐ 저는 경제학을 전공했습니다.	I studied economics in college.
☐ 당신의 강점과 약점은 무엇입니까?	What are your strengths and weaknesses? Tell us about your strengths and weaknesses.
☐ 저는 활발하고 성실하며 끈기가 있습니다.	I'm very active, sincere, and patient.
☐ 저는 일중독 성향이 있습니다.	I could be a workaholic.
☐ 대학 생활은 어땠나요?	How was your school life? *school life = campus life
☐ 많은 친구들을 사귀었습니다.	I've made lots of friends.
☐ 왜 이 회사를 선택했나요?	Why did you choose our company? Is there any reason why you picked our company?
☐ 이곳은 제가 꿈에 그리던 직장입니다.	It's my dream job. I always wanted to work for the company like this.

194

☐ 이곳의 기업 활동을 주시해 왔습니다.	I've been paying attention to your corporate activities.
☐ 입사하면 해 보고 싶은 일이 있나요?	What would you like to do if you enter this company?
☐ 제 아이디어를 실현시켜 보고 싶어요.	I'd like to try my own idea and see if it works.
☐ 이전 직장에 대해 말해 보세요.	Let us know about your previous work.
	Tell us about your previous work.
☐ 마케팅 회사에서 3년간 일했습니다.	I worked for the marketing company for three years.
☐ 왜 그만두었나요?	Why did you quit?
	Why did you leave your previous work?
☐ 자신의 경력에 대해 말해 보세요.	Would you please tell me about your career?
☐ 수출입 업무에 경험이 많습니다.	I have a lot of experience in importing and exporting.
☐ 요즘 경제에 대해 어떻게 생각하나요?	What do you think about the economic situation these days?
	What is your opinion on the recent economic situation?
☐ 본인이 창의적인 사람이라고 생각해요?	Do you consider yourself a creative person?
	Do you think you're creative?
☐ 창의적이 되려고 노력합니다.	I try to be creative.
☐ 면접 어땠어?	How was the interview?
	How did the interview go?
☐ 너무 떨렸어.	I was extremely nervous.
☐ 침착해지려고 애썼어.	I tried to be calm.

*calm = cool

📑 **Notes**

neat and tidy 깔끔하고 단정한 corporate 기업의, 회사의 work 제대로 작용하다 career 경력, 직업으로의 성
공과 출세 import 수입하다 export 수출하다 recent 최근의, 근래의 go (일이) 되다, 되어가다

03 첫 출근

first day at work(첫 출근 날)에는 함께 일할 직원들을 소개 받고 간단히 사무실 투어를 합니다. staff training(직원 교육)을 통해 회사 규칙 등을 배우고 자리도 배정 받죠. probie(수습사원)로서 회의에 참석하거나 다양한 경험들을 하게 됩니다.

원어민 발음 듣기 ☑□   회화 훈련 □□   듣기 훈련 □□

□ 입사를 환영합니다.	Welcome aboard! Nice to have you with us.
□ 입사 첫날 어때요?	How is your first day going (so far)?
□ 모든 것이 너무 빨라요.	Everything's moving very fast.
□ 곧 익숙해져요.	You'll get used to it. You'll be comfortable with it.
□ 잘 보고 배우세요.	Watch and learn.
□ 선배를 잘 따라 하세요.	Just follow what your seniors do.
□ 그는 당신보다 1년 먼저 입사했어요.	He joined this company one year before you. *join = enter
□ 그가 당신보다 선임입니다.	He has more seniority than you.
□ 그가 우리 사무실 최고 고참입니다.	He has the most seniority in the office.
□ 우리는 입사 동기예요.	We joined the company the same year.
□ 회사 규칙을 잘 따르세요.	Please respect the company rules.
□ 수습 기간은 3개월입니다.	Your probation will be for three months. You will be a probie for three months.
□ 직원 교육에 참석하세요.	Please participate in staff training.
□ 어려운 점은 상사와 의논하세요.	If you have difficulties, talk to your boss.
□ 어려울 땐 저에게 오세요.	If you feel difficult, come to me.
□ 신입 사원을 소개합니다.	Let me introduce our new employees. Here are our new members of the staff.

잘 부탁합니다.	I depend on all of you.
뭐든지 시켜 주세요.	I'm at your service.
자리가 여기예요.	This is your desk. *desk = cubicle
간단히 사무실 투어를 하겠습니다.	Let me give you a quick office tour. I'll give you a quick tour. Let me show you the office.
직원들을 소개시켜 드릴게요.	Allow me to introduce you to people you'll be working with.
업무 시작합시다.	Let's get started. Let's get to work. Everyone, let's work.
오늘 주간 회의 있습니다.	We have a weekly staff meeting today.
모두 회의에 참석하세요.	All staff members make sure to attend the meeting.
오늘이 마감 날입니다.	Today is the deadline. We have the deadline today.
야근할 각오하세요.	Get ready to work late. *Get ready = Be ready

DIALOGUE

A Welcome aboard! I'm sure you'll like it here.

B It's so great to be here. I'll do my very best.

A 입사를 환영해요! 여기서 일하는 게 마음에 들 거예요.

B 여기 입사하게 돼서 정말 좋습니다. 최선을 다해 노력하겠습니다.

📑 **Notes**

aboard 새로운 멤버로서, 신입자로서 **move fast** 빠르게 움직이다(돌아가다) **get used to** ~에 익숙해지다 **join the company** 회사에 입사하다(= enter the company) **seniority** 선임, 선배 **probation** 수습(견습) 기간 **probie** 견습생, 수습 사원 **cubicle** 칸막이가 쳐진 좁은 장소 **office tour** 사무실 둘러보기 **staff meeting** 직원 회의 **make sure** 확실히 해 두다 **work late** 늦게까지 일하다, 야근하다

04 회의 및 보고

conference(회의)에서는 주요 issues(안건)에 대한 의견을 나누고 찬성과 반대를 결정합니다. 업무 진행 과정에 대한 간단한 briefing(브리핑)이나 상세한 presentation(프레젠테이션)이 이뤄지기도 하죠. 복잡하고 어려운 문제에 대해서는 이를 철저히 분석하고 맡아서 처리할 사람을 결정하기도 합니다.

원어민 발음 듣기 ☑☐　회화 훈련 ☐☐　듣기 훈련 ☐☐

☐ 회의합시다.	Let's have a meeting.
	Let's start a meeting.
☐ 화상 회의가 있어요.	We have a video conferencing.
☐ 전화 회의가 있어요.	We have a conference call.
☐ 회의 주제가 뭡니까?	What are the issues for the meeting?
	What are you covering on the meeting?
☐ 논의할 세 가지 안건이 있습니다.	We have three issues to discuss.
	*issues = items, topics, matters, agendas
☐ 첫 번째 안건은 이것입니다.	First is this.
☐ 다음 안건은 이것입니다.	The next matter is this.
☐ 마지막 안건은 이것입니다.	And the last one is this.
☐ 다음 안건입니다.	Move on to the next topic.
	Can we go on to the next item?
	Next agenda, please.
☐ 만장일치입니다.	It's a unanimous decision.
	We've unanimously agreed on this.
☐ 쉽게 결론이 났네요.	That was easy.
	It was an easy decision.
☐ 반대하는 사람 있나요?	Is there anyone who doesn't agree?
	Anyone who opposes this?
☐ 이 건에 대해선 다시 회의합시다.	Let's talk more about this later.
	Let's have another meeting later.
☐ 브리핑하세요.	Give us a briefing.

□ 브리핑을 받았어요.	I've been briefed.
□ 프레젠테이션을 시작하겠습니다.	I'll start my presentation.
	Let me start my presentation.
□ 건의사항 있습니까?	Do you have any suggestions? *suggestions = recommendations
□ 문제점이 무엇입니까?	What seems to be the problem?
	What are the problems?
□ 상대편의 입장은 무엇입니까?	What's the other part's position?
	What's their position?
□ 해결책이 있나요?	Do we have any answers? *answers = solutions
□ 이 문제를 처리할 사람?	Does anyone want to handle this problem?
	Does anyone want to take care of this?
□ 제가 해 보겠습니다.	I'll do it.
	I'll give it a shot.
	I think I can take care of it.
□ 변동 사항은 즉시 보고하세요.	If there are any changes, report to me right away. *right away = immediately

DIALOGUE

A We have a meeting tomorrow.
B What are the issues for the meeting?
A We have three issues to discuss so far.
   But we might have a few more. I'll let you guys know later.

A 내일 회의가 있습니다.
B 안건이 무엇입니까?
A 논의할 안건이 세 가지 있습니다.
   하지만 몇 가지 안건이 더 있을지도 모르겠군요. 나중에 여러분께 알려 드릴게요.

📑 Notes

conferencing 회의, 회담, 협의(= conference) unanimous 만장일치의 brief 요점을 간략하게 보고하다 take care of ~을 처리(해결)하다 give it a shot 한번 시도해 보다 let ~ know ~에게 알려 주다

05 업무 지시

상사는 부하 직원에게 보고서나 기획안 작성, 자료 정리, 프로젝트 진행 및 중간 점검과 같은 giving orders(업무 지시)를 합니다. 부하 직원의 실수를 지적하고 바로잡는 것도 이들의 주요 역할이죠. 부하 직원은 상사의 지시를 받아 review(검토), check(확인) 업무를 하게 됩니다.

원어민 발음 듣기 ☑□ 회화 훈련 □□ 듣기 훈련 □□

잠시 들어오세요.	Could you please come in?
바로 가겠습니다.	Sure, I'll be right in.
지금 외부에 있습니다.	I'm outside now.
바로 올라가겠습니다.	I'll be right up.
저를 찾으셨다고요.	You wanted to see me? Did you want to see me?
보고서 작성하세요.	Make a report.
기획안을 만드세요.	Make a plan. *make = set up
여기 보고서입니다.	Here is the report.
승인해 주십시오.	I need your approval on this project. I need you to approve this project.
수치가 안 맞잖아요.	These numbers are wrong. *numbers = figures These numbers don't add up.
다시 검토하세요.	Review again. *review = check
재확인하겠습니다.	I'll double-check. I'll recheck.
수정하세요.	Make it correct. Fix it.
다시 하세요.	Do it again. Do it over.
자료를 수집, 정리하세요.	Gather and organize the materials. *materials → information (정보)

□ 복사해서 팀원에게 돌리세요.	Make copies of these materials and hand them to the staff.
□ (저에게) 팩스로 보내세요.	Fax it (to me). Send it (to me) by fax.
□ 사내 게시판에 올리세요.	Post it on the company Intranet.
□ 신입 사원에게 시키세요.	Let our new employee do the job.
□ 신입 사원을 보내세요.	Send our new employee.
□ 심부름 좀 다녀와요.	Do some errands for me.
□ 시킬 일이 있어요.	I have something for you. You have work to do.
□ 그 프로젝트는 어떻게 진행되고 있나요?	How is the project going?
□ 얼마나 진행됐나요?	How far are you with the project?
□ 언제 마무리할 수 있나요?	When can you finish it? When will it be done?
□ 곧 마무리하겠습니다.	I'll be done soon. I'll finish it as fast as I can.
□ 확실히 알아들었어요?	Crystal clear? Did I make myself clear?
□ 확실히 해 두겠어요.	Let me be clear.
□ 잘 알아들었습니다.	Crystal clear.
□ 그렇게 하겠습니다.	You got it. You bet. Sure thing.
□ 당장 하겠습니다.	Right away.

📝 **Notes**

approve 승인하다, 허가하다 add up 계산이 맞다, 말이 앞뒤가 맞다 double-check 재점검하다 do over 다시 하다 hand ~에게 건네주다 let ~하게 시키다, ~하게 하다 do errands 심부름하다 as fast as I can 가능한 한 빨리 crystal clear 아주 명확한, 의미가 선명한 make oneself clear 의사를 정확히 전하다

06 식사, 휴식 시간

바쁜 오전 업무가 끝나고 점심시간이 되면 항상 "무엇을 먹을까?", "어디서 먹을까?" 고민합니다. 보통 cafeteria(구내식당)을 이용하지만 회사 밖에 있는 restaurants (음식점)에 가는 경우도 있습니다. 식사 후에는 coffee break(커피를 마시며 휴식하는 시간)을 가지기도 합니다.

원어민 발음 듣기 ☑☐ 회화 훈련 ☐☐ 듣기 훈련 ☐☐

☐ 오늘 점심 뭘 먹을까요?	What should we eat for lunch? *eat = have
☐ 어디에서 먹을까요?	Where should we eat?
☐ 구내식당 갈까요?	Shall we eat in the cafeteria?
☐ 나가서 먹어요.	Let's eat outside. Why don't we go out for lunch?
☐ 회사 근처 새로 생긴 음식점에 가 볼까?	Shall we try a new restaurant outside the office?
☐ 난 도시락을 싸 왔어.	I've brought my lunch.
☐ 샌드위치 싸 왔어.	I've brought sandwiches for my lunch.
☐ 식당 음식에 질렸어.	I'm sick and tired of the restaurant dishes.
☐ 점심 약속이 있어요.	I already have a lunch plan. I'm going to have lunch with someone.
☐ 쉬었다 합시다.	Let's take a break. Let's take 5.
☐ 커피 한잔 합시다.	Take a coffee break? How about some coffee?
☐ 식곤증 나요.	I feel drowsy after lunch.
☐ 잠시 외출할게요.	I'll be out for a minute.
☐ 누가 찾으면 문자 주세요.	If anyone wants me, please text me.
☐ 쉴 틈도 없어.	We don't have time for a break.
☐ 다시 일합시다.	Let's get back to work.

07 지각, 결근, 휴가

being late for work(지각)나 day-off(결근)를 할 때, 혹은 taking vacation(휴가 신청) 할 때에는 회사에 합당한 이유를 밝혀야 합니다. 무단으로 회사를 나오지 않을 경우 심각한 문제에 직면할 수도 있습니다. 몸이 아프거나 출산을 앞둔 경우라면 sick leave(병가)나 maternity leave(출산 휴가)를 냅니다.

원어민 발음 듣기 ☑□   회화 훈련 □□   듣기 훈련 □□

□ 늦어서 죄송합니다.	I'm sorry I'm late.
□ 그는 또 지각이야.	He's late again.
□ 그는 항상 늦게 출근해.	He's always late for work.
□ 다시는 이런 일이 없도록 하겠습니다.	It won't happen again.
	I promise it will never happen again.
□ 내일 조금 늦게 출근하겠습니다.	I'll be coming in a little late tomorrow.
	Can I come in a little late tomorrow?
□ 이유가 뭡니까?	What's the reason?
	Tell me why.
□ 내일 아침에 건강 검진이 있어요.	I have a physical exam tomorrow morning.
□ 저 오늘 조퇴하겠습니다.	Can I go home early today?
	Can I take the rest of the day off?
	May I leave early today?
□ 몸이 안 좋아요.	My condition is not so good.
	I don't feel good today.
□ 집에 급한 일이 생겼어요.	I have an urgent matter at home.
□ 삼촌이 돌아가셨어요.	My uncle passed away.
□ 집에 가세요.	Go home.
	You can go.
	*go = leave
□ 하필이면 오늘입니까?	Why today?
□ 오늘 출근 못하겠습니다.	I don't think I can make it today.
□ 그는 오늘 무단결근했어.	He took a day off without notice.
	He didn't come in without calling.

□ 월차를 내고 싶습니다.	I'd like to take a day off.	
□ 내일 병가를 내겠습니다.	I'd like to get sick leave tomorrow.	
□ 여름휴가 일정을 잡고 싶어요.	I'd like to schedule my summer vacation.	
□ 출산 휴가를 내겠습니다.	I'm going to take maternity leave.	
□ 내일부터 휴가야.	My vacation starts from tomorrow.	
□ 휴가 때 어디 가?	Are you going somewhere during your holidays?	
□ 해외여행 가려고.	I'm planning an overseas trip. I'm preparing for a trip abroad.	
□ 집에서 푹 쉬려고.	I'm going to relax at home.	
□ 잠이나 실컷 자려고.	I'm going to oversleep.	
□ 바닷가에 가려고.	I'm going to the beach.	
□ 휴가 때 전화하지 마.	Don't call me while I'm on my vacation.	
□ 휴대폰 꺼 놓을 거야.	My cell phone will be off.	

DIALOGUE

A You're late again. Tell me why.
  You'd better have a good excuse.
B Well, you know I worked late yesterday.
  And I couldn't get up early this morning.
  I'm very sorry. It won't happen again.

A 또 지각이네요. 이유를 말해 보세요. 그럴듯한 변명인지 들어 봅시다.
B 그게요. 아시다시피 어제 제가 야근을 해서요. 아침에 일찍 일어날 수가 없었어요.
  정말 죄송합니다. 다시는 이런 일이 없도록 하겠습니다.

Notes

come in 회사에 출근하다   physical exam 건강 검진(= general check-up)   rest of the day 남은 하루
urgent 긴급한, 응급의   pass away 죽다, 돌아가시다   make it 해내다, 성공하다   take a day off 월차를 내다(쓰
다), 하루 쉬다   maternity leave 출산 휴가   overseas trip 해외여행(= trip abroad)   oversleep 늦잠 자다, 지
나칠 정도로 자다   had better ~하는 게 낫다

08 거래처 방문, 손님 접대

working outside(외근)의 종류는 다양하지만 흔히 거래처를 방문하는 일이 많습니다. 손님으로서 다른 회사를 찾아가는 경우와 반대로 외부 손님을 자신이 근무하는 회사에서 접대하는 경우에 쓸 수 있는 표현을 알아보겠습니다.

원어민 발음 듣기 ☑☐   회화 훈련 ☐☐   듣기 훈련 ☐☐

☐ 오늘 외근합니다.	I'll work outside today.
	I'll be out today.
☐ 거래처에 다녀올게요.	I'll visit our client's office.
☐ 거래처에서 부르네요.	Our client wants to see me.
☐ 다른 업무도 처리하고 올게요.	I'll take care of other things, too.
☐ 외근 뒤 바로 퇴근하겠습니다.	After that, I'll go straight home.
	After that, I'll go home without coming in.
☐ 사무실에 들어오세요.	Come back in, please.
	Come back to the office.
☐ 손님이 오셨어요.	We have clients here.
☐ 접견실로 모셔 주세요.	Why don't you guide them to the reception room?
☐ 마실 것을 대접해 주세요.	Would you serve drinks to them?
☐ 이쪽입니다.	This way, please.
☐ 들어가세요.	Go right in.
☐ 오늘 손님 접대가 있습니다.	We have clients to comfort.
	*comfort = entertain
☐ 누가 접대합니까?	Who's going to comfort them?
☐ 중요한 손님입니다.	They're very important clients.
☐ 정중히 대접하세요.	Take extra good care of them.

📑 **Notes**

straightly 바로, 곧바로   come back in 사무실에 다시 들어오다   guide 안내하다, 인도하다   serve 대접하다
go in 들어가다   comfort 접대하다, 기분 좋게 대접하다(=entertain)

출장

회사 생활에서 국내 또는 해외로의 business trip(출장)이 불가피할 때가 있습니다. 특히 해외 출장의 경우 빡빡한 출장 일정뿐만 아니라 장거리인 경우 jet lag(시차증)로 고생하기도 하죠.

원어민 발음 듣기 ☑☐ 회화 훈련 ☐☐ 듣기 훈련 ☐☐

저 출장 갑니다.	I'm going for a business trip.
며칠 사무실을 비웁니다.	I'll be away from the office for a few days.
	I'm out of town for a couple of days.
그는 지금 부산으로 출장 중입니다.	He's on a business trip to Busan.
출장 준비 다 되셨어요?	Are you ready for the business trip?
며칠간 출장이십니까?	How long will you be gone?
	How long will you be on a business trip?
이틀이요.	I'll be on a business trip for two days.
출장 일정이 아주 빡빡해요.	The schedule is very tight.
	You'll have a very tight schedule.
누구와 동행하십니까?	Who will you go with?
혼자 갑니다.	I'll go alone.
상사를 모시고 갑니다.	I'll go with my boss.
잘 다녀오셨어요?	Welcome back!
출장 어땠어요?	How was your business trip?
아주 바빴어요.	I was crazily busy.
한숨도 못 잤어요.	I couldn't sleep at all.
시차증이 있어요.	I have the jet lag.
	I'm jet-lagged.
보고하셨어요?	Did you report to the boss?
출장비 내역 올렸어요?	Did you report your travel expenses?

10 퇴근, 회식

업무를 마무리하고 퇴근할 때 I'm going home.(퇴근하겠습니다.) 또는 I'll see you tomorrow.(내일 봅시다.)와 같은 인사를 합니다. 퇴근 후 dinner party(회식)도 빠질 수 없는 회사 생활의 일부입니다.

원어민 발음 듣기 ☑□   회화 훈련 □□   듣기 훈련 □□

☐ 퇴근 시간 다 됐네.	It's almost time to go home.
☐ 업무 마무리합시다.	Let's call it a day.
	Let's wrap things up.
☐ 퇴근하겠습니다.	I'm going home.
	I'm out of here.
	I'm taking off.
☐ 칼퇴근이네.	You're leaving on time.
☐ 야근 안 좋아해요.	I don't like working late.
☐ 제 일 다 끝냈어요.	I have my work done.
	I've finished my work.
☐ 회식이 있어요.	Let's go to dinner.
	We have a dinner plan tonight.
☐ 일차는 내가 삽니다.	The first round is on me.
☐ 일차만 하고 집에 갑시다.	Let's go home after the first round.
	Let's go home after dinner.
☐ 신입 사원 환영회가 있어요.	We have the welcome party for our new employees.
☐ 송년 모임이 있어요.	We have a year-end party.
☐ 부장님 생일 파티가 있어요.	We have a birthday party for our boss.
☐ 비용은 각출합시다.	Let's chip in.

📑 **Notes**

call it a day 일을 마무리하다, 퇴근하다 wrap things up 하던 일을 마무리하다, 정리하다 take off 자리를 뜨다, 퇴근하다 be on ~ ~가 지불하다 first round 술자리에서 처음 술을 돌리는 것, 일차 chip in 각자 조금씩 내다

11 급여

pay slip(급여 명세서), base pay(기본금), annual pay(연봉), bonus(상여금), overtime work pay(초과 근무 수당), severance pay(퇴직금) 등 급여와 관련된 기본 표현들과 급여 인상, 인상 요청 등에 관한 표현들을 살펴보겠습니다.

원어민 발음 듣기 ☑☐ 회화 훈련 ☐☐ 듣기 훈련 ☐☐

☐ 월급날이 언제야?	When is your payday?
☐ 월급날이 일주일 남았어.	My payday is a week away.
☐ 월급날은 매달 20일이야.	My payday is on the 20th of every month.
☐ 급여 명세서 받았어?	Did you get your pay slip?
☐ 기본금이 얼마야?	How much is your base pay?
☐ 상여금 얼마 받았어?	How much bonus did you get paid?
☐ 초과 근무 수당 받았어?	Did you get paid for the overtime work?
☐ 기대했던 것보다 적어.	It's lower than I expected. *lower ↔ higher(더 많은)
☐ 연말 보너스가 나올까?	I wonder if we get our year-end bonuses. Does our boss give us a year-end bonus?
☐ 이번 달부터 급여가 인상됐어.	My pay has increased from this month.
☐ 급여 인상을 요청해 봤어?	Have you asked for a raise (in salary)?
☐ 급여 인상해 주세요.	I want a raise.
☐ 급여 통장에 입금됐어?	Has your pay been deposited to your bank account?
☐ 연말 정산 했어?	Did you get your tax refund filing done?
☐ 퇴직 급여는 얼마나 될까?	How much severance pay will we get? *get = receive
☐ 연봉 얼마 받아?	How much do you get paid annually?
☐ 시급으로 돈을 지급 받아.	We get paid by hour.

Chapter 14

음식
Food

01 좋아하는 음식

서로 다른 취향, 특히 좋아하는 음식에 대해 이야기하다 보면 처음 만난 사이라도 어색함이 금방 사라집니다. 어떤 종류의 음식을 좋아하는지, 요리를 할 줄 아는지, 잘하는 요리가 있는지 등을 어떻게 물어보는지 알아봅시다.

원어민 발음 듣기 ☑□　회화 훈련 □□　듣기 훈련 □□

□ 어떤 음식 좋아해?
What kind of food do you like?
*food = dish, meal

□ 가장 좋아하는 음식은 뭐니?
What's your favorite food?
What do you like the most?

□ 한식은 다 좋아해.
I like all Korean foods.

□ 난 이탈리아 음식이 좋아.
I love Italian foods.

□ 특별한 날엔 어떤 음식을 먹어?
What do you eat on a special day?

□ 요리 잘해?
Are you a good cook?
Do you cook well?

□ 가장 잘하는 요리는 뭐야?
What's your specialty?

□ 레시피 좀 가르쳐 줘.
Can I have the recipe?
Do you mind if you give me the recipe?

□ 나도 만들어 보고 싶어.
I'd like to try it by myself.

□ 손님을 치를 땐 어떤 음식을 준비하니?
What do you usually cook when you have guests at home?

□ 간식을 좋아하니?
Do you like snacks?

□ 난 과일을 즐겨 먹어.
I enjoy eating fruits.

□ 주로 어떤 차를 마시니?
What do you usually drink?

□ 커피와 녹차를 주로 마셔.
I drink coffee and green tea.

□ 과일 주스가 최고야.
Fruit juices are my favorite.

📋 Notes

favorite 특히 좋아하는 (것)　cook 요리사　specialty 특히 잘하는 것　recipe 요리의 조리법　(Do you) mind if ~? ~해도 싫지 않으세요?　by oneself 혼자 힘으로

02 음식점 선택

음식점은 어디를 가나 즐비하지만 내 입에 맞는 '맛있는 집'을 찾기란 결코 쉽지 않습니다. 보통 음식점에 대해 평가할 때는 taste(맛), portion(양), price(가격) 등을 기준으로 하는데 요즘에는 소위 '맛집'으로 소문난 음식점을 찾아가더라도 신통치 않은 경우도 있습니다.

원어민 발음 듣기 ☑□　회화 훈련 □□　듣기 훈련 □□

☐ 어느 음식점에 갈까? | Which restaurant should we go?

☐ 새로 생긴 음식점 가 볼까? | Let's try a new restaurant.
Do you want to try a new one?

☐ 네가 골라. | You choose.
*choose = pick
It's up to you.

☐ 인터넷으로 '맛집' 검색해 보자. | Let's search some famous restaurants on the Internet.
*search = find

☐ 그 음식점 맛있대. | The dish at that restaurant is delicious.

☐ 그 음식 아주 유명해. | The dish is very famous.

☐ 이 식당 내 친구가 추천한 곳이야. | My friend recommends this restaurant.

☐ 저번에 한 번 먹었는데 맛있더라. | I tried it once and it was delicious.

☐ 이 음식이 내 입에 맞아. | This food suits my taste.
It tastes perfect for me.

☐ 가격은 괜찮은 것 같은데. | Prices seem reasonable.

☐ 늘 가던 데로 가자. | Let's go to the restaurant where we usually go.
Let's go to our usual place.

☐ 거기서는 우리가 단골손님이잖아. | We are patrons there.

☐ 양이 푸짐하잖아. | They give us generous portions.
I like their big portions.

☐ 주인 인심이 후하잖아. | The owner is very generous.
I like the owner's generosity.

03 식사 주문하기

식당에서 음식을 주문할 때는 I'll have ~. 또는 I'm going to have ~.(~을 먹을게요.)라고 합니다. 식사 중간에 필요한 것을 요청할 때, 취향에 따라 직접 골라야 하는 경우, 테이블 정리를 부탁할 때 어떻게 말하는지 살펴봅시다.

원어민 발음 듣기 ☑☐ 회화 훈련 ☐☐ 듣기 훈련 ☐☐

☐ 어서 오세요.

Welcome.
Come right in.

☐ 일행이 몇 분이세요?

How many are with you?
How many (are) in your party?

☐ 네 명 자리 주세요.

We need a table for four.
A table for four, please.

☐ 창가 자리로 주시겠어요?

I'd like a table by the window.
A window table, please.

☐ 조용한 자리로 주시겠어요?

I'd like quiet seats.
Quiet seats, please.

☐ 메뉴판 주세요.

Can I see the menu?
Can we have the menu?
The menu, please.

☐ 어떤 음식을 주문할까?

What should we order?
Let's order.

☐ 각기 다른 메뉴를 시키자.

Let each of us order a different dish.

☐ 나눠서 먹자.

Let's share the food.
Shall we share the food?

☐ 주문할게요.

We're ready to order.
We're going to order.

☐ 주문하시겠어요?

Would you like to order?
May I take your order?
Are you ready to order?

☐ 한 사람이 더 올 거예요.

I'm expecting someone.

잠시 후에 주문할게요.	We'll order a little later.
여기는 어떤 음식을 잘 하나요?	What's your specialty? What's good here?
네가 먹는 것(같은 것)으로 할래.	I'll have what you're having. I'll have the same.
새로운 것을 먹어 볼래.	I'll try something new.
아직 결정 못했어요.	We haven't decided yet.
결정되면 부를게요.	We'll call you when we're ready.
스테이크로 먹을게요.	I'll have steak. I'll try steak. I'm going to have steak.
스테이크는 어떻게 해 드릴까요?	How would you like your steak done?
완전히 익혀 주세요.	(I like it) Well-done, please. *well-done → medium well-done(적당히 익힌), medium(중간 정도 익힌), medium rare(적당히 날것의), rare(날것의)
바로 가져다 드리겠습니다.	Coming right up. They'll be ready soon.
음식 나왔습니다.	Here are your dishes.
스테이크는 어느 분이 시키셨죠?	Who ordered steak?
우리가 주문한 것이 아닌데요.	This isn't what we ordered.
음식이 아직 안 나왔어요.	I haven't got my food yet.
식탁 좀 치워 주세요.	Could you please clear the table?
필요한 것 있으면 버튼을 눌러 주세요.	Ring me if you need anything. *ring = buzz
물 좀 더 주세요.	Can I get some more water? I want some more water.
반찬 좀 더 주세요.	I'd like to have more of this side dish.
후식은 무엇으로 하시겠어요?	What would you like for dessert? Would you like dessert?

☐ 커피 주세요.	(Just) Coffee, please.
☐ 남은 음식은 싸 주시겠어요?	Could you please wrap this up?
	Can I have a doggie bag?
☐ 스테이크 두 개 포장이요.	I'd like two steaks to go.
	Can I have two steaks for take-out?
☐ 빈자리가 없어요.	We don't have any tables available now.
☐ 20분 정도면 자리가 납니다.	We'll have a table available in 20 minutes.
	*available = ready

DIALOGUE

A We don't have any tables available now.

B Oh, we should have made a reservation.

How long do we have to wait?

A I think we'll have a table available in 20 minutes.

B That's not so bad. We'll wait.

A 지금 빈 자리가 없어요.

B 저런. 예약을 할 걸 그랬네요. 얼마나 기다려야 하죠?

A 아마 20분 정도면 자리가 날 것 같습니다.

B 그다지 오래는 아니네요. 기다릴게요.

 Notes

share the food 음식을 함께 나눠 먹다　take order 주문을 받다　clear the table 식탁을 치우다　ring 벨을 울
리다　wrap up 포장하다. 싸다　doggie bag 남은 음식을 싸는 봉지　to go (식당에서) 가져가기 위한　take out
사 가지고 가는 음식

04 술자리에서

식사 자리에서 술을 권할 때는 Want a drink?라고 하면 됩니다. 술을 한잔 사겠다고 할 때는 I'll buy you a drink.라고 하고, 주량을 물어볼 때는 How much do you drink?라고 하죠. 이 밖에도 건배 제의하기, 취했을 때 등의 표현들을 배워 보겠습니다.

원어민 발음 듣기 ☑☐　회화 훈련 ☐☐　듣기 훈련 ☐☐

☐ 술 한잔 하고 싶다.	I'd like to have a drink. I feel like drinking.
☐ 술 한잔 할래?	Would you like to have a drink? Want a drink? How about a drink?
☐ 내가 한잔 살게.	I'll buy you a drink.
☐ 술을 주문할까?	Let's order some alcohol.
☐ 맥주 주세요.	Can I have a beer?
☐ 와인 한 병 주세요.	Can I have a bottle of wine?
☐ 어떤 와인으로 드릴까요?	What kind of wine would you like?
☐ 가장 인기 있는 것으로 주세요.	The most popular wine here, please.
☐ 건배!	Let's toast. / Cheers! / Chin-chin!
☐ 모두들, 원샷!	Everybody, bottoms up!
☐ 건강을 위하여!	To our health!
☐ 성공을 위하여!	To our success!
☐ 잔이 비었네.	Your glass is empty.
☐ 한 잔 더해.	You need another shot.
☐ 한 잔 따라 줄게.	Let me pour you a drink.
☐ 술 좋아해?	Do you like drinking? Do you enjoy drinking?
☐ 주량이 보통 얼마야?	How much do you usually drink? What's your limit?

☐ 맥주 두 병 마셔.	I drink two bottles of beer.
☐ 난 술이 세.	I drink like a fish. I'm a heavy drinker.
☐ 난 술이 약해.	I'm a lightweight.
☐ 전혀 못 마셔.	I don't drink. Not even a drop.
☐ 난 사람이 좋아서 술을 마셔.	I'm a social drinker. I love drinking with people.
☐ 술을 천천히 마시는 편이야.	I'm a slow drinker.
☐ 가능하면 안 마시려고 해.	I try not to drink.
☐ 술 마시는 거 좋아하지 않아.	I don't like drinking.
☐ 나 술 끊었어.	I quit drinking.
☐ 일주일에 두 번 마셔.	I drink twice a week.
☐ 나 취하는 것 같은데.	I think I'm getting drunk.
☐ 나 안 취했어.	I'm not drunk.
☐ 이제 그만 마셔야겠다.	I think I should stop here. That's it for me.
☐ 다리에 힘이 없어.	My legs are shaky. I can't walk straight.
☐ 토할 것 같아.	I don't feel good. I think I'm going to throw up. *throw up = puke
☐ 머리가 핑핑 돌아.	I feel dizzy. *dizzy = tipsy My head is spinning.
☐ 그는 엄청 취했어.	He's totally wasted.
☐ 그는 주사가 심해.	He's out of control when he gets drunk.
☐ 어젯밤에 나 필름 끊겼어.	I blacked out last night. *black out = pass out

216

05 음식의 맛 표현

음식의 맛은 sweet(단), salt(짠), bitter(쓴), sour(신), spicy(매운)의 '오미(五味)' 외에 입 안에서 씹히는 느낌이나 질감, 향 등에서도 영향을 받습니다. '고소한', '바삭한', '비린', '텁텁한', '개운한' 등의 음식의 맛을 어떻게 표현하는지 알아보겠습니다.

원어민 발음 듣기 ☑□   회화 훈련 □□   듣기 훈련 □□

□ 밥이 잘 됐어.
This rice is perfect for me.

□ 밥이 질어.
This rice is sticky.

□ 밥이 덜 됐어.
This rice is not done yet.

□ 찌개가 너무 짜.
The stew is too salty.
*is = tastes
There's too much salt.

□ 국이 심심해.
This soup tastes bland.
*bland = weak
This soup needs salt.
This soup isn't salty enough.

□ 도넛이 너무 달아.
Doughnuts are too sugary.
*sugary = sweet

□ 김치가 정말 맵다.
Kimchi is very spicy.
*spicy = hot

□ 국물 맛이 쓰다.
This soup is bitter.

□ 크림소스가 새콤하다.
Cream sauce tastes sour.

□ 비린내가 나.
Fish smell.
I smell something fishy.

□ 참기름 냄새가 고소하다.
Sesame oil smells savory.

□ 견과류가 들어서 쿠키가 바삭바삭해.
Cookies are crunchy and nutty.
*crunchy = crispy

□ 계란찜이 아주 부드러워.
Steamed eggs are soft.

□ 소시지가 느끼해.
Sausages are greasy.
*greasy = oily

□ 맛이 텁텁하다.
It tastes thick.

□ 입 안이 텁텁해.	I have an unpleasant taste in my mouth.	
□ 사과가 입 안을 개운하게 해.	Apple makes your mouth fresh.	
□ 감이 떫어.	This persimmon is astringent.	
□ 이거 맛이 이상해.	This tastes strange.	
	*strange = funny, odd, weird	
□ 상한 것 같아.	It's gone bad.	
	It's rotten.	
□ 고기가 질겨.	This meat is tough.	
□ 고기가 부드러워.	This meat is tender.	

Notes

sticky 끈적끈적한, 질척한 bland 맛이 밋밋한, 싱거운 fishy 생선 비린내의, 의심스러운 nutty 견과류가 많이 든
greasy 기름진, 느끼한 thick 두꺼운, 액체가 걸쭉한, 맛이 텁텁한 go bad 상하다, 나쁘게 변질되다

06 식당 평가

식당에 가면 그 집의 taste(맛)와 service(서비스)를 평가하게 됩니다. 아무리 famous restaurant (맛집)이라도 그 reputation(명성)과 달리 실망스러운 경우도 있지요. 음식의 맛과 서비스에 대한 표현은 어떤 것이 있는지 살펴보겠습니다.

원어민 발음 듣기 ☑□　회화 훈련 □□　듣기 훈련 □□

□ 음식이 맛있다.	The food is delicious.
	It tastes wonderful.
	*wonderful = tasty, superb, fabulous
□ 처음 먹어 보는 맛이야.	I've never tasted like this before.
□ 역시 소문대로야.	It has lived up to its reputation.
□ 음식이 형편없어.	The food is horrible.
	*horrible = awful
□ 유명한 집 맞아?	Is this really a famous restaurant?
□ 서비스가 최고야.	The service here is great.
□ 서비스가 엉망이야.	The service here is really bad.
□ 너무 불친절해.	They are very rude.
□ 너무 비싸다.	It's too expensive.
□ 멀리서 찾아왔는데.	We came from a long way.
□ 거기 다시는 안 갈 거야.	I'll never go there again.
□ 인터넷에 평가글 올려야지.	I'm going to post some comments on the Internet.
□ 음식에서 머리카락이 나왔어요.	There's a piece of hair in my food.
□ 컵에 립스틱 자국이 있어요.	There's a lipstick mark on my cup.
□ 위생적이지 않아요.	It's not sanitary.
	*sanitary = hygienic, clean
□ 매니저 불러 주세요.	Call your manager, please.
	I'd like to have a word with your manager.

07 계산하기

미국에서는 같이 먹은 음식 값을 계산할 때 보통 go Dutch(각자 내다)하지만 특별한 경우 I'll get this. 혹은 I got it.(내가 살게.)이라고 말하는 때도 있습니다. 반반씩 부담할 경우에는 간단히 Go 50-50.라고 하면 됩니다.

원어민 발음 듣기 ☑☐   회화 훈련 ☐☐   듣기 훈련 ☐☐

☐ 계산서 주세요.	**Check, please.** *check = bill **Can we have the bill?**
☐ 내가 살게.	**It's on me.** **My treat.** **I'll get this (one).** **I got it.**
☐ 아냐. 내가 살게.	**No, let me.** **Please, allow me.**
☐ 다음에 사 줘.	**Next meal is on you.** **Why don't you buy me next time?**
☐ 디저트는 네가 사.	**Dessert is on you.** **Why don't you buy me dessert?**
☐ 각자 내자.	**Let's go Dutch.** **Let's pay separately.** **Let's split it.**
☐ 반씩 내자.	**Let's go fifty-fifty.** *fifty-fifty = halves
☐ 어디서 계산하죠?	**Where can I pay?**
☐ 계산이 이상해요.	**I think there's a mistake on the bill.**
☐ 다시 확인해 주세요.	**Would you please check again?**
☐ 이 음식 주문하지 않았어요.	**We didn't order this food.**
☐ 주문에 착오가 있었습니다.	**There was a mix-up in orders.**

08 식사 준비와 정리

집에서 식사를 할 때에는 cooking(요리)에서부터 setting the table(식탁 차리기), washing the dishes(설거지)까지 여러 일을 하게 됩니다. 손이 모자랄 때는 식탁 차리는 것을 도와달라고 부탁할 수도 있죠. 식사 준비와 정리에 관련된 다양한 표현들을 배워 보겠습니다.

원어민 발음 듣기 ✔☐   회화 훈련 ☐☐   듣기 훈련 ☐☐

☐ 배고프다.
I'm hungry.
*hungry = starving, starved

☐ 배고파 죽겠어.
I'm starving to death.
My stomach is growling.

☐ 요즘 식욕이 엄청 나.
I have such a big appetite these days.

☐ 점심을 굶었어.
I didn't have lunch.
I skipped lunch.

☐ 나 하루 종일 굶었어.
I haven't eaten anything all day.

☐ 저녁 식사 준비할게.
I'll make dinner.
*make = prepare for

☐ 저녁 식사 준비 도와줄래?
Could you help me make dinner?

☐ 야채 좀 씻어 줘.
Wash vegetables, please.

☐ 야채 껍질을 벗겨 줘.
Peel them off, please.

☐ 야채를 잘게 썰어 줘.
Chop them up, please.

☐ 식탁 차려 줘.
Could you set the table?

☐ 국을 데울게.
I'm going to heat up the stew.
*heat up = warm up

☐ 저녁 식사 준비 거의 다 됐어.
Dinner's almost ready.

☐ 10분만 더 기다려 줘.
Wait ten more minutes.

☐ 식사 준비 끝!
Dinner's ready!

☐ 식사 대령이요.
Dinner is served.

☐ 먹자.
Let's eat.
Let's dig in.

▢ 그릇을 싱크대로 옮겨 줘.	Move your dishes into the sink, please.
▢ 설거지는 내가 할게.	I'll wash the dishes.
▢ 내가 나중에 할게.	I'll do it later.
▢ 그릇의 물기 좀 닦아 줘.	Dry the dishes, please.
▢ 식탁을 닦아 줘.	Clear the table, please.

📖 요리법(cooking)

끓이다 boil, heat, warm
삶다 boil, simmer
데치다 blanch, parboil
굽다 grill, bake, broil, toast
튀기다 fry
찌다 steam
볶다 roast, stir-fry
곁들이다 add, garnish
소금에 절이다 be salted

발효시키다 be fermented
양념에 재우다 marinate
양념을 치다 add(= sprinkle) seasoning,
　　　　　give flavor
썰다 cut, chop, slice
다지다 mince
깍뚝 썰다 dice, cube
채 썰다 shred

 Notes

starve 몹시 배고프다, 굶주리다　growl (몹시 배고파서) 배에서 소리가 나다　big appetite 왕성한 식욕　skip 건너 뛰다, 넘기다　make dinner 저녁을 차리다　peel off 껍질을 벗기다　chop up 잘게 다 썰다, 다지다　warm up 데우다, 따뜻하게 하다(= heat up)　stew 큼직한 건더기가 있는 수프, 국, 찌개　dig in 식사하기 시작하다　wash the dishes 설거지하다

09 배달 음식

미국에서 order in(배달시키다)해서 먹는 음식의 메뉴는 우리와 크게 다르지만, 미국에서도 중국 음식과 피자는 대표적인 배달 음식입니다. 전화로 음식을 주문하는 것부터 주문한 음식을 받는 것까지 다양한 표현을 배워 보겠습니다.

원어민 발음 듣기 ☑☐ 회화 훈련 ☐☐ 듣기 훈련 ☐☐

☐ 여기 주소는 ~인데요.
The address here is ~.
My address is ~.

☐ 주소를 말씀해 주시겠어요?
Can I have your address, please?

☐ 영업 시작하셨나요?
Are you open?

☐ 배달되나요?
Do you deliver?

☐ 피자 라지 사이즈 2판 배달해 주세요.
I'd like to order two large pizzas.
Can you deliver two large pizzas, please?

☐ 피클과 딥핑 소스도 주세요.
I need pickles and dipping sauces, too.

☐ 자장면은 곱빼기로 주세요.
Can I get a double portion of jajangmyeon?

☐ 주문이 밀렸어요.
Orders have piled up.
Orders are backed up.

☐ 30분 정도 기다리셔야 합니다.
You need to wait for about 30 minutes.
Can you wait for 30 minutes?

☐ 기다릴게요.
I'll wait.
I can wait.

☐ 면이 불지 않게 해 주세요.
I don't like soggy noodles.

☐ 가능한 빨리 배달해 드리겠습니다.
We'll have them delivered as fast as we can.

☐ 피자 왔습니다.
Your pizzas are here.

☐ 아주 따끈따끈하네요.
They're really hot.

☐ 그릇은 문밖에 둘게요.
I'll put the dishes right outside the door.

10 식탁 예절

입 안에 음식을 넣고 말을 하는 것은 동서양을 막론하고 식탁 예절에서 벗어나는 행동입니다. 그리고 상대방이 정성껏 차린 음식을 먹을 때는 '잘 먹었다'는 인사도 잊지 말아야겠죠. 식탁에서 음식이나 식사 태도에 관해 할 수 있는 표현을 알아봅시다.

원어민 발음 듣기 ☑□   회화 훈련 □□   듣기 훈련 □□

☐ 맛있겠어요.	It looks delicious.
☐ 입에 침이 고여요.	My mouth is watering.
	It makes my mouth watery.
☐ 한 상 차려 놓으셨네요.	You put on quite a spread.
☐ 차린 것은 없어요.	It's not much.
☐ 맛있게 (많이) 드세요.	Help yourself.
	Enjoy!
	Eat up!
	(I hope) You enjoy the food.
☐ 입에서 살살 녹아요.	It melts in my mouth.
☐ 최고예요.	It's the best.
☐ 더 드릴까요?	(Do you) Want some more?
☐ 더 드세요.	Have (some) more.
☐ 감사하지만 괜찮습니다.	Thanks, but no.
☐ 저는 소식가입니다.	I'm not a big eater.
	I eat like a bird.
☐ 디저트가 준비됐어요.	Dessert is ready.
☐ 거절할 수 없죠.	I can't say no to that.
☐ 배불러요.	I'm full.
	*full = stuffed
	I'm up to here.
☐ 잘 먹었습니다.	It was (really) delicious.
	The food was delicious.

The dinner was delicious.
Everything was so delicious.
I enjoyed the dinner very much.

☐ 바른 자세로 식사하세요.	Sit straight when you eat.
☐ 입 안에 음식을 넣고 말하지 마세요.	Don't talk with your mouth full.
☐ 트림은 삼가세요.	Please don't belch.
☐ 재채기가 날 때는 입을 가리세요.	Cover your mouth when you sneeze.
☐ 다른 사람 앞으로 손을 내밀지 마세요.	Don't reach your hands to other people.
☐ 식사 중에 담배를 피우지 마세요.	Don't smoke while eating.
☐ 음식을 후후 불지 마세요.	Don't blow on your plates.
☐ 먹을 때 소리 내지 마세요.	Don't make noise when you eat.

📋 **Notes**

watering 입에 침이 고이는, 군침을 흘리는 put on a spread 음식을 잔뜩 차려놓다, 한 상 크게 차리다 eat up
많이 먹다, 다 먹어 치우다 big eater 대식가 eat like a bird 새처럼 아주 조금 먹다, 소식하다 stuffed 꽉 찬, 배
가 잔뜩 부른 sit straight 똑바로 앉다 belch 트림하다 sneeze 재채기하다 reach 뻗다, 닿다 blow 불다
plate 접시, 요리 make noise 시끄럽게 하다, 소리를 내다

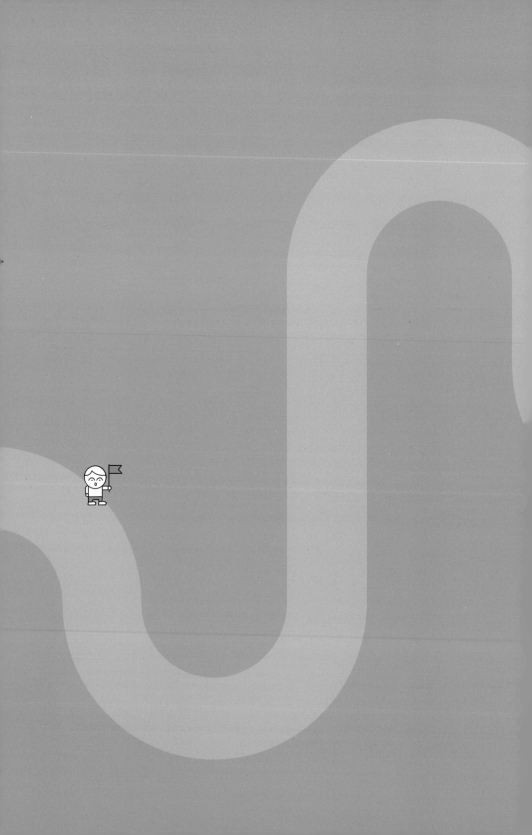

Chapter 15

병원
Hospital

01 진료 예약과 접수

병원 진료 예약 및 접수에 필요한 표현들을 알아보겠습니다. "진료 예약해 주세요."는 I'd like to make an appointment.라고 하고, 특정 의사에게서 진료를 받고 싶다면 I'd like to see Dr. ~.라고 말하면 됩니다.

원어민 발음 듣기 ☑☐   회화 훈련 ☐☐   듣기 훈련 ☐☐

☐ 진료 받으러 왔어요.

I'm here to see a doctor.
I'd like to see a doctor.

☐ 처음 오셨나요?

Is this your first time?

☐ 여기에 진료 기록이 있나요?

Do you have your medical records here?

☐ 여기에서 진료 받은 적 있나요?

Have you seen a doctor here?

☐ 기록을 찾아보겠습니다.

I'll check your records.
Let me check your records.

☐ 의사와 지금 상담할 수 있나요?

Can I see a doctor now?

☐ 먼저 접수처로 가세요.

Go to the reception desk first, please.

☐ 진료 예약해 주세요.

I'd like to make an appointment.

☐ 김 선생님에게 진료 받고 싶습니다.

I'd like to see Dr. Kim.

☐ 지금 다른 환자를 진료 중입니다.

He's seeing another patient.
He's with another patient now.

☐ 김 선생님은 이번 주 일정이 꽉 찼어요.

Dr. Kim's schedule has been fully booked for this week.

☐ 다음 주 진료 예약은 가능합니다.

You can see him next week.

☐ 예약해 주세요.

Book me with him, please.
Make an appointment with him, please.

☐ 다음 차례입니다.

You're next.

☐ 이제 의사 선생님과 상담 가능합니다.

The doctor will see you now.

📄 Notes

see a doctor 의사와 상담하다, 의사에게 진료 받다   make an appointment ~와 약속을 잡다   patient 환자
be fully booked (예약, 스케줄 등이) 다 잡히다   book 예약하다, 약속해 두다

02 건강 검진 받기

건강을 위해서 정기적으로 general check-up(종합 건강 검진)을 받는 것이 좋죠. 검진을 실시하는 병원에 전화해서 날짜를 예약하면 검진 전 준비 사항을 알려 주는데, 검진 전날 "밤 9시 이후로는 금식하세요."는 영어로 Don't eat anything after 9.이라고 합니다.

원어민 발음 듣기 ☑☐   회화 훈련 ☐☐   듣기 훈련 ☐☐

Chapter 15

병원

☐ 건강 검진을 받고 싶어요.	I'm here for a check-up. *check-up = physical exam
☐ 11월 30일에 검진을 받고 싶습니다.	I'd like to get a physical on Nov 30th.
☐ 이틀 전에 문자메시지 드리겠습니다.	We'll text you two days before your physical.
☐ 검진비는 언제 지불하나요?	When should I pay for a physical exam?
☐ 검진 당일에 지불하시면 됩니다.	You can pay it on the day you get a physical.
☐ 밤 9시 이후로는 금식입니다.	Don't eat anything after 9. You're not supposed to eat anything after 9.
☐ 물도 마시지 마세요.	Don't even drink water.
☐ 껌, 담배, 격렬한 운동은 피해 주세요.	Try to avoid chewing gums, smoking, or hard exercise. *hard = intense
☐ 대변을 받아오세요.	You need to bring your stool.
☐ 검진 시간은 얼마나 걸리나요?	How long does it take for a check-up?
☐ 위장 내시경을 하고 싶어요.	I'd like to get an (stomach) endoscopy.
☐ 대장 내시경을 해야 할까요?	Do I need a colonoscopy?
☐ 결과는 일주일 후에 나옵니다.	You will know the result in a week.
☐ 아주 정상입니다.	You're perfectly normal. *normal = healthy
☐ ~에 문제가 있는 것 같습니다.	You seem to have a problem with ~.
☐ 진료 받으세요.	Why don't you see a specialist? You need to see a doctor.

03 내과에서

stomachache(복통), headache(두통), bad cold(독감) 등이 있을 때 internal department(내과)를 찾습니다. internist 혹은 physician(내과 의사)에게 어디가 아픈지, 어떤 증상이 있는지를 상세히 설명해야 합니다. 내과 질병의 증상들을 설명하는 기본적인 표현들을 정리했습니다.

원어민 발음 듣기 ☑□   회화 훈련 □□   듣기 훈련 □□

□ 배가 아파요.

I have a stomachache.
I have an upset stomach.
My stomach hurts.

□ 설사가 나요.

I've got diarrhea.
I have diarrhea.
My bowels are loose.

□ 변비가 있어요.

I'm constipated.
My bowels have stopped.

□ 설사와 변비를 반복해요.

I have sensitive bowels.
I have diarrhea and constipation.

□ 가스가 차요.

I've got gas in my bowels.

□ 위가(속이) 쓰려요.

I have a sore stomach.
I have heartburn.
I have a burning feeling in my stomach.

□ 속이 더부룩해요.

I feel bloated.
My stomach is heavy.
*is = feel
Food sits heavy on my stomach.
*sit = lie

□ 매스꺼워요.

I feel nauseous.
I feel sick (to my stomach).

□ 구토가 나요.

I feel like throwing up.

□ 머리가 아파요.

I have a headache.
My head hurts.

□ 편두통이 있어요.

I have a migraine.

□ 머리가 깨질 듯이 아파요.	I have a splitting headache.
□ 머리를 두드려 맞은 듯 아파요.	I have a pounding headache.
□ 현기증이 나요.	I feel dizzy.
□ 감기에 걸렸어요.	I've got a cold.
	I have a cold.
	I think I'm coming down with a cold.
	I'm catching a cold.
□ 독감에 걸렸어요.	I've got a bad cold.
	*bad = nasty
	I've got the flu[influenza].
	*influenza에는 the를 쓰지 않는다.
□ 감기가 안 떨어져요.	I can't shake off the cold.
□ 미열이 있어요.	You're a little feverish.
□ 열이 높아요.	I have a high fever.
	*fever = temperature
□ 밤만 되면 열이 나요.	I have a fever at night.
□ 오한이 나요.	I feel cold.
	I've got chills.
□ 온 몸이 아파요.	My body is aching.
	My body is sore.
□ 몸살이 났어요.	I've got fatigue.
□ 재채기가 나요.	I sneeze.
	I keep sneezing.
□ 콧물이 줄줄 나요.	I've got a runny nose.
	My nose is running.
□ 코가 막혔어요.	My nose is stopped up.
	*stopped up = stuffed up
□ 숨 쉬기가 힘들어요.	I can't breathe well.
	It's hard to breathe.
□ 기침이 계속 나요.	I cough constantly.
	I keep coughing.

목이 아파요.	I have a sore throat.
	My throat hurts.
	My throat is sore.

(감기로) 목이 쉬었어요.	My voice is hoarse (from a cold).
	I've got a hoarse voice.
	*hoarse = husky

| 목소리가 안 나와요. | I've lost my voice. |

| 편도선이 부었어요. | I've got swollen tonsils. |
| | My tonsils are swollen. |

| 기운이 없어요. | I feel weak. |
| | *weak = feeble |

| 식욕을 잃었어요. | I've lost my appetite. |

| 갑자기 체중이 줄었어요. | I've lost weight suddenly. |
| | I've had a sudden weight loss. |

| 갑자기 체중이 늘었어요. | I've gained weight suddenly. |
| | I've had a sudden weight gain. |

| 혈색이 안 좋군요. | You look pale. |
| | You have no color. |

| 물을 많이 드세요. | Drink plenty of water. |
| | *water = fluid |

| 충분한 수면을 취하세요. | Sleep enough. |

| 처방약을 드세요. | Take a prescribed medicine. |

| 좀 더 두고 봅시다. | Let's wait and see. |
| | Let's see how things will shape up. |

📋 Notes

upset 속이 불편한, 속이 아픈 bowel 장, 대장 loose 설사하는, 설사가 나는 constipated 변비의 sensitive 민감한, 예민한 get gas 가스가 차다 sore 쓰린, 아픈 heartburn 속 쓰림 burning feeling 속이 화끈거림, 속 쓰림 bloated 속이 더부룩한, 소화가 잘 안 되는 sit heavy on 음식이 소화되지 않고 위에 괴어 있다(= lie heavy on) nauseous 매스꺼운 splitting 깨지는 듯한 pounding 두드리는, 타격하는 듯한 come down with 병에 걸리다 shake off 털어내다, 떨어내다 feverish (미)열이 있는 chills 오한, 오싹함 fatigue 심신의 피로, 몸살 runny nose 콧물이 줄줄 흐름 be stopped up 꽉 막히다(= be stuffed up) hoarse 목이 쉰, 쉰 소리가 나는 feeble 연약한, 무기력한 lose weight 체중이 줄다 gain weight 체중이 늘다 pale 얼굴이 창백한, 핏기 없는 fluid 액체, 물, 수분 shape up 잘 되다, 뜻대로 되다

04 외과에서

팔이나 다리의 dislocation(골절), muscle pain(근육통), abrasion(찰과상), burn(화상), infection(염증) 등으로 고생할 때는 surgery department(외과)에 가서 치료를 받습니다.

원어민 발음 듣기 ☑️□ 회화 훈련 □□ 듣기 훈련 □□

Chapter 15
응급실

☐ 발목을 삐었어요.

I sprained my ankle.

I've got a sprained ankle.

*ankle → wrist(손목)

☐ 뼈마디가 탈구됐어요.

My joints are dislocated.

☐ 팔이 탈구됐어요.

My arm is out of joint.

☐ 발목이 (퉁퉁) 부었어요.

My ankle is (all) swollen.

☐ 발을 땅에 못 디디겠어요.

I can't step on the ground.

*step = tread

☐ 다리가 부러졌어요.

I broke my leg.

I have a broken leg.

☐ 팔이 부러졌어요.

I broke my arm.

☐ 찰과상이 심해요.

I've got a serious scratch.

*scratch = abrasion

☐ 어깨 (심한) 통증이 있어요.

I have (severe) pain in my shoulders.

☐ 팔을 들 수가 없어요.

I can't raise my arms.

*raise = lift up, hold up

☐ 근육통이 심해요.

I have serious muscle pain.

☐ 갈수록 통증이 더 심해요.

It's getting worse (and worse).

☐ 허리가 아파요.

I have waist pain.

My waist hurts.

☐ 다리가 당겨요.

My legs are cramping.

I've got a cramp in my leg.

☐ 다리에 쥐가 자주 나요.

My legs are often asleep.

☐ 다리를 들어 올릴 수가 없어요.

I can't lift up my leg.

233

□ 목 뒤가 아파요.	I have pain in the back of my neck.	
□ 멍이 잘 생겨요.	I get bruises easily.	
□ 화상을 입었어요.	I got burnt.	
□ 햇볕에 심하게 탔어요.	I got sunburn.	
□ 물집이 생겼어요.	I've got blisters.	
□ 고름이 나요.	Pus is coming out of the wound.	
	I have pus.	
□ 염증이 있군요.	You have an infection.	
	*infection = inflammation	
□ 항생제를 처방할게요.	I'm going to prescribe antibiotics.	
□ 골절이 심하군요.	You have a severe dislocation.	
□ 깁스를 해야 합니다.	You need to cast it.	
	You need a cast.	
□ 회복하는 데 얼마나 걸릴까요?	How long will it take to recover?	
	How long will it take to get better?	
□ 한 달 정도 걸립니다.	It will take about a month.	
□ 왜 이제야 오셨어요?	Why didn't you come sooner?	
	You should've seen a doctor earlier.	
□ 수술을 해야 합니다.	You need a surgery.	
□ 수술 동의서가 필요합니다.	We need you to sign on the surgery consent form.	
□ 척추 디스크가 의심됩니다.	I suspect that you have disc herniation.	
□ 2도 화상입니다.	You've got a second-degree burn.	
□ 물집을 터뜨리지 마세요.	Don't burst blisters.	

📑 Notes

sprain (발목, 손목 등을) 삐다 joint 관절 dislocate 관절을 탈구시키다, 틀어지게 하다 step on ~에 발을 디디다(= tread on) severe 심한, 심각한 hold up 팔을 들어 올리다, 쳐들다 cramp 당기는 통증을 느끼다 legs are asleep 다리에 쥐가 나다, 저리다 bruise 멍 get burnt 화상을 입다, 불에 데다 wound 상처 prescribe 약을 처방하다 cast 깁스, 깁스로 고정시키다 recover 회복하다, 낫다 should have+과거분사 ~했어야 했다 consent 동의, 허가 disc herniation 척추 디스크

05 피부과에서

갈수록 심해지는 환경 오염 때문인지 dermatology(피부과)를 찾는 사람들이 부쩍 늘고 있다고 합니다. 아토피 피부염으로 고생하는 아기에서부터 뾰루지나 알레르기성 발진을 앓는 어른에 이르기까지 다양합니다. dermatologist(피부과 의사)에게 증상을 설명할 때 필요한 표현들을 알아보겠습니다.

원어민 발음 듣기 ☑□   회화 훈련 □□   듣기 훈련 □□

□ 피부가 가려워요.

My skin is itchy.
I've got itchy skin.

□ 피부가 빨갛고 아파요.

My skin is red and sore.

□ 발진이 있어요.

I've got a rash.

□ 땀띠가 심해요.

I've got a terrible heat rash.

□ 얼굴에 뾰루지(여드름)가 심해요.

My face is covered with pimples.
Pimples have broken out on my face.

□ 여드름을 짜지 마세요.

Don't squeeze the pimples.

□ 발에 습진이 있어요.

I've got eczema on my feet.

□ 습진은 전염되지 않아요.

Eczema is not contagious.

□ 알레르기성 발진입니다.

It's an allergic rash.

□ 면역력 약화 때문입니다.

Your immune system is weaker than usual.
Your level of immunity has dropped.

□ 아토피입니다.

It's atopic dermatitis.
You've got atopy.

□ 아이가 홍역에 걸렸습니다.

Your kid has measles.
*measles → chickenpox (수두), rubella (풍진)

□ 대상포진입니다.

You've been infected by herpes virus.
You've got herpes.

□ 곰팡이입니다.

You've got a fungus.
You've been infected by a fungus.

□ 연고를 처방할게요.

I'm going to prescribe an ointment.

06 치과에서

cavity(충치) 치료, wisdom tooth(사랑니)를 뽑거나 scaling(치석 제거), teeth whitening(치아 미백) 등을 위해 치과를 찾습니다. 치과 의사는 dentist 혹은 oral surgeon이라고 부르죠.

원어민 발음 듣기 ☑☐ 회화 훈련 ☐☐ 듣기 훈련 ☐☐

☐ 이가 (많이) 아파요. I have a bad toothache.

☐ 잘 씹을 수 없어요. I can't chew properly.

☐ 충치가 있는 것 같아요. I think I have a cavity.
　　　　　　　　　　　I think I have a decayed tooth.
　　　　　　　　　　　I have a bad tooth.

☐ 이가 부러졌어요. My tooth broke off.
　　　　　　　　　I have a broken tooth.

☐ 이가 흔들려요. My tooth is loose.
　　　　　　　　I have a loose tooth.

☐ 이가 빠졌어요. I've lost my tooth.
　　　　　　　　A tooth has come out of itself.

☐ 사랑니를 뽑아 주세요. I'd like you to pull out my wisdom tooth.
　　　　　　　　　　　Can you pull my wisdom tooth out?

☐ 잇몸이 붓고 피가 나요. My gums are swollen and bleeding.

☐ 치석 제거를 해 주세요. I need scaling.
　　　　　　　　　　　Can I get scaling?

☐ 치아 미백을 해 주세요. I want teeth whitening.

☐ 임플란트 시술이 필요할까요? Do I need a dental implant?

☐ 틀니를 사용하세요. You need a denture.

☐ 치아 엑스레이를 봐야겠어요. I need to check your dental X-ray.

☐ 필링을 해야 합니다. You need filling.

☐ 신경 치료를 해야 합니다. You need a root canal treatment.

07 안과에서

시력이 떨어져 안경을 써야 하거나 안구 질환이 있을 때는 ophthalmology(안과)를 찾습니다. nearsighted (근시), farsighted(원시), astigmatic(난시)이 있다면 이에 맞는 시력 교정이 필요하죠. 안과 의사는 ophthalmologist인데, eye doctor 라고도 부릅니다.

원어민 발음 듣기 ☑□   회화 훈련 □□   듣기 훈련 □□

☐ 시력이 나빠지고 있어요.	My vision is getting worse.
	I'm losing my vision.
	*vision = eyesight
☐ 눈이 침침해요.	I can't see things clearly.
	My eyes are blurry.
☐ 사물이 두 개로 보여요.	I have double vision.
☐ 눈이 충혈됐어요.	My eyes are red.
	My eyes are bloodshot.
☐ 눈이 가려워요.	My eyes are itchy.
☐ 눈이 따끔거려요.	My eyes are stinging.
☐ 눈물이 자꾸 나요.	My eyes are watery.
☐ 눈곱이 자주 껴요.	I have gum.
	*gum = eye wax
☐ 눈이 아파요.	My eyes hurt.
☐ 안구 건조증이 심해요.	My eyes are very dry.
	I have dry eyes.
☐ 콘택트렌즈를 끼고 싶어요.	I want to wear contact lenses.
☐ 라식 수술을 받고 싶어요.	I want the Lasik procedure.
	*Lasic → Lasek (라섹)
	*procedure = surgery, operation
☐ 근시입니다.	You're nearsighted.
	*nearsighted = shortsighted
	You can't see things from a far distance.
☐ 난시입니다.	You are astigmatic.
	You have astigmatism.

□ 원시입니다.	You're farsighted.
□ 노안입니다.	You have old eyes. You've become farsighted.
□ 안경을 쓰세요.	You need to wear eye glasses. Why don't you wear eye glasses?
□ 돋보기를 쓰세요.	You need reading glasses. Why don't you use reading glasses?
□ 콘택트렌즈는 눈을 건조하게 합니다.	Contact lenses will make your eyes dry. You will have dry eyes if you wear contact lenses.
□ 점안액을 사용하세요.	You need to use eye drops.
□ 30분마다 눈을 감고 쉬세요.	Close your eyes and relax every 30 minutes.
□ 수술을 권장하지 않습니다.	I don't recommend the surgery.

DIALOGUE

A My eyes are itchy and watery.
  They are red, too.
B Let me see your eyes first.
  Open your eyes wide.

A 눈이 가렵고 눈물이 나요. 충혈도 됐어요.
B 한번 봅시다. 눈을 크게 뜨세요.

📖 Notes

see clearly 명확히 보다　blurry 뿌연, 명료하지 않은　double vision 복시, 물건이 이중으로 보이는 현상
bloodshot 눈이 충혈된, 핏발이 선　sting 따끔따끔하다, 콕콕 찌르다　watery 눈물 나는, 눈물이 고이는　gum 끈적
끈적한 점성 물질, 눈곱(= eye wax)　procedure 의학적 조치　far distance 먼 거리　old eyes 나이 든 눈, 노안
eye glasses 안경　reading glasses 독서용 안경, 돋보기　eye drops 안약

08 산부인과에서

산부인과는 ob/gyn, obstetrics, gynecology 등으로 불립니다. 여성 환자를 보기 때문에 obstetrician(산부인과 의사)을 ladies' doctor라고도 부르죠. 임신을 원하지 않는 경우 올바른 birth control(피임) 방법을 알려 주고 임신이 되지 않는 여성에게는 artificial insemination(인공 수정)을 권하기도 합니다.

원어민 발음 듣기 ☑□   회화 훈련 □□   듣기 훈련 □□

□ 임신 테스트를 해 봤어요. I took a (home) pregnancy test.

□ 양성 반응 나왔어요. It was positive.
*positive → negative(음성)

□ 임신인 것 같아요. I think I'm pregnant.

□ 임신 3개월입니다. You're three months pregnant.

□ 임신이 아닙니다. You're not pregnant.

□ 상상 임신입니다. It's an imaginary pregnancy.
It's a phantom pregnancy.

□ 당신은 불임입니다. You're infertile.
*infertile = sterile, barren
You can't have a baby.

□ 임신이 안 돼요. I can't get pregnant.
It's difficult to get pregnant.

□ 인공 수정을 원해요. I want artificial insemination.
*artificial insemination = in vitro fertilization

□ 당신은 지금 배란기입니다. You're ovulating now.

□ 지금이 임신 적기입니다. It's the perfect time to conceive a baby.

□ 피임하고 싶어요. I don't want to be pregnant.
I want to avoid pregnancy.

□ 피임을 하고 있어요. I'm taking birth control pills.
I'm using a diaphragm.

□ 피임의 부작용을 알려 주세요. What are the side effects of a contraceptive?

□ 유산의 위험성이 있어요. You might have a chance to miscarry your baby.

239

☐ 아들입니다.	It's a boy.
☐ 예정일은 언제인가요?	When is the due date? When will I be expecting my baby?
☐ 출산일이 일주일 지났어요.	My baby is a week overdue.
☐ 입덧이 심해요.	I have severe morning sickness.
☐ 진통이 시작됐어요.	Her contractions have started. She's having contractions. She's in labor.
☐ 방금 양수가 터졌어요.	Your water (just) broke.
☐ 힘주세요.	Push! You've got to push.
☐ 아기 손, 발가락 모두 10개씩입니다.	Your baby has ten fingers and ten toes.
☐ 아기가 정상입니다.	Your baby is perfectly normal. *normal = healthy
☐ 생리가 불규칙해요.	I have irregular (menstrual) periods. I skip my periods time to time.
☐ 생리통이 너무 심해요.	I have severe (menstrual) cramps.

📑 **Notes**

imaginary 상상의, 공상의   phantom 가공의, 허깨비의   infertile 생식력이 없는, 불임의(= sterile, barren)
ovulate 배란하다   conceive 아이를 배다, 임신하다   diaphragm 다이어프램, 여성용 피임 도구   side effects 부
작용   contraceptive 피임약, 피임 기구   might have a chance ~할지 모른다, ~할 가능성이 있다   miscarry
유산하다   due date 마감일, 출산일   overdue 기한이 지난, 출산 예정이 지난   morning sickness 아침 구역질,
입덧   contractions 출산을 위한 진통   be in labor 출산 중에 있다   labor 출산, 분만   toe 발가락   menstrual
월경의   time to time 때때로, 가끔씩

09 이비인후과에서

ear(귀), nose(코), throat(목)이 아플 때는 이비인후과에서 치료를 받습니다. 이비인후과는 귀, 코, 목의 맨 앞 철자만 따서 ENT clinic이라고 부릅니다. 이비인후과 의사는 ENT doctor라고 하면 되겠죠.

원어민 발음 듣기 ☑□   회화 훈련 □□   듣기 훈련 □□

☐ 소리가 안 들려요.	I can't hear properly. I have a hearing problem.
☐ 귀에서 소리가 나요.	My ears are buzzing. *buzzing = ringing
☐ 귀에서 고름이 나와요.	Pus is coming out of my ear(s).
☐ 이물질이 들어갔어요.	There's something in my ears.
☐ 귀에 물이 들어갔어요.	There's water in my ears. Water got in my ears.
☐ 귀 모양이 기형이에요.	I have a deformed ear. My ears are deformed.
☐ 냄새를 못 맡겠어요.	I can't smell.
☐ 누런 콧물이 나와요.	I have yellow nasal mucus.
☐ 콧물과 재채기가 나요.	I have a runny nose and sneeze a lot.
☐ 저는 코를 골아요.	I snore.
☐ 코피가 자주 나요.	I often have a nosebleed. I often have a bloody nose.
☐ 코에서 악취가 나요.	I have a bad smell inside of my nose.
☐ 목에 생선 가시가 걸렸어요.	I've got a fish bone in my throat.
☐ 알레르기성 비염입니다.	You have allergic rhinitis.
☐ 꽃가루 알레르기입니다.	You're allergic to pollen.

📋 **Notes**

deformed 기형의, 변형의, 불구의   nasal 코의   mucus 끈적끈적한 점액물질   nosebleed 코피(가 남)   be allergic to ~에 알레르기가 있다, 알레르기 반응을 일으키다   pollen 꽃가루

10 정신과에서

depression(우울증) 또는 insomnia(불면증)가 지속될 때, phobias(공포증)나 스트레스가 심할 때도 psychiatry(정신과)에서 치료를 받습니다. psychiatrist(정신과 의사)는 머릿속을 치료하는 의사라는 의미에서 head doctor 혹은 shrink라고도 부릅니다.

원어민 발음 듣기 ☑□   회화 훈련 □□   듣기 훈련 □□

□ 우울해요.
I feel depressed.
I feel so down.

□ 자살 충동을 느껴요.
I feel suicidal.
I have urges to commit suicide.
I want to kill myself.

□ 불면증이 있어요.
I have insomnia.
I have sleeplessness.
I can't sleep.

□ 늘 긴장 상태에 있어요.
I'm always tense.

□ 스트레스가 심해요.
I'm stressful.
I'm stressed out.

□ 대인 기피증이 심해요.
I have a fear of being around people.
I have a social phobia.

□ 환청이 들려요.
I hear sounds.

□ 헛것이 보여요.
I see things.

□ 여러 공포증에 시달리고 있어요.
I'm suffering from many phobias.

□ 늘 자기 비하에 시달려요.
I always put myself down.
I have zero confidence.

□ 공황 상태에 빠져요.
I have panic disorder.

□ 당신은 우울증입니다.
You have depression.

□ 당신은 조울증입니다.
You have manic-depression.
You're manic-depressive.

11 진료 받기

병원에서 진료를 받을 때 필요한 기본적인 표현들을 알아보겠습니다. 정확한 병의 진단을 위해 병원에서는 보통 채혈을 하고 body temperature(체온)와 blood pressure(혈압) 등을 체크하죠.

원어민 발음 듣기 ☑□   회화 훈련 □□   듣기 훈련 □□

☐ 윗옷을 올려 주세요.   Pull your shirt up, please.

☐ 소매를 올려 주세요.   Roll up your sleeves, please.

☐ 숨을 크게 들이쉬세요.   Take a deep breath.
Breathe deeply in.

☐ 이제 숨을 내쉬세요.   Now, breathe out.

☐ 입을 벌려 보세요.   Open your mouth.

☐ 여기 누워 보세요.   Lie down here.
Why don't you lie down here?

☐ 배를 눌러 보겠습니다.   I'm going to press your abdomen.

☐ 체온을 재겠습니다.   I'll take your temperature.
*take = check
Let me take your temperature.

☐ 혈압을 재겠습니다.   I'll take your blood pressure.
Let me take your blood pressure.

☐ 채혈을 하겠습니다.   I'll take your blood.

☐ 혈당을 체크하겠습니다.   I'll check your blood sugar.

☐ 부분, 아니면 전신 마취 하시겠어요?   Which one would you prefer? General or local anesthetic?

☐ 상처 부위를 봅시다.   Let me see your wound.

☐ 시력 검사를 해 봅시다.   Let me check your eye vision.

☐ 초음파 검사를 해 봅시다.   Let's do an ultrasound.

12 입원과 퇴원, 문병

병이 심각하지 않다면 outpatient(외래 환자)로 통원하며 치료를 받지만 그렇지 않다면 inpatient(입원 환자)가 되어야 합니다. 문병하러 병원에 갈 때에는 visiting hours(면회 시간)를 확인하고 환자에게 무리가 되지 않도록 해야 하겠죠.

☐ 입원하세요.	You need to be hospitalized.
	You need hospital treatment.
☐ 입원 안 하셔도 됩니다.	You don't need to be in the hospital.
	You're an outpatient.
☐ 그를 입원시켜야 합니다.	We need to keep him in the hospital.
☐ 일주일 더 입원하세요.	You need to be in the hospital for another week.
☐ 입원 수속을 밟으세요.	Go through formalities, please.
☐ 상태가 좋군요.	Your condition is great.
☐ 내일 퇴원하세요.	You can leave the hospital.
	You can be discharged.
	You are well enough to leave the hospital.
☐ 너 입원했다면서?	I heard you're in the hospital.
	I heard you're sick in the hospital.
☐ 문병하러 갈게.	I'll go and visit you.
☐ 무슨 병원 몇 호실이야?	Which hospital and what (sick)room are you in?
	Which hospital? What (sick)room?
	What (sick) ward are you in?
☐ 면회 시간이 언제야?	When are the visiting hours?
	When am I allowed to visit you?
☐ 몸은 좀 어때?	How are you feeling?
	How's your condition?

□ 그냥 누워 있어.	Just lie down.
	Don't get up.
□ 어쩌다 그랬어?	What happened?
	How did it happen?
□ 안 와도 되는데.	You don't have to come.
	You shouldn't have (come).
□ 몸조리 잘해.	Take care.
	Take good care of yourself.
□ 빨리 회복해.	Get well (real) soon.

DIALOGUE

A (Visiting a friend who is sick in the hospital) Hey, how're you feeling?
B I'm okay. You don't have to come.
A Please don't get up. Just lie down.

A (병원에 입원에 있는 친구를 방문하며) 이봐, 좀 어때?
B 나 괜찮아. 일부러 안 와도 되는데.
A 제발 일어나지 마. 그냥 누워 있어.

 Notes

be hospitalized 입원하다 hospital treatment 병원 치료 formalities 규정, 절차 be discharged 퇴원하다 go and visit 가서 방문하다, 가 보다 ward 병동, 병실 shouldn't have+과거분사 ~하지 말았어야 했다, ~ 안 해도 되는데…… take care of oneself 스스로를 잘 돌보다, 건강 관리를 잘하다

245

13 응급 구조 전화

emergency(응급 상황)에 처하면 우리나라에서는 119번에 전화를 걸어 도움을 청하지만, 미국의 응급 전화 구조 센터는 911번입니다. ambulance(응급차)로 병원에 도착하기 전까지 paramedic(응급 구조 요원)이 first aid(응급 처치)를 합니다.

원어민 발음 듣기 ☑□   회화 훈련 □□   듣기 훈련 □□

☐ 아이가 숨을 쉬지 않아요.	My kid is not breathing.
☐ 할머니가 쓰러졌어요.	An old lady fell. *fall = collapse
☐ 다친 사람이 길에 누워 있어요.	The injured person is lying on the street. *injured = wounded Someone's hurt and she is lying on the street.
☐ 출혈이 심해요.	He is bleeding a lot. He is overbleeding.
☐ 약물을 과다 복용했어요.	She had a drug overdose.
☐ 아이가 발작 증상을 보여요.	My kid is having a seizure.
☐ 물에 빠졌어요.	A woman is drowning.
☐ 높은 곳에서 떨어졌어요.	He fell from a height.
☐ 심장 마비를 일으켰어요.	He is having a heart attack.
☐ 응급차가 이미 출동했습니다.	An ambulance is already on the way.
☐ 응급 처치 들어갑니다.	I'm going to administer first aid.
☐ 의식이 있는지 확인하세요.	Check the patient if she is conscious.
☐ 숨을 쉬는지 확인하세요.	Check the patient if she is breathing.
☐ 환자를 안전한 곳으로 옮기세요.	Move the patient to the safe place.
☐ 심폐 소생술을 안내하겠습니다.	I'm going to guide you through CPR.

📋 Notes

overbleed 피를 많이 흘리다, 과다 출혈하다   overdose 약의 과다 복용, 치사량, 유해량   seizure 발작   on the way 가는(오는) 중인   administer 행하다, 실시하다, 약을 투여하다   first aid 응급 처치, 구급 요법   guide through ~을 처음부터 끝까지 안내하다   CPR 심폐 기능 소생술(= cardiopulmonary resuscitation)

14 한의학, 민간 요법

Chinese acupuncture and herbal clinic(한의원)에서는 acupuncture(침술)와 herbal medicine (한약)으로 환자를 치료합니다. cupping(부항)이나 moxa(뜸)를 뜨기도 하죠. 한의사는 oriental (medical) doctor라고 부릅니다.

원어민 발음 듣기 ☑☐   회화 훈련 ☐☐   듣기 훈련 ☐☐

☐ 진맥하겠습니다.
Let me get your pulse.

☐ 침을 놓겠습니다.
I'm going to give you an acupuncture treatment.

☐ 한약을 드세요.
Take oriental medicine.
*oriental = herbal

☐ 부항을 뜨겠습니다.
I'm going to apply cupping treatment.

☐ 뜸을 뜨겠습니다.
Let me cauterize your skin.
I'm going to burn moxa on your skin.
I'm going to give you moxa treatment.

☐ 민간요법은 효과가 있어.
Home remedies work well.
*Home remedy = Folk remedy
Home remedies have proven to be effective.

☐ 체했을 때는 손을 따 봐.
When you have an upset stomach, prick under your thumbnail and draw blood.

☐ 코감기엔 코로 증기를 쐐.
When you have a cold, get steam through your nose.

☐ 딸꾹질엔 설탕 한 티스푼을 먹어.
When you can't stop your hiccup, try a teaspoon of sugar.

☐ 잇몸 염증은 소금물로 씻어내.
When you have an infection in your mouth, wash it off with salty water.

📑 **Notes**

pulse 맥박, 고동   get pulse 맥박을 재다, 진맥하다   acupuncture 침술; 침을 놓다   oriental 동양의   herbal 풀의, 약초의   apply cupping 부항을 뜨다   cauterize 상처에 뜸을 뜨다   burn moxa 뜸을 뜨다   prick (가시, 바늘 등으로) 콕 찌르다, 쑤시다   thumbnail 엄지손가락   draw blood 피를 뽑아내다, 피를 흘려 내보내다   get steam 증기를 쐬다

247

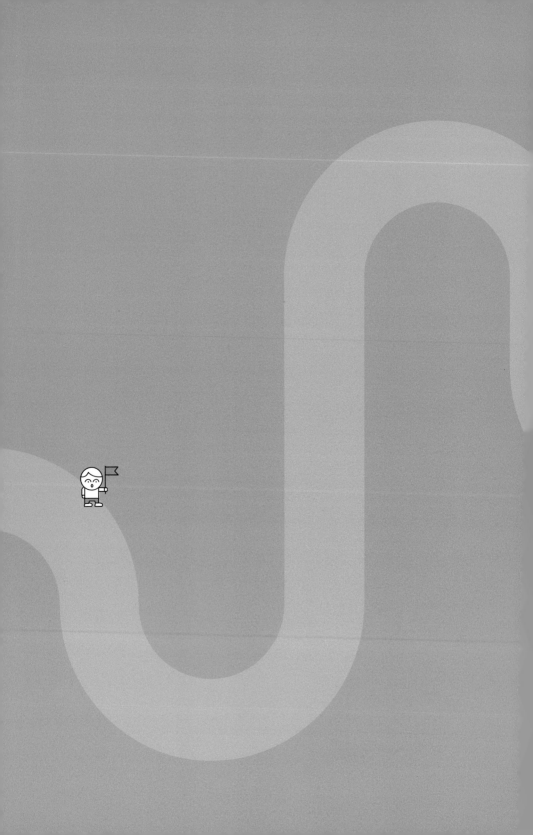

Chapter 16

여행
Travel

여행지 선택

여행을 가기로 마음먹었다면 domestic travel(국내 여행)을 갈지 overseas travel (해외여행)을 갈지 결정해야 합니다. 가까운 곳으로 one day trip(당일 여행)을 떠나는 것도 좋은 방법이지요. 요즘에는 각양각색의 취향을 만족시키려는 노력으로 문화 체험, 자연 관광, 맛집 순례, 쇼핑 등 다양한 여행 상품이 개발되어 있습니다.

원어민 발음 듣기 ☑☐   회화 훈련 ☐☐   듣기 훈련 ☐☐

☐ 여행 가고 싶다.	I want to travel.
	I'd like to take a trip.
☐ 어딘가 가고 싶다.	I want to go somewhere.
☐ 여기저기 여행하고 싶다.	I want to travel around.
	I want to take a tour.
☐ 여행 못 한 지 오래 됐다.	It's been a while to travel.
☐ 여행 가자.	Let's take a trip.
	Let's go somewhere.
☐ 가까운 곳이라도 가자.	Let's take a short trip.
☐ 긴 여행을 하자.	Let's take a long journey.
☐ 무작정 떠나자.	Let's just leave.
☐ 어디로 갈까?	Where should we go?
☐ 국내여행 아니면 해외여행?	Domestic or international travel?
	Domestic or overseas travel?
☐ 며칠 동안 갈까?	How long will we travel?
☐ 2박 3일 어때?	How about two nights and three days?
☐ 당일 여행 어때?	Do you want to take a day trip?
☐ 패키지 상품을 알아볼까?	Shall we look for package tours?
☐ 2박 3일 여행지로 어디가 좋을까요?	Where is the perfect place for a three-day trip?
☐ 어떤 여행을 하고 싶으세요?	What kind of trip do you want?
	What do you want to experience from the trip?

☐ 문화 체험을 해 보고 싶어요.	I'd like culture experiences.
☐ 관광 명소를 둘러보고 싶어요.	I'd like to look around tourist attractions.
☐ 자연을 만끽하고 싶어요.	I'd like to enjoy nature.
	*enjoy = see
☐ 신나는 모험을 원해요.	I'm looking for adventures.
☐ 맛집을 순례하고 싶어요.	I want to go to famous restaurants.
☐ 쇼핑하고 싶어요.	I want to go shopping.
☐ 온천을 즐기고 싶어요.	I want to enjoy hot springs.
☐ 푹 쉬다 오고 싶어요.	I just want to relax.
☐ 딱 맞는 상품이 있습니다.	We have the perfect one for you.
☐ 특별 할인가입니다.	It's our special offer.
	It's our special travel rate.

 여행(trip, travel) 종류

기차 여행 train travel	허니문 honeymoon trip
유람선 여행 cruise	골프 여행 golf trip
배낭여행 backpack trip	성지 순례 pilgrimage
트래킹 trekking	에어텔 airtel(airplane+hotel) trip
패키지 여행 package trip	건강 여행 travel for health

 Notes

take a trip 여행하다 travel around 여기저기 여행하며 돌아다니다 domestic 가정의, 국내의 overseas 해외의, 바다 건너의 tourist attractions 관광객을 끄는 장소, 관광 명소 hot springs 온천 special offer 특별 제안(판매) special rate 특별 할인율

02 비자와 여권

해외여행을 하기 위해서는 passport(여권)와 tourist visa(관광 비자)가 필요합니다. 여행 전에 미리 신청해야 함은 물론이고, 여권의 경우 expiration date(여권 만료일)를 꼭 확인해야 합니다. 비자와 여권 발급에 필요한 표현을 알아보겠습니다.

원어민 발음 듣기 ☑□   회화 훈련 □□   듣기 훈련 □□

☐ 관광 비자가 필요한가요?	Do I need a tourist visa?
☐ 비자 신청은 어떻게 하나요?	How do I apply for a visa?
☐ 비자 신청했어요?	Have you applied for a visa?
☐ 비자 신청에 무엇이 필요한가요?	What do I need for a visa application?
☐ 먼저 비자 신청서를 작성하세요.	First, you have to fill out an application.
☐ 비자용 사진 1장 주세요.	You need a visa-sized photo.
☐ 3개월 여행은 비자가 필요 없습니다.	You don't need a visa for a three month trip.
☐ 여행사에 알아서 해 줍니다.	Your travel agency will take care of everything.
☐ 여권 신청은 어떻게 하나요?	How do I apply for a passport?
☐ 여권 신청서와 사진 1장이 필요합니다.	You need a filled-out application and a photo.
☐ 여권 발급 수수료는 얼마인가요?	How much is a passport application fee? How much do you charge for a passport application?
☐ 여권 있어?	Do you have your passport?
☐ 여권 만료일 확인했어?	What is the expiration date of your passport? Did you check the expiration date of your passport?
☐ 여권은 항상 소지하도록 하세요.	You should carry your passport all the time.
☐ 만일의 경우를 대비해 여권을 복사해 둬.	Just in case, make a copy of your passport.

252

03 교통편과 숙소 예약

travel agency(여행사)에 일괄적으로 맡길 것이 아니라면 여행 시 교통편과 숙소 예약 정도는 직접 챙겨야 합니다. 요즘은 인터넷 예약 서비스로 더욱 편하게 여행할 수 있게 되었죠. flight ticket(항공권)과 accommodation(숙소) 예약에 필요한 표현을 살펴보겠습니다.

원어민 발음 듣기 ☑☐   회화 훈련 ☐☐   듣기 훈련 ☐☐

Chapter 16
여행

☐ 인터넷으로 비행기 표 예약할게.	I'll reserve airline tickets. I'll make a reservation for airline tickets.
☐ 할인 항공권을 찾아볼게.	I'll look for discounted flight tickets. I'll find discounted air tickets.
☐ 비행기 표를 예매하고 싶어요.	I'd like to reserve plane tickets.
☐ 일본행 두 사람 왕복 항공권 주세요.	I need two round-trip plane tickets to Japan.
☐ 유효 기간이 얼마나 되죠?	How long will the ticket be valid? When will the ticket be expired?
☐ 일주일 안에 결제하세요.	You have to pay for the ticket within a week.
☐ 그렇지 않으면 예약이 취소됩니다.	If you don't, your reservation will be canceled. If you don't, you'll lose your reservation.
☐ 노쇼와 환불 규정을 확인하세요.	Check no-show and refund policies, please. *예약하고 나타나지 않는 손님을 no-show라고 한다.
☐ 결제가 확인되었습니다.	Your payment has been confirmed.
☐ 전자 티켓이 이메일로 발송되었습니다.	Your e-ticket has been sent by email.
☐ 전자 티켓을 출력하세요.	Print out your e-ticket, please.
☐ 탑승권 수령 시 전자 티켓을 보여 주세요.	Show your e-ticket when you get your boarding pass.
☐ 어디를 경유하나요?	Where's the stopover?
☐ 어린이 비행기 표는 할인되나요?	Do you have a discounted plane ticket for children?

☐ 지금 방이 있나요?	Do you have a room?
	Is there a room available?
☐ 하루 숙박비가 얼마죠?	How much is the room for a day?
	How much is your hotel bill for a day?
	*bill = charge
☐ 숙박비에 아침 식사도 포함되나요?	Does this hotel bill include breakfast?
	Is breakfast included in this hotel charge?
☐ 호텔 시설은 무엇이 있죠?	What are your hotel facilities?
☐ 스파가 있나요?	Do you have a spa in your hotel?
☐ 이틀간 2인용 침실을 예약하고 싶어요.	I'd like (to reserve) a room with a double-sized bed for two people for two days.
☐ 전망이 좋은 방을 주세요.	I'd like a room with a nice view.
☐ 예약을 확인하겠습니다.	Let me confirm your reservation.
☐ 그 날은 방이 없습니다.	We don't have any rooms available on that day.
☐ 성수기라 추가 요금이 있습니다.	You have to pay extra charge during the peak season.
	*peak season = busy season
☐ 호텔과 공항 사이에 셔틀버스가 있나요?	Is there a shuttle bus available between the airport and the hotel?
☐ 버스 시간표를 알고 싶어요.	I'd like to know the shuttle bus schedule.

📑 **호텔 객실**(hotel room)

1인실 : 싱글(single room)
2인실 : 세미 더블(semi-double room),
　　　　더블(double room), 트윈(twin room)

3인실 : 트리플(triple room)
고급 : 스위트(suite room)

📃 **Notes**

make a reservation 예약하다 discounted 할인된 round-trip 왕복, 왕복표 valid 유효한, 효력 있는 expire 만기가 되다, 효력이 다하다 no-show 교통편의 좌석을 예약하고도 나타나지 않는 승객 refund 환불; 환불하다 confirm 재확인하다, 확실시하다 boarding pass 항공기 탑승권 stopover 도중 하차, 경유 facilities 편의 시설 peak 최고 절정기, 가장 많은 때

04 공항에서

공항에 도착하면 boarding pass(탑승권)를 받고 짐을 부쳐야 합니다. 짐은 weight limit(무게 제한)이 있기 때문에 초과 무게에 대해서는 extra charge(추가 요금)를 지불해야 하죠. security check(보안 검색)가 엄격해져 탑승까지 절차가 복잡하니 공항에는 여유 있게 가는 것이 좋습니다.

원어민 발음 듣기 ✔☐   회화 훈련 ☐☐   듣기 훈련 ☐☐

출발 3시간 전엔 공항에 도착해야 해.	We need to get to the airport three hours before our departure.
보안 검색이 강화됐어.	Security checks have been reinforced. *reinforced = beefed up
탑승권을 받자.	Let's get our boarding pass.
창문쪽 좌석 주세요.	I'd like a window seat. A window seat, please. *window seat → aisle seat (통로쪽 좌석)
탑승 시간과 탑승구를 확인하세요.	Check your boarding time and boarding gate, please.
탑승 30분 전에는 탑승구로 가세요.	You need to be at your boarding gate thirty minutes before your boarding.
짐부터 부치자.	Let's check in our luggage. *luggage = baggage Why don't we check in our luggage?
부칠 가방이 두 개입니다.	We have two pieces of luggages to check in.
무게가 초과됐어요.	Your luggage is overweight.
추가 요금을 내셔야 합니다.	You need to pay extra charge for it.
여권과 탑승권을 보여 주시겠어요?	May I see your passport and boarding pass?
짐을 검색대에 올리세요.	Put your bags on the X-ray scanner.
신발을 벗어 주세요.	Take off your shoes, please.
가방 검사를 하겠습니다.	Let me check your luggage. Open your luggage, please.

Chapter 16

여행

255

□	비행기는 정시에 출발합니다.	Your flight will depart right on time.
□	출발이 10분 지연될 예정입니다.	Your flight will depart ten minutes late.
□	불편을 드려 대단히 죄송합니다.	I'm sorry for your inconvenience.
		I apologize for the late departure.
□	연결 편 비행기는 어디서 타나요?	Where is the connecting flight?
		Where can I catch the connecting flight?
□	비행기를 놓쳤어요.	I missed my flight.
□	다음 편 탑승이 가능한가요?	Can I get a seat on the next flight?
□	다음 편 비행기는 언제인가요?	When is the next flight?
□	하루를 기다려야 합니다.	You have to wait for a day.
□	근처에 호텔이 있나요?	Is there a hotel near here?

 Notes

reinforce 강화하다, 증강하다(= beef up) overweight 중량 초과의 X-ray scanner 보안 검색대 take off (옷 등을) 벗다 inconvenience 불편함, 번거로움 connecting flight 연결 편 비행기

05 기내에서

비행기에 탑승하면 자리를 찾아 큰 짐은 overhead compartment(머리 위 짐칸)에 넣고 작은 짐은 의자 밑에 놓습니다. taking off(이륙) 또는 landing(착륙) 전에는 의자를 바로 세우고 좌석 앞 접이식 테이블을 잠금 위치에 두어야 합니다. 착륙 전에 입국(세관) 신고서 작성도 잊지 마세요.

원어민 발음 듣기 ☑☐   회화 훈련 ☐☐   듣기 훈련 ☐☐

□ 자리를 찾아 주세요.
Please help me find my seat.
Could you help me find my seat?

□ 제 자리에 누군가가 앉아 있어요.
Somebody is sitting in my seat.

□ 제 자리에 앉아 계신 것 같아요.
I think you're sitting in my seat.

□ 자리를 바꿀 수 있나요?
Can I change my seat?

□ 우리 자리를 바꿀까요?
Shall we change seats?
Let's change seats.

□ 신문이나 잡지를 드릴까요?
Would you like the newspapers or magazines?

□ 가방을 선반에 올려 주시겠어요?
Could you please place my bag in the overhead compartment?

□ 곧 이륙합니다.
We're about to take off.
This flight is about to take off.

□ 의자를 바로 세워 주세요.
Please put your seat (back) up?

□ 의자를 앞으로 해 주시겠어요?
Could you put your seat forward?

□ 접이식 테이블이 잠겨 있는지 확인해 주세요.
Please make sure your tray tables are in the lock position.

□ 짐은 좌석 아래에 두세요.
Put your bags under the seat, please.

□ 좌석 벨트를 착용하세요.
Fasten your seatbelt, please.

□ 식사는 무엇으로 하시겠어요?
What would you like to have?

□ 저는 비빔밥 주세요.
I'd like to have bibimbap.
I'll have bibimbap.

□ 그 밖에 필요한 것이 있으신가요?
Do you need anything else?

Chapter 16 여행

☐ 마실 것 좀 주시겠어요?	Can I get something to drink?
	I'd like some drinks.
☐ 담요를 한 장 더 주시겠어요?	Can I get an extra blanket?
☐ 도착하려면 얼마나 남았나요?	How long before we land?
☐ 곧 착륙합니다.	We'll be landing shortly.
	We're about to land.
☐ 10분 내로 도착할 예정입니다.	We'll be landing in ten minutes.
☐ 입국, 세관 신고서를 작성해 주세요.	Fill out your landing and customs declaration form, please.

*landing = arrival, disembarkation

DIALOGUE

A (On the plane) Excuse me, can I have something to drink?

B Sir, I'm terribly sorry, but we'll be landing in 20 minutes.
We can't serve anything to the passengers while the pilot is preparing for a landing.

A Okay. No problem.

A (비행기 내에서) 저기요, 마실 것 좀 주실 수 있나요?

B 손님, 대단히 죄송합니다만 비행기가 20분 후에 착륙합니다.
기장이 착륙 준비를 하는 동안에는 탑승객에게 어떤 서비스도 제공할 수 없습니다.

A 알겠어요. 괜찮습니다.

 Notes

change seats 자리를 맞바꾸다   place (물건 등을) 놓다, 자리하다   overhead compartment 머리 위에 있는 수납 칸   be about to 막 ~하려고 하다   take off (비행기 등이) 이륙하다, 뜨다   put (back) up 제자리로 세워 놓다, 바르게 놓다   put forward 앞으로 놓다   tray tables 접이식 테이블   fasten ~에 단단히 고정시키다, 동여매다   land (비행기 등이) 착륙하다, 내리다   shortly 바로, 즉시, 곧   landing declaration form 입국 신고서   customs declaration form 세관 신고서   disembark (비행기 등이) 내리다, 착륙하다

06 입국 심사, 짐 찾기, 세관 검사

비행기에서 내리면 입국 심사를 받습니다. immigration officer(입국 심사관)가 얼마 동안 체류할 것인지, 어디서 머물 것인지, 방문 목적은 무엇인지 등을 간단히 묻습니다. 심사가 끝나면 baggage claim(수화물 찾는 곳)에서 짐을 찾고 customs(세관)를 거친 후 입국합니다.

원어민 발음 듣기 ☑□   회화 훈련 □□   듣기 훈련 □□

□ 얼마 동안 체류하시나요?	How long will you be staying? How long do you plan to stay?
□ 일주일간 체류할 예정입니다.	I'll be staying for a week.
□ 어디서 머무르시나요?	Where will you be staying?
□ 호텔에 머물 것입니다.	I'll be staying at a hotel.
□ 어느 호텔입니까?	Which hotel, sir?
□ 방문 목적은 무엇입니까?	What's your purpose of this visit?
□ 업무차 왔습니다.	I'm here for business.
□ 관광차 왔습니다.	I'm here for sightseeing.
□ 가족을 방문하러 왔어요.	I'm visiting my family.
□ 짐은 이게 전부입니까?	Is this luggage all you have?
□ 짐은 어디에서 찾죠?	Where can I find my luggage? *find = claim Where should I go to pick up my baggage?
□ 어느 항공편을 타고 오셨나요?	Which fight did you fly in here?
□ 3번 짐 찾는 곳으로 가세요.	Go to the luggage carousel number 3, please.
□ 제 짐이 아직 안 나왔네요.	My luggage hasn't come out yet.
□ 수화물 표를 보여 주시겠어요?	Can I see your baggage claim ticket?
□ 세관에 신고할 것이 있나요?	Do you have anything to declare?
□ 가방을 열어 봐도 될까요?	Can I open your luggage?
□ 이것은 무엇입니까?	What are these? Can I ask what this is?

07 숙소 체크인과 숙박하기

예약한 숙소에 도착하면 가장 먼저 check in(체크인)을 해야 합니다. 자신의 이름으로 예약을 한 것이 확인되면 바로 입실이 가능하죠. 룸서비스를 이용하거나 숙소 내 시설 이용에 대한 도움을 청할 때 유용한 표현들을 알아보겠습니다.

원어민 발음 듣기 ☑☐ 회화 훈련 ☐☐ 듣기 훈련 ☐☐

☐ 체크인 하려고요.	I'd like to check in.
	Check in, please.
☐ 예약자명은 크리스털로 되어 있습니다.	My reservation is under the name of Crystal.
☐ 그 이름으로는 예약이 없습니다.	I can't find your reservation by that name.
☐ 그럴 리가요.	It can't be.
	It's impossible.
☐ 고객님의 방은 101호실입니다.	You'll be staying in room number 101.
	Your room number is 101.
☐ 고객님의 짐을 이미 방으로 옮겼습니다.	Our porter has already taken your bags to your room.
	Your bags are already taken to your room.
☐ 서비스가 정말 좋네요.	What a nice service!
☐ 룸서비스 시키려고요.	I'd like to order some room service.
☐ 샌드위치 두 개와 맥주 주세요.	Can I have a sandwich and a beer?
☐ 몇 호실이시죠?	What room are you staying in?
☐ 바로 가져다 드리겠습니다.	We'll have your order delivered right away.
☐ 옆방이 너무 시끄러워요.	My next door is making too much noise.
☐ 방이 너무 추워요.	My room is too cold.
☐ 난방기를 어떻게 사용하는 거죠?	I don't know how to use the heater.
☐ TV가 안 켜져요.	My TV isn't working.
☐ 사람을 (당장) 보내겠습니다.	We'll send someone up (right away).

☐ 체크아웃 할게요.	I'd like to check out.
	Check out, please.
☐ 내일 정오까지 체크아웃 하셔야 합니다.	You'll have to check out tomorrow morning by noon.
☐ 방을 바꿀 수 있나요?	Can I change rooms?
	*change=switch
☐ 전망이 좋은 방으로 주세요.	I'd like to have a room with a nice view.
☐ 아침에 모닝콜 되나요?	Can I get a wake-up call in the morning?
☐ 몇 시에 모닝콜 해 드릴까요?	What time do you need your wake-up call?
	When should we give you a wake-up call?
☐ 하루 연장하고 싶습니다.	I'd like to stay one more day.
	Can I extend my staying one more day?
☐ 숙박비는 총 70달러입니다.	Your room charge would be $70.
☐ 이건 팁이에요.	Here's a tip for you.

📑 **Notes**

check in 호텔의 숙박 수속   porter 운반인, 짐꾼, 사환   make noise 시끄럽게 하다, 소란 피우다   wake-up call (호텔 등에서의) 모닝콜   extend 연장하다   room charge 숙박비

08 사진 촬영

여행 후 '남는 것은 사진'이라는 말처럼 좋은 사진을 찍는 것은 매우 중요한 일입니다. 관광지에서는 낯선 이에게 사진을 찍어 줄 것을 부탁하거나 부탁 받기도 합니다. 마음에 안 들면 다시 찍어 달라고도 할 수 있죠.

원어민 발음 듣기 ☑☐   회화 훈련 ☐☐   듣기 훈련 ☐☐

☐ 여기서 사진 찍을까?	Let's take a picture here.
	Shall we take pictures here?
☐ 내가 사진 찍어 줄게.	I'll take a picture of you.
	Want me to take a picture of you?
☐ 내 사진 좀 찍어 줄래?	Will you take a picture of me?
☐ 한 장 더 찍어 줘.	Will you take another picture of me?
	One more picture, please.
☐ 인상 쓰지 말고 웃어.	Don't make faces. Smile!
☐ (멋지게) 포즈 취해 봐.	Pose for the camera.
	Pose like a model.
☐ (기억보다) 오래 남는 것은 사진이야.	Pictures last longer (than our memories).
☐ 여기를 누르시면 돼요.	You can press this button here.
	Press here, please.
☐ 저 건물이 나오게 찍어 주세요.	I'd like to have that building in a picture.
☐ 한번 보세요.	Take a look at the picture.
	Why don't you check it out?
☐ 마음에 안 드시면 다시 찍어 드릴게요.	If you don't like it, I can take a picture of you again.
	If you don't like it, I'll try again.
☐ 사진 잘 찍으셨네요.	You take good pictures.
	You photograph well.
☐ 사진 잘 받으시네요.	You're very photogenic.

09 길 찾기와 안내하기

초행길에서는 다른 사람에게 길을 물어 찾아갈 때가 있습니다. '~에 가려고 하는데요', '~를 찾고 있는데요.'라는 표현은 I'd like to ~. 또는 I'm looking for ~.라고 하면 됩니다. "그곳을 어떻게 가는지 알려 주시겠어요?"라고 묻는 표현은 Can you give me a direction to get there?입니다.

원어민 발음 듣기 ☑□　회화 훈련 □□　듣기 훈련 □□

□ '타임 스퀘어'에 가려고 하는데요.	I'd like to go Times Square.
□ '센트럴 파크'를 찾고 있는데요.	I'm looking for Central Park.
□ '북촌'이라고 하는 곳을 찾고 있는데요.	I'm looking for the place called Bukchon.
□ 방향 감각이 통 없어요.	I don't have any sense of direction.
□ 길을 잃었어요.	I'm lost. We've got lost.
□ 어떻게 가야 하나요?	How can I get there?
□ 그곳에 가는 길을 알려 주시겠어요?	Could you give me a direction to get there?
□ 걸어서 갈 수 있나요?	Can I walk there? Can I go there by foot?
□ 걸어서 10분 거리입니다.	It's only ten minutes walk. It'll take only ten minutes by foot.
□ 직진해서 우회전하세요.	Go straight and turn right. Go straight and make a right turn.
□ 길을 건너서 좌회전하세요.	Cross the street and turn left. Cross the street and make a left turn.
□ 두 블록 가면 왼편에 있습니다.	Go two blocks and it's on your left.
□ 이 건물 돌아가시면 돼요.	Just go around this building.
□ (바로) 보일 거예요.	You'll see it. It's (right) there. You can't miss it.
□ 데려다 드릴게요.	I'll walk you there.

Chapter 16 여행

▢ 태워 줄게요.	I'll give you a ride.
▢ 걷기에는 멀어요.	It's too far to walk.
▢ 버스나 지하철을 타세요.	Take a bus or the subway.
	Why don't you take a bus or the subway?
▢ 버스 정류장은 바로 저기에 있습니다.	A bus stop is right there.
▢ 지하철역은 모퉁이만 돌면 있어요.	The subway station is just around the corner.
▢ 저는 여기 대중교통에 익숙하지 않아요.	I'm not familiar with any public transportation here.
▢ 그러면 택시를 타세요.	Then, take a cab. *cab = taxi Then, why don't you take a cab?
▢ 택시 기사가 잘 데려다 줄 겁니다.	A taxi driver will take you there safely.

DIALOGUE

A I'd like to go to Bryant Park.
   Could you give me a direction?
B Sure. Take a taxi on this side.
   It will take only 15 minutes to get there.
A A taxi? I was thinking to go there by walking.
B No way. It's too far to walk. Trust me.

A 브라이언트 파크에 가려고 하는데요. 가는 길을 알려 주시겠어요?
B 물론이죠. 이쪽에서 택시를 타세요. 15분이면 도착할 겁니다.
A 택시요? 저는 걸어갈까 생각했는데요.
B 말도 안 돼요. 걸어가기에는 너무 멀어요. 제 말을 믿으세요.

 Notes

a sense of direction 방향(길, 지리) 감각 **be lost** 길을 잃다, 어찌할 바를 모르다(= get lost) **give ~ a direction** ~에게 길(방향)을 가르쳐 주다 **cross** 길을 가로지르다, 건너다 **go around** 돌아가다 **give ~ a ride** ~를 차에 태워 주다, 태워서 바래다주다 **be familiar with** ~에 익숙하다, 편하다 **safely** 안전하게, 무사히, 탈 없이

10 관광지에서

낯선 곳을 여행하며 관광지에 가면 The view is spectacular.(경치가 좋다.), The air is so fresh.(공기가 맑다.), This city is clean.(도시가 깨끗하다.), This place looks exotic.(여기 이국적이다.) 등과 같은 감상을 나눕니다. 이런 표현들은 영어로 어떻게 하는지 알아보겠습니다.

원어민 발음 듣기 ☑□ 회화 훈련 □□ 듣기 훈련 □□

Chapter 16 여행

경치가 장관이다.	The view is spectacular.
	The view is breathtaking.
물이 너무 깨끗해.	The water is clear to the bottom.
공기가 정말 맑다.	The air is so fresh.
건물들이 굉장해.	The buildings are magnificent.
도시가 아주 깨끗해.	This city is very clean.
도시가 지저분해.	This city is filthy.
	*filthy = dirty
이국적이다!	How exotic!
	*exotic = outlandish
이색적인 물건이 많아.	There are many unique things.
	*unique = different, eye-catching
여기 물가가 싸다.	Prices here are low.
여기 물가가 비싸다.	Prices here are high.
오길 잘했어.	It's good to be here.
	Great to come here.
다음에 (여기) 또 오자.	Let's come (here) again next time.
거리가 너무 붐벼.	The street is too busy and crowded.
바가지 쓴 것 같아.	I think we have been overcharged.
	I think we have been ripped off.
관광객이 봉이야.	Tourists are an easy target.
	*easy target = easy mark

265

11 관광 에티켓

여행 중에 쓰레기를 아무 데나 버리거나 공공장소의 물건을 함부로 집어 오는 몰상식한 행동을 하는 사람들이 있습니다. 외국에서는 특히 더 타인을 배려하고 우리와 다른 문화를 존중해 줄 필요가 있습니다. 기본적인 관광 에티켓에 대한 표현을 알아보겠습니다.

원어민 발음 듣기 ☑☐ 회화 훈련 ☐☐ 듣기 훈련 ☐☐

☐ 쓰레기를 버리지 마세요.
Don't dump trash.
Don't leave trash behind.
No litter in public places.

☐ 머무는 동안 숙소를 깨끗이 쓰세요.
Keep your hotel room clean and tidy while staying.

☐ 담배꽁초를 함부로 버리지 마세요.
Don't throw away your cigarette butts.

☐ 공공장소에서는 침을 뱉지 마세요.
Don't spit in public areas.

☐ 꽃을 꺾지 마세요.
Don't pick the flowers.

☐ 나무에서 열매를 따지 마세요.
Don't pick fruit from a tree.

☐ 과음하지 마세요.
Don't drink heavily.
Don't drink too much.

☐ 공공장소에서 큰 소리 내지 마세요.
Don't yell in public places.

☐ 음식은 먹을 만큼만 주문하세요.
Take only food as much as you can eat.

☐ 상대방을 배려하세요.
Be considerate.
*considerate = thoughtful

☐ 과도한 쇼핑은 삼가세요.
Avoid excessive shopping.

☐ 우리말로 외국인을 욕하지 마세요.
Don't call foreigners names in Korean.

☐ 사람을 향해 삿대질하지 마세요.
Don't point your finger at people.

☐ 위기 상황에서는 침착하게 행동하세요.
In an emergency, act cool and calm.
Act calmly at a time of crisis.

📑 Notes

leave behind 뒤에 남기다, 버려놓다 litter (물건 등으로) 어지르다, 주변을 더럽게 만들다 butt 담배꽁초 pick (꽃, 열매 등을) 꺾다, 따다 excessive 과도한, 과다한 call ~ names ~에게 욕하다 point one's finger at ~에게 손가락질하다, 삿대질하다

Chapter 17

쇼핑
Shopping

01 쇼핑에 대해 이야기하기

새로운 쇼핑몰이 생기면 Let's go and check it out.이라고 말합니다. "쇼핑 가자."는 뜻이죠. 세일에 대한 정보도 중요합니다. When does the sale start?(세일이 언제 시작이야?), Are they having a sale now?(지금 세일 기간이야?), The shop is having a sale up to 30%.(최고 30%까지 세일이야.) 등의 표현이 주로 사용됩니다.

원어민 발음 듣기 ☑□   회화 훈련 □□   듣기 훈련 □□

☐ 쇼핑은 (주로) 어디에서 하니?	Where do you (usually) shop?
	Where do you go shopping?
	When you shop, where do you go?
☐ 난 주로 백화점에 가.	I usually go to the department store.
☐ 시장에 가.	I go to the market.
☐ 시장은 잘 안 가.	I don't usually go to the market.
☐ 난 충동구매를 해.	I'm an impulsive buyer. *buyer = shopper
☐ 누구와 함께 가니?	Who do you go with?
☐ 항상 혼자 가.	I go shopping alone.
☐ 늘 친구와 함께 가.	I go shopping with friends.
☐ 쇼핑몰이 새로 생겼어.	There's a new shopping mall.
	There's a shopping mall newly opened.
☐ 쇼핑 가자.	Let' go shopping.
	Let's go and check it out.
☐ 구경이라도 하자.	Let's window-shop.
	Let's look around.
☐ 그 쇼핑몰 위치가 어디야?	Where is the mall (located)?
☐ 버스로 갈 수 있어?	Can we go there by bus?
☐ 바로 지하철역 근처야.	It's just near the subway station.
☐ 지하철역과 연결되어 있어.	It's connected to the subway station.
☐ 상품권을 준대.	They're giving us a gift certificate.

더블 포인트 행사도 한대.	We can get a double-points, too.
거기에는 어떤 브랜드들이 있어?	What brands do they have?
너는 어떤 브랜드를 좋아해?	What brands do you like?
유명 브랜드들이 다 모여 있어.	Famous brands are all there.
	Well-known brands are all gathered there.
신규 브랜드들이 많아.	Many new brands are launched in the mall.
그 매장은 거기밖에 없어.	You can find that shop only there.
꼭 가 보고 싶어.	I'd really like to go and check it out.
	I'm dying to go there.
그 매장은 세일 중이야.	That shop is on sale.
최고 30%까지 세일이야.	That shop is having a sale up to 30%.
세일이 언제 시작이야?	When does the sale start?
	When will the sale begin?
세일이 언제까지야?	When does the sale end?
	When will the sale end?
지금 세일 기간이야?	Are they having a sale now?

📖 **세일(sale) 종류**

재고 정리 세일 clearance sale	샘플 세일 sample sale
점포 정리 세일 going-out-of business sale	하나 값으로 두 개 구입 two for one sale
균일가 세일 one-price sale	벼룩시장 flea market
창고 세일 wholesale discount,	차고 세일 garage sale
warehouse sale	마당 세일 yard sale

📝 **Notes**

shop 물건을 사다, 쇼핑하다 impulsive 충동적인, 감정에 끌리는 newly 새롭게, 새로이 window-shop 윈도쇼핑, 사지 않고 눈으로만 구경하는 것 well-known 잘 알려진, 이름난, 유명한 be dying to ~하고 싶어 죽을 지경이다, 안달나다 up to (최고) ~까지

02 매장에서

매장을 찾거나 매장 내에서 원하는 물건을 찾을 때 I'm looking for ~. (~를 찾고 있어요.)라고 말합니다. store clerk(점원)은 new arrivals(신상품)와 sale items(세일 상품)가 진열된 곳으로 안내해 주기도 하고 일시 품절된 상품을 order in advance(선주문)해 주기도 합니다.

원어민 발음 듣기 ☑□   회화 훈련 □□   듣기 훈련 □□

□ 여성 옷은 몇 층에 있나요?

Which floor is women's clothing?
Where can I find women's wear?
*wear = apparel

□ 5층으로 가세요.

It's on the fifth floor.
Go to the fifth floor, please.

□ 중앙의 에스컬레이터를 이용하세요.

Use the escalator in the middle.

□ '샤넬' 매장을 찾는데요.

I'm looking for Chanel.
I'd like to find Chanel.

□ 그 매장은 없어졌어요.

That shop is no longer here.
You can't find that shop here.

□ 특별히 찾으시는 상품이 있나요?

Are you looking for something in particular?

□ 도와드릴까요?

Can I help you?
Can I help you find something?

□ 카디건을 찾는데요.

I'm looking for a cardigan.

□ 신상품은 이쪽입니다.

New arrival items are displayed here.
You can check out new items here.

□ 매대에서 만 원 균일가 세일 중입니다.

Items on this stand are on 10,000 won one-price sale.
*stand = rack

□ 이 신발 245mm 있나요?

Do you have these shoes in size 245?
*사이즈 245mm = 7 ½

□ 창고에 가서 확인해 보겠습니다.

I'll check in our stock room.
Let me check our storage room.

□ 있으면 가져다 드릴까요?

If we have it, should I bring them?

□ 그 상품은 일시 품절입니다.	The item is not available right now. *item = product	
□ 다 팔렸습니다.	We're sold-out.	
□ 재고가 없습니다.	We're out of stock. We're out of it at the moment.	
□ 일주일 후면 재입고 됩니다.	The item will be restocked in a week. The item will be available in a week.	
□ 선 주문하시겠어요?	Would you like to order in advance?	
□ 도착하면 배송해 드리겠습니다.	When it arrives, we'll deliver the item to your house.	
□ 그런 상품은 없는데요.	We don't have that item. *have = sell, carry	
□ 여기 매장에서 본 적 있어요.	I've seen the item in your store.	
□ 이것도 세일인가요?	Is this a sale item, too?	
□ 그것은 세일 제외 상품입니다.	That is excluded from the sale.	
□ 그 상품은 판매하기는 아직 이릅니다.	It's too early to have that item. *have = sell, carry	
□ 인터넷 쇼핑몰에 들어가 보세요.	Why don't you check out the Internet shopping mall? Visit our on-line shopping mall.	
□ 재고 정리 세일이 진행 중입니다.	We're having a clearance sale now.	

DIALOGUE

A Can I help you find something?
B That would be great.
   I'm looking for winter boots.
A Oh, I'm sorry. It's only September.
   It's too early to sell those items.

A 도와드릴까요?
B 그래 주시면 감사하겠어요. 겨울 부츠를 찾고 있는데요.
A 아, 죄송합니다. 아직 9월이라서요. 겨울 부츠를 팔기에는 시기가 너무 이릅니다.

271

03 상품 비교, 선택하기

구매 전 상품을 비교해 볼 때 쓸 수 있는 표현들을 알아봅시다. 옷 고를 때는 I like the design.(디자인이 마음에 들어요.), You have quite a variety.(제품이 다양하네요.), Can I see the item over there?(저쪽에 있는 상품 보여주세요.) 등의 말을 할 수 있겠죠. 너무 비싸서 다시 생각해 보고 싶으면 I'll think about it. 하고 말하면 됩니다.

원어민 발음 듣기 ☑☐   회화 훈련 ☐☐   듣기 훈련 ☐☐

☐ 이 옷 디자인이 마음에 들어요.

I like the design of this cloth.
*like 대신 love를 쓰면 '매우 좋다'는 의미가 된다.

☐ 다른 색깔은 없나요?

Do you have other colors?

☐ 검정색과 회색, 두 가지뿐입니다.

We have only black and grey.

☐ 두 색 다 잘 어울리시네요.

You look great in black and grey.

☐ 입어 보세요.

Why don't you try it on?

☐ 탈의실이 어디예요?

Where is the fitting room?
*fitting room = changing room

☐ 밝은 색이 있으면 좋을 텐데요.

I wish you had brighter colors.

☐ 제품이 더 다양하면 좋을 텐데요.

I wish you had more varieties.
I wish you had a wide selection.

☐ 제품이 다양하네요.

You have quite a variety.

☐ 이 상품은 어떠세요?

How would you like this one?

☐ 그 디자인은 별로예요.

I don't like the design.

☐ 저쪽에 있는 상품을 보여 주세요.

Let me see the product over there.
Can I see the item over there?

☐ 마네킹이 입은 옷을 입어 보고 싶어요.

I'd like to try on the clothes that a mannequin is wearing.

☐ 처음 상품이 제일 낫네요.

First one is the best for me.

☐ 볼수록 마음에 들어요.

The more I look at it, the more I like it.
I like it more and more.

☐ (이것보다) 저것이 더 나아요.

That one is better (than this one).

☐ 저라면 검정색을 사겠어요.

If I were you, I would buy a black one.

☐ 둘 다 주세요.	I'll take (them) both.
☐ 재킷이 약간 작네요.	This jacket is a little small (for me).
☐ 이 옷은 너무 꽉 껴요.	This is too tight.
☐ 이 옷은 너무 커요.	This is too loose.
☐ 사이즈가 딱 맞네요.	It's a perfect fit for you. It fits you perfectly. It's just right for you.
☐ 요즘 유행이에요.	This is in style now. This is the trend at the moment. It's the most popular these days.
☐ 날씬해 보이세요.	You look thin in those clothes.
☐ 한 치수 작은 것으로 할게요.	I'd like to have this in a smaller size. Can I have a smaller one?
☐ 스웨터와 함께 입으려고요.	I'm going to wear this with this sweater.
☐ 이 재킷과 어울리는 스웨터가 있나요?	Do you have a sweater to go with this jacket?
☐ 손님에게 딱 맞는 게 있어요.	I've got what you need. I know what you're looking for.
☐ 이 화장품은 비싸지만 품질이 좋아요.	This cosmetics brand is expensive but has good quality.
☐ 이건 가격은 괜찮은데 품질이 그냥 그래.	This is reasonable but has average quality.
☐ 누가 쓰실 건가요?	Who is this for? Who will be using this?
☐ 이건 품질이 최고예요.	This is the best.
☐ 좀 더 생각해 볼게요.	I'll think about it. I need more time to think.
☐ 좀 더 둘러볼게요.	I want to look around more.
☐ 다시 들를게요.	I'll come back later. I'll come by later.

04 가격 흥정하기

가격 흥정을 할 때는 주로 Can you give me a discount?(깎아 주시면 안 돼요?)라고 말합니다. 물건을 살 때 현금으로 지불하면 할인을 받을 수 있는지, 여러 개를 구입하면 싸게 살 수 있는지 등 가격을 흥정할 때 쓰는 여러 가지 표현을 알아보겠습니다.

원어민 발음 듣기 ☑☐   회화 훈련 ☐☐   듣기 훈련 ☐☐

☐ 가격이 얼마예요?	How much (is this)? How much does it cost?
☐ 가격표가 없네요.	I can't find the price tag on this.
☐ 너무 비싼 것 같아요.	I think it's too expensive. It's way out of my price range. It's over my limit.
☐ 깎아 주시면 안 돼요?	Can you give me a discount? Can you give me a better price?
☐ 얼마나 할인해 주실 건데요?	How much discount can you give me?
☐ 두 개 사면 싸게 주시나요?	If I take two, can I get a discount? *take = buy
☐ 현금으로 지불하면 할인되나요?	If I pay in cash, can I get a discount?
☐ 정찰가 판매입니다.	It's a fixed price.
☐ 이미 할인된 가격이에요.	It's already discounted. The price has already been dropped.
☐ 밑지고 파는 겁니다.	We're making no profit out of it. We're selling them below cost. *cost = price
☐ 싸게 사시는 거예요.	It's a good deal.
☐ 살 거예요, 말 거예요?	Are you going to buy it or not? Take it or leave it?
☐ 안 팔아요.	I don't want to sell it to you.

05 계산, 포장하기

카드 결제 시에는 pay in a single payment(일시불)로 할 것인지 아니면 pay in installments(할부)로 할 것인지를 물어봅니다. no interest(무이자) 기간을 확인하여 결제하는 것이 현명한 구매 방법이겠죠. 환경을 위해 plastic bag(비닐)이나 paper bag(종이 가방) 대신 가져온 장바구니를 사용하는 것이 좋겠습니다.

원어민 발음 듣기 ☑□   회화 훈련 □□   듣기 훈련 □□

□ 계산해 주세요.	I'd like to pay for this.
□ 어떻게 계산하시겠어요?	How would you like to pay?
□ 현금, 아니면 카드로 하시겠습니까?	Cash or (credit) card? Cash or charge?
□ 현금 드릴게요.	I'll pay in cash. Cash.
□ 현금 영수증 주세요.	Can I have a cash receipt? Cash receipt, please.
□ 카드로 할게요.	I'll pay by credit card. Card. Charge. Do you take credit cards?
□ 일시불로 계산할게요.	I'll pay in a lump sum. I'd like to pay in a single payment. I'll pay all at once.
□ 할부로 계산할게요.	I'll pay in installments. I'll pay in the installment plan.
□ 몇 개월로 하시겠어요?	How many months would you like?
□ 3개월 무이자 할부로 해 주세요.	No interest for three months, please.
□ 종이 가방이나 비닐봉지 필요하세요?	Do you need a paper or plastic bag?
□ 환경부담금 50원을 내셔야 합니다.	You have to pay 50 won for a bag. It's Environ-mental Improvement Fund(EIF).
□ 장바구니 있어요.	I have my own shopping bag.

Chapter 17

쇼핑

□ 선물용 포장해 주세요.	Can I get this gift-wrapped?	
	Could you gift-wrap it?	
	Giftwrap, please.	
□ 가격표는 떼 주세요.	Remove the price tag, please.	
□ 상품 교환권을 주세요.	Can I get the exchange coupon for it?	
□ 이 주소로 배송해 주세요.	Can you deliver it to this address? *deliver＝ship	
	Please have it delivered to this address.	
□ 며칠 정도 걸릴까요?	How long will it take?	
	When will it be delivered?	
□ 내일 배송됩니다.	It will be delivered tomorrow.	
□ 휴일이라 4~5일 걸립니다.	It will take 4~5 days during holidays.	

DIALOGUE

A I'd like to pay for these items.
B How would you like to pay for them?
A I'll pay by credit card.
   No interest for three months installments, please.
B No problem.
   Can I have the first three digits of your credit card password?

A 이 물건들 계산할게요.
B 어떻게 계산하시겠어요?
A 신용 카드로 계산할게요. 3개월 무이자 할부로 해 주세요.
B 그렇게 하겠습니다. 카드 비밀번호 앞의 세 자리를 말씀해 주시겠어요?

Notes

in a lump sum 전부 한 묶음으로, 한 번에 all at once 전부를 한 번에 installment 할부, 할부금 gift-wrap
선물용으로 포장하다, 선물용 포장 remove 제거하다, 없애다 have ~ delivered ~을 배달해 주다 ship 물건을 보
내다, 옮기다 digit 아라비아 숫자

06 상품의 질과 상태 확인하기

옷은 주로 fabric(원단), stitches(바느질) 상태, texture(질감), pattern(무늬) 등을 평가하고, 화장품은 피부에 발랐을 때의 느낌이나 향으로 상품을 평가할 수 있습니다. 식료품은 freshness(신선함)이나 sweetness(당도) 등으로 품질을 평가하겠죠.

원어민 발음 듣기 ☑☐ 회화 훈련 ☐☐ 듣기 훈련 ☐☐

☐ 원단이 고급스럽다.	**This fabric is fine.** *fine = luxurious, high quality
☐ 질감이 부드러워.	**The texture is soft.** *soft = silky **This fabric has a silky texture.**
☐ 이 치마는 무늬가 독특해.	**The pattern on this skirt is unique.** **The design on this skirt is unusual.**
☐ 이 치마는 바느질이 꼼꼼하게 잘 됐어.	**The stitches on this skirt are very fine.** *fine = even
☐ 유행을 안 타겠어.	**It doesn't follow the trends.** *trends = fashions **It's a classic.**
☐ 요즘 입기에 딱이야.	**It's perfect for this kind of season.**
☐ 봄, 가을에 입기 딱이야.	**It's perfect for the spring and fall.**
☐ 이 화장품 향이 좋다.	**This cosmetic smells good.**
☐ 산뜻한 느낌이야.	**It refreshes my skin.**
☐ 피부를 촉촉하게 해 줘.	**It moisturizes my skin.** *moisturizes = hydrates
☐ 저자극성이야.	**It's hypoallergenic.** **It doesn't seem to cause skin trouble.**
☐ 지성인 내 피부에 맞아.	**It's perfect for my oily skin.**
☐ 건성인 내 피부에 (딱) 맞아.	**It's (just) right for my dry skin.**
☐ 민감성인 내 피부에 좋아.	**It's good for my sensitive skin.**
☐ 이 가구는 디자인이 현대적이야.	**The design of this furniture is modern.**

Chapter 17

쇼핑

277

☐ 이건 고풍스러워.	It's antique.
☐ 빈티지 스타일이야.	It has a vintage style.
☐ 원목으로 만들어져 따뜻한 느낌이야.	The furniture is made of natural woods. It feels warm.
☐ 그건 자리를 너무 많이 차지해.	It takes up too much space.
☐ 휴대폰 기능이 전보다 훨씬 다양해졌어.	Cell phones have more functions than before. *cell phones = cellular phones, mobiles
☐ 디자인이 세련됐어.	The design is quite stylish.
☐ 부속품이 다양해.	It has many accessories.
☐ 이게 최신 모델이야?	Is this the latest model? *model = fashion
☐ 배터리 수명도 꽤 길어.	Battery life is pretty good. It has pretty good battery life.
☐ 야채가 신선해 보여.	Vegetables look fresh.
☐ 생선이 싱싱해 보여.	Fish seems fresh.
☐ 고기에 비계가 많다.	Meat has a lot of fat.
☐ 요즘 사과가 제철이야.	Apples are now in season.
☐ 제철이 지났어.	They're out of season.
☐ 과즙이 풍부해.	They're juicy.
☐ 당도가 높아.	They're high in sugar.
☐ 사각사각해.	They are crunchy.

📑 Notes

silky 부드러운, 촉감이 좋은 unusual 희한한, 독특한 even 바른, 고른 spring and fall 봄과 가을 refresh 산뜻하게 하다, 생기 넘치게 하다 hydrate 수분을 주다, 촉촉하게 하다 hypoallergenic 알레르기를 적게 일으키는, 저자극성의 cause 일으키다, 야기하다 antique 예스러운, 고풍스러운(= vintage) take up 자리를 차지하다 accessories 장신구, 액세서리 fat 지방, 비계 in season 유행하는, out of season 한물간, 유행이 지난 juicy 과즙이 많은, 싱싱한 crunchy 사각사각한, 오독오독하는

07 교환, 환불하기

구입한 상품을 exchanges(교환), refunds(환불)할 때는 보통 구입 후 일정 기간 내에 상품의 하자가 없는 상태에서 상품과 영수증을 가져가면 됩니다. 교환의 경우 difference(차액)가 발생할 수 있습니다.

원어민 발음 듣기 ☑☐ 　 회화 훈련 ☐☐ 　 듣기 훈련 ☐☐

☐ 환불과 교환 규정이 어떻게 되나요?	What's your policy on refunds and exchanges?
☐ 구입 후 일주일 안에 환불, 교환됩니다.	Purchased items can be refunded or exchanged within a week after the purchase of the item.
☐ 구입하신 물건과 영수증이 필요합니다.	You need the purchased item and the receipt. Don't forget to bring the purchased item and the receipt.
☐ 물건을 교환하고 싶어요.	I'd like to exchange this.
☐ 물건에 하자가 있어요.	The item is damaged. It has defects.
☐ 제가 그런 게 아니에요.	I didn't do this.
☐ 영수증은 가져오셨어요?	Do you have the receipt (on you)?
☐ 물건을 확인할게요.	Let me check the item. Let me check whether the item is fine.
☐ 어떤 것으로 교환하고 싶으세요?	What would you like to exchange?
☐ 차액은 환불해 주세요.	I'd like to get the rest in cash, please.
☐ (초과된) 차액을 지불할게요.	I'll pay the difference.
☐ 이 물건을 환불하고 싶어요.	I'd like to refund this.
☐ 카드 결제가 취소되었습니다.	The transactions have been cancelled.
☐ 착용한 옷은 교환이나 환불이 안 됩니다.	The clothes you've already worn can't be exchanged or refunded.
☐ 세일 품목은 교환이나 환불이 안 됩니다.	Sale items cannot be exchanged or refunded.

Chapter 17

쇼핑

279

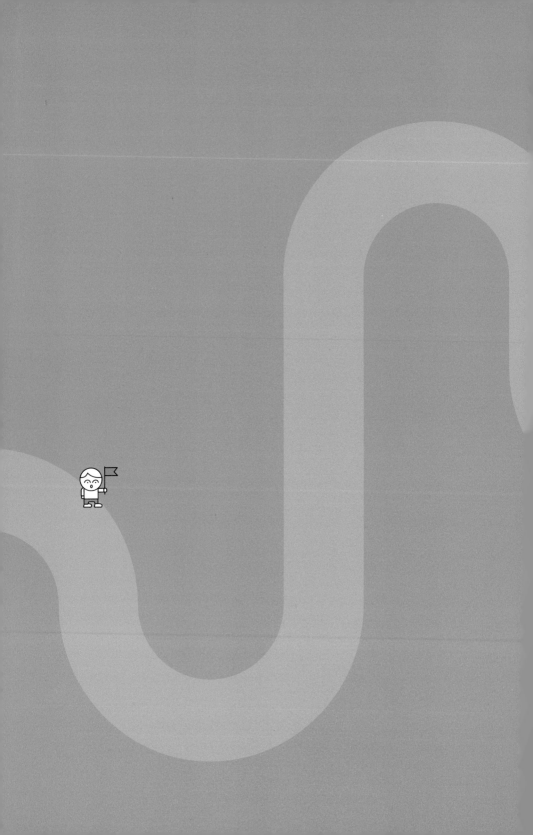

Chapter 18

취미
Hobby

01 문화, 취미에 대해 이야기하기

대표적인 취미 활동으로는 reading(독서), listening to music(음악 감상), watching movies(영화 감상)가 있죠. 요즘은 여럿이 모여 같이 취미를 즐기는 스포츠나 댄스 club(동호회)도 많아졌습니다. 다양한 취미 활동에 대해 알아봅시다.

원어민 발음 듣기 ☑☐   회화 훈련 ☐☐   듣기 훈련 ☐☐

□ 취미가 뭐야?
What's your hobby?
What are you interested in?

□ 쉴 때는 주로 뭐해?
What do you usually do in your free time?

□ 난 친구들과 어울려.
I hang out with my friends.

□ 난 주로 영화를 봐.
I go to the movies.
I watch movies.

□ 난 독서를 좋아해.
I read books.
I like reading.

□ 난 연극과 뮤지컬 광이야.
I'm a huge fan of plays and musicals.

□ 첨단 소형 전자 제품 사는 재미로 살아.
I live for getting high-tech gadgets.

□ 그는 주말마다 축구를 해.
He plays soccer every weekend.

□ 그녀는 거의 모든 전시회에 가.
She goes to almost every exhibition.

□ 콘서트는 정말 신나.
Music concerts really excite me.

□ 인디밴드 공연은 색다른 맛이야.
Indie bands concerts are unconventional.

□ 난 클래식 음악회를 좋아해.
I love classical music concerts.

□ 발레 공연은 너무 멋져.
Ballet is so fantastic.

□ 댄스 동호회에 가입했어.
I joined the dance club.

□ 나는 파티 여는 것을 좋아해.
I love having a party.

□ 나는 바에 즐겨 가.
I hang out in a bar.

□ 배우는 것을 좋아해.
I enjoy learning.
I like taking classes.

02 영화 관람, 영화관에서

가장 대중적인 문화생활 중 하나로 '영화 관람하기'가 있습니다. 영화의 종류가 워낙 다양해 취향에 따라 골라 보기도 하고, 관람 전 movie review(영화 관람평)를 읽으며 영화를 선택하는 경우도 있습니다. "아주 훌륭해.", "스토리가 좋아.", "영상이 끝내줘.", "마지막 반전이 압권이야." 등의 소감을 나눌 수도 있겠죠.

원어민 발음 듣기 ☑☐　회화 훈련 ☐☐　듣기 훈련 ☐☐

☐ 요즘 무슨 영화 상영하지?	What movies are on these days? *movies = films
☐ 요즘 어떤 영화가 가장 재미있어?	What's the best movie lately?
☐ 그 영화는 언제 개봉하지?	When will the movie open? When will the movie come out? When will the movie be released?
☐ 그 영화 언제 개봉했지?	When did it open? *open = come out
☐ 10월 31일에 개봉 돼.	It will be released on Oct 31.
☐ 그 영화제에서 개봉작으로 상영됐어.	It was screened at the movie festival.
☐ 가을엔 멜로 영화가 최고야.	In fall, romantic movies are the best.
☐ 여름엔 공포 영화가 최고야.	Horror movies are perfect for the summer.
☐ 너무 기대된다.	I can't wait. I'm looking forward to it.
☐ 그 영화는 엄청나게 히트 칠 것 같아.	The movie's going to be a huge hit.
☐ 예고편이 멋있어.	I like the trailer of the movie.
☐ 영화평이 좋아.	The movie has a great review.
☐ 시사회 관람권이 있어.	I've got preview tickets.
☐ 친구들이 강력 추천했어.	My friends strongly recommend it.
☐ 친구들이 절대 보지 말래.	My friends told me not to watch it.
☐ 내가 영화 보여 줄게.	Let me take you to the movies. The movie is on me.
☐ 그 영화 상영 끝났어?	Did the movie close?

Chapter 18　취미

	Did the movie stop running?
☐ 아직 상영 중일걸.	I think it's still on.
	I think it's still running.
☐ 그 영화 봤어?	Did you see the movie?
☐ 어땠어?	How was it?
☐ 아직 안 봤어.	I haven't seen it yet.
☐ 지난 주말에 봤어.	I saw it last weekend.
☐ 아주 훌륭했어.	It was great.
	*great = wonderful, superb, exceptional
☐ 스토리가 좋았어.	The movie has a great story.
	*story = plot
☐ 내용은 별로야.	It doesn't have a great story.
	Not much of a story.
☐ 그래픽이 환상적이야.	The images are fantastic.
☐ 배우들이 연기를 잘했어.	The actors played well.
	*played = performed
☐ 참신했어.	It was new.
	*new = fresh, different
☐ 감동적이었어.	It was heartwarming.
	*heartwarming = touching
	It touched my heart.
☐ 이런 영화 전에 본 듯해.	I've seen this kind of movie before.
☐ 특수 효과가 압권이야.	The special effects are outstanding.
☐ 영상과 음악이 끝내줬어.	The images and music are amazing.
☐ 마지막 10분 반전이 끝내줬어.	The last ten minutes reversal was great.
	*reversal = twist
☐ 이야기하지 마.	Don't tell me.
	I'm not listening.
☐ 스포일러 경고야!	Spoiler alert!
☐ 속도감 있어.	It's speedy.
☐ 너무 처져.	It's too slow.

☐ 긴장감을 늦추지 않아.	It has a lot of suspense.
☐ '킹콩'을 리메이크한 영화야.	It's a remake of King Kong.
☐ '배트맨'을 리부트한 영화야.	It's a reboot of Batman.
☐ 그 영화는 실화를 바탕으로 만들었어.	The movie is based on the true story. *true = real
☐ 그 영화는 소설을 영화화했어.	The movie was made based on a novel. A novel was made into a movie.
☐ 그 영화는 소설만 못해.	The novel is better than the movie. The movie isn't as good as the novel.
☐ 그 영화는 소설을 능가해.	The movie is better than the novel.
☐ 그 영화는 그 사건을 생생히 재현했어.	The movie re-creates the event realistically. *realistically = vividly
☐ 형편없었어.	The movie was awful. *awful = terrible, horrible
☐ 섬뜩했어.	It's terrifying.
☐ 찝찝했어.	It's uncomfortable.
☐ 지루했어.	It's boring.
☐ 내용이 기억조차 안 나.	I don't even remember the story.
☐ 100점 만점에 몇 점 줄 거야?	What's your score out of 100?
☐ 85점 줄 수 있어.	I can give it 85. I'll say 85.
☐ 그 영화 또 봐야지.	I'm going to see the movie again.
☐ 그는 그 영화로 떴어.	The movie's made him rich and famous. He's got fame in the movie. The movie was a big break for him.
☐ 영화가 흥행에 성공했어.	The movie has commercially succeeded. The movie did great at the box office.
☐ 영화가 흥행에 실패했어.	The movie was a total failure. The movie failed at the box office.
☐ 유명 배우가 총출연 했음에도 실패했어.	Despite an all-star cast, the movie failed.

◻ 가장 재미있게 본 영화가 뭐야?	What's your favorite movie? What's your all time favorite? What movies do you like the most?
◻ 어떤 종류의 영화를 좋아해?	What kind of movies do you like?
◻ 난 공포 영화 좋아해.	I like horror movies.
◻ 영화관에 얼마나 자주 가?	How often do you go to the movie theater?
◻ 한 달에 한두 번 정도.	Once or twice a month.
◻ 주로 영화를 다운로드 해.	I download the movies from the Internet.
◻ 누구와 영화 보러 가?	When you see a movie, who do you go with?
◻ 주로 친구와 함께 가.	I usually go with my friends.
◻ 먹으면 영화에 집중이 안 돼.	I can't concentrate on a movie while eating.
◻ 인터넷으로 티켓 예매했어.	I've got tickets on the Internet.
◻ 좌석이 네 맘에 들 거야.	You'll like the seat.
◻ 좌석표 확인하자.	Let's check a seating layout. Let's check out our seats.
◻ 스크린에 너무 가깝다.	It's too close to the screen.
◻ 머리가 어질어질해.	It gives me a headache.
◻ 좌석이 편안했어.	My seat was very comfortable.
◻ 좌석이 좁아서 불편했어.	My seat was too small for me.

📋 영화(movies) 종류

멜로 romance(=romantic)	특수 효과 special effects
로맨틱 코미디 romantic comedy(rom-com)	무협 martial arts(=Kung Fu)
가족 family	공포 horror
액션 action	스릴러 thriller
공상 과학 science fiction(=sci-fi)	컬트 cult
다큐멘터리 documentary	독립 영화 independent(=indie) films
애니메이션 animation	

03 독서, 서점에서

주제별로 다양한 책들이 출판되고 있는 가운데 사람마다 책을 고르는 기준도 다릅니다. 책을 고르는 기준으로는 '베스트셀러', '유명 작가', '언론 매체의 추천' 등이 있을 수 있겠죠. 요즘에는 paper book(종이책) 외에도 e-book(전자책)도 보편화되는 추세입니다.

원어민 발음 듣기 ☑☐   회화 훈련 ☐☐   듣기 훈련 ☐☐

☐ 어떤 종류의 책을 좋아해?

What kind of books do you like?
*kind = sort

☐ 난 역사 소설을 좋아해.

I love history novels.

☐ 왜 역사 소설이야?

Why do you like them?

☐ 역사 속 인물들 이야기가 좋아.

I love to read about people in history.

☐ 난 모든 종류의 책을 다 읽어.

I read all kinds of books.

☐ 난 책을 많이 읽어.

I read a lot.
I'm a big reader.

☐ 한 달에 책은 몇 권 읽어?

How many books do you read for a month?

☐ 한 달에 3~4권 읽어.

I read three or four books a month.

☐ 거의 못 읽어.

I barely read books.
I don't have time to read.

☐ 읽고 감상문을 써야 해.

We have to write about what we think about the book.

☐ 책을 고르는 기준은 뭐야?

How do you choose books?

☐ 유명한 작가의 책을 읽어.

I read famous writer's books.

☐ 신인 작가의 책을 읽어.

I read books written by young writers.
*young writer = new writer

☐ 대형 출판사의 책을 읽어.

I read books published by big publishers.

☐ 베스트셀러를 주로 읽어.

I read bestselling books.

☐ 보통 친구들이 추천해 줘.

My friends usually recommend me books.

☐ 언론 매체에서 추천하는 도서를 읽어.

I read books recommended by the media.
*recommended = reviewed, selected

☐ 디자인이 잘 된 책에 역시 시선이 가.	Well-designed books definitely get my attention.
☐ 도서는 어디에서 구입해?	Where do you buy books?
☐ 인터넷상으로 구입해.	I buy books on the Internet. I shop in the online book store.
☐ 서점에 직접 가.	I go to the (off-line) bookstore.
☐ 판타지 소설을 찾는데요.	I'm looking for fantasy novels.
☐ 책을 찾을 수 없네요.	I can't find the book.
☐ 제가 찾아 드릴게요.	Let me find the book for you.
☐ 책 제목이 뭐죠?	What's the title of the book?
☐ 저자명이 뭐죠?	Who wrote it? Who's the writer?
☐ 책 제목을 정확히 몰라요.	I don't remember the title exactly.
☐ 그런 책은 없습니다.	We don't have the book by that title.
☐ 서점 멤버십 카드가 있으세요?	Do you have the membership card of this bookstore? Are you a member of this bookstore?
☐ 없으면 만드시겠어요?	If you don't, do you want to register? If you aren't, do you want to register?
☐ 어떤 혜택이 있나요?	What are the benefits?
☐ 구매액의 5%가 포인트로 적립됩니다.	You can save 5% of purchase amount as points. *save = collect
☐ 포인트는 현금처럼 쓰세요.	You can use those points like cash.
☐ 사인회에도 초대됩니다.	You will be invited to book signing events. *book signing = autograph signing
☐ 생일날 구매 시 할인 받습니다.	You will get a discount on your birthday purchase.
☐ 그 책 읽어 봤어?	Did you read the book? Have you read the book?
☐ 아니, 아직.	No, not yet.

읽고 있는 중이야.	I'm reading it now.
거의 다 읽었어.	I'm almost done.
작가가 명석해.	He is a brilliant writer.
내 상상력을 자극해.	The book stimulates my imagination.
도입부는 조금 지루해.	The beginning is a little boring.
결론이 통쾌해.	The ending is quite satisfying. *satisfying = gratifying
순식간에 다 읽었어.	I read it at a stretch. I read it at a sitting.
책을 덮을 수가 없었어.	I couldn't stop reading in the middle. I had to finish reading it.
처음부터 끝까지 다 읽었어.	I read it cover to cover.
나 오디오북을 들어.	I listen to audio books.
언제 주로 들어?	When do you usually listen?
운전하면서 들어.	I listen to it while driving.
운동하면서 들어.	I listen to it while exercising.
잠자리에서 들어.	I listen to it in bed.
e-book은 주로 어디에서 다운 받아?	From where do you download e-books?
무료 사이트를 뒤져서 받아.	I look through free e-book download websites.
e-book은 종이책의 절반 값이야.	E-books are half price of paper books.
e-book은 값이 저렴해.	E-books are cheaper.
난 종이책이 (여전히) 더 좋아.	I (still) prefer paper books.
종이 냄새가 좋아.	I like the smell of paper books.

문학의 장르(type of literature)

시 poet, poetry	평론 critique, review
소설 novel	수필 essay
희곡 drama, play	동화 children's story, fairy tale

04 TV 시청

드라마나 최근 들어 큰 인기를 몰고 있는 survival show(서바이벌 쇼)는 addictive(중독성이 강한)하여 계속 보게 됩니다. 혹시라도 놓친 경우 친구에게 Did you see it?(어제 그 프로그램 봤어?), How did the story end?(어떻게 됐어?) 하고 묻기도 하지요.

원어민 발음 듣기 ☑☐   회화 훈련 ☐☐   듣기 훈련 ☐☐

☐ TV를 많이 보니?	Do you watch TV a lot?
☐ 틈만 나면 봐.	I watch TV whenever I can.
	Every chance I get.
☐ 거의 못 봐.	I barely watch TV.
☐ 어떤 프로그램을 좋아해?	What programs do you like?
☐ 뉴스와 교양 프로그램을 좋아해.	I like the news and culture programs.
☐ 가장 좋아하는 채널은 뭐야?	What's your favorite channel?
☐ 13번 채널이야.	I like channel 13.
☐ 13번을 고정해 놓고 봐.	I stay tuned for channel 13.
☐ 어제 일일 연속극 봤어?	Did you see the daily drama yesterday?
	*drama = soap opera
☐ 다른 프로그램 봤어.	I watched a different program.
☐ 어떤 내용이었어?	How did the story turn out?
	How did the story go?
	What was that about?
☐ 그 프로그램 좋아하니?	Do you like the program?
☐ 그 프로그램 정말 재미없지 않니?	Isn't the program boring?
☐ 그거 중독성이 강해.	It's very addictive.
☐ 시시한데 자꾸 보게 돼.	It's boring, but I can't stop watching it.
☐ 꼭 챙겨 보는 프로그램이야.	I never miss the program.
☐ 그 프로그램 정말 좋아해.	I really love the program.
☐ 그 프로그램 그냥 별로야.	I don't like the program so much.

☐ 가족이 보니까 함께 봐.	My family watches it. So I watch it, too.
☐ 그 프로는 장수 프로그램이야.	It's a long-running show. The program has legs.
☐ 그 프로그램을 연장하기로 했대.	They've decided to extend their show.
☐ 그 프로그램은 엄청난 인기야.	The program is very popular. The program is a huge hit.
☐ 시청률이 20%가 넘었대.	It shows over 20% viewer ratings.
☐ 사상 초유의 시청률 기록이래.	It's recorded the highest ratings.
☐ 그 드라마는 해외로 수출됐어.	The program has been exported to overseas.
☐ 그 드라마 촬영지는 관광 명소가 됐어.	The locations for the drama have become tourist attractions.
☐ 그 프로그램은 아무도 안 볼 거야.	No one will watch that program.
☐ 시작부터 말 많은 프로그램이야.	The program has many controversial issues.
☐ 금방 종영될 거야.	I guess it will end very soon.
☐ 생방송 중에 방송 사고가 났어.	There was an incident during the live (broadcast).
☐ 출연자가 말실수를 했어.	One of the guests made a tongue slip.
☐ 그 서바이벌 프로그램 우승자는 누굴까?	Who's going to be the winner of the survival show?
☐ 참가자들이 모두 쟁쟁해.	Contestants are all qualified. *qualified = outstanding
☐ 막상막하야.	It's neck and neck. It's nip and tuck.
☐ 결과를 예견하기 힘들어.	No one can predict the end. It's hard to predict how it ends.
☐ 우승 상금이 얼마야?	How much is the prize money? *prize = award
☐ 저 배우 TV에서 오랜만에 본다.	I haven't seen her on TV for a while.

☐ 그 여자 많이 늙었다.	She looks old.
☐ 그는 오히려 젊어졌어.	He looks even younger (than before).
☐ 그 배우는 몸값이 높아.	The star is expensive.
☐ 그 배우는 스캔들에 휘말렸어.	She has got involved with some scandal.
☐ 두 배우가 열애 중이라는 소문이 있어.	There's a rumor that they're having a romantic relationship.
☐ 방송 활동을 잠시 중단하고 싶대.	He wants to stop making TV appearances for a while.
☐ 그녀는 은퇴 선언을 했어.	She has announced her retirement.

📋 TV 프로그램(TV programs) 종류

뉴스 news	영화 movies
드라마 drama, soap opera	오락 entertainment show
게임 프로그램 game show	취미 프로그램 hobbies
음악 프로그램 music show	의료 프로그램 medical show
퀴즈 프로그램 quiz show	스포츠 sport
토크 프로그램 talk show	리얼리티 reality show
다큐멘터리 documentary	서바이벌 프로그램 survival show

📝 Notes

stay tuned 채널 고정하다 turn out ~의 결과가 되다, 결국 ~이 되다 addictive 중독성이 강한 long-running 장기간 지속되는 legs TV 쇼나 영화 등의 관객 동원력, 인기 지속력 extend (기간을) 연장하다 viewer ratings TV 프로그램의 시청률(= viewership) controversial 논쟁의 여지가 있는 make a tongue slip 말실수를 하다 neck and neck 막상막하의, 경쟁이 치열한(= nip and tuck) predict 미래(결과)를 예견하다 get involved with ~와 연관되다, ~에 휘말리다 There's a rumor that ~ ~라는 소문이 있다 make TV appearances TV에 출연하다

05 인터넷, 통신 관련 취미

인터넷을 기반으로 한 통신 서비스나 컴퓨터, 휴대폰 등은 요즘 최고의 화젯거리입니다. 인터넷 기반 서비스로는 Social Networking Service(소셜 네트워크 서비스)와 instant messaging service(인스턴트 메시지), texting service(문자) 등이 있습니다.

원어민 발음 듣기 ☑□　　회화 훈련 □□　　듣기 훈련 □□

□ 새 스마트폰 샀어.	I've got a new smart phone.
□ 세련됐다.	It's sleek.
□ 월 서비스 이용료가 얼마야?	How much do you pay for the service for a month?
□ 어떤 기능이 있어?	What functions does it have?
□ 주로 어떤 용도로 사용해?	How do you use it?
□ 인터넷 사용 목적으로 이용해.	I use it for the Internet service.
□ 내비게이션으로 이용해.	I use it as a navigator.
□ 스마트폰의 장점이 뭐야?	What are the strong points of a smart phone?
□ 쉽고 편리해.	It's easy and convenient.
□ 가볍게 볼일 볼 때 편리해.	It's convenient to run some errands.
□ 업무 처리를 쉽게 도와줘.	It helps my work get done easily.
□ 태블릿 PC를 갖고 싶어 죽겠어.	I'm dying to have a tablet PC.
□ 태블릿 PC만 쓰게 돼.	I only use my tablet PC.
□ 하루 종일 태블릿 PC에만 매달려 있어.	I'm on my tablet PC all the time.
□ SNS 쓰니?	Do you use SNS service?
□ 옛 친구와 다시 연락하게 됐어.	I've reconnected to my old friends.
□ 친구 추천 받았어.	My friends introduce me to their friends.
□ 친구들이 빠르게 늘고 있어.	The number of my friends is increasing fast.
□ 인스턴트 메시지 보내고 있어.	I'm sending instant messages.

Chapter 18

취미

☐ 간단한 업무는 인스턴트 메시지를 사용해.	I use instant messaging for simple work-related communication.
☐ 친구들과 문자를 많이 해.	I'm texting a lot with my friends.
☐ 답 문자가 없어.	I haven't gotten any text back yet.
☐ 개인 정보 유출이 걱정돼.	I'm worried about leaking my private information.
☐ 사생활이 노출되는 게 싫어.	I don't want my private life to be exposed.
☐ 재미있는 사진 올렸어.	I've posted some funny pictures.
☐ 동영상 찍어서 올렸어.	I've uploaded some video clips.
☐ 내 블로그 방문해 줘.	Visit my blog.
☐ 미니홈피를 만드는 중이야.	I'm creating my mini-homepage now.
☐ 인터넷 카페를 추천해 줄까?	Do you want me to recommend you an Internet café?
☐ 휴대폰 없이는 못 살겠어.	I can't live without my cell phone.
☐ 휴대폰이 성가셔.	I'm sick of my mobile.

DIALOGUE

A I've got a new smart phone.
B Let me see. Wow, it's sleek.
　I'm dying to get a tablet PC.
A Do you want to check out electronics stores?
B Sure, why not?

A 나 스마트폰 샀다.
B 어디 봐. 와 세련됐다. 나는 태블릿 PC가 너무 갖고 싶어.
A 전자 제품 상가를 좀 둘러볼래?
B 물론. 왜 아니겠어!

Notes

sleek 세련된, 미끈한　run errands 용무를 처리하다　reconnect 다시 연락하다, 연락이 닿다　work-related 업무와 관련된　leak 새다, 누출하다　expose 노출시키다

06 연극, 뮤지컬 관람

play(연극)와 musical(뮤지컬)은 영화와는 다른 매력으로 많은 사람들을 불러 모읍니다. 공연을 감상한 후에는 autograph event(팬 사인회)를 통해 배우와 직접 만나는 기회를 잡을 수도 있죠.

원어민 발음 듣기 ☑□   회화 훈련 □□   듣기 훈련 □□

☐ 요즘 어떤 연극이 재미있어?	What play is good these days?
☐ 예전보다 다양한 작품들이 공연 중이야.	There's more variety than before.
	Plays offer more variety than before.
	*plays → musicals (뮤지컬)
☐ 그건 외국 작품이야.	It's a foreign play.
☐ 그건 창작극이야.	It's an original play.
☐ 열성팬들이 많아.	There are many enthusiastic fans.
☐ 티켓 값이 저렴해.	Ticket prices are reasonable.
	*reasonable = cheap
☐ 학생이나 커플은 할인 혜택이 많아.	They offer students or couples a discount.
☐ R석 4장 주세요.	Can I get four R seats?
☐ 좌석은 어디를 원하세요?	Where would you like to sit?
	What seat would you like to have?
☐ 맨 앞줄 가운데 자리 주세요.	I'd like seats in the front row.
☐ 공연 후 팬 사인회가 있습니다.	There will be an autograph event after the play.
☐ 공연 소감을 올려 주세요.	Write us about how you feel about our performance.
☐ 좌석 사이가 너무 좁아.	The space between seats is too narrow.
☐ 배우들이 열연했어.	Actors played their roles passionately.
☐ 브로드웨이 뮤지컬 팀의 공연이야.	It's the Broadway team's performance.
☐ 자막 보느라 바빴어.	I was busy reading subtitles.

등산

mountain-climbing(등산)은 몸과 마음이 건강해지는 활동으로 사계절 어느 때나 즐길 수 있습니다. 요즘은 bag pack(배낭), hiking boots(등산화), climbing equipments(등산 장비) 등의 등산 용품들로 보다 안전하고 편하게 등산을 즐길 수 있죠.

원어민 발음 듣기 ☑□ 회화 훈련 □□ 듣기 훈련 □□

□ 등산 가자.	Let's go to the mountains. Let's go climbing. *go climbing = go hiking
□ 주말마다 등산 다녀.	I go to the mountains every weekend.
□ 등산하기 좋은 날씨야.	It's the perfect weather for climbing.
□ 등산하기 좋은 날이야.	It's a perfect day for hiking.
□ 등산하기 좋은 계절이야.	It's a perfect season for mountain-climbing.
□ 온 산이 단풍으로 물들었어.	The whole mountain is covered with autumn leaves. Autumn leaves are great these days.
□ 등산하기 좋은 산이 어디야?	Which mountain is good for climbing?
□ 서울에서 등산하기 좋은 산은 어디야?	Which mountain in Seoul is good for climbing?
□ 초보자에게 적격인 산은 어디야?	What mountain is perfect for a beginner?
□ 정상까지 얼마나 걸려?	How long does it take to the top? *to the top = to go up
□ 등산이 왜 좋아?	Why is climbing good for us?
□ 정신적, 신체적으로 모두 건강해져.	It makes your body and mind strong and healthy.
□ 우울증에도 효과가 있어.	It's also good for someone who has depression. *depression = the blues
□ 등산갈 때 준비물은 뭐야?	What do I need to prepare? What do I need for mountain-climbing?
□ 배낭과 등산화가 필요해.	You need a bag pack and hiking boots.

□	다양한 등산 장비가 있어.	There are various climbing equipment.
□	등산복 브랜드가 매우 많아.	There are many different brands for mountain-climbing clothes.
□	가격대가 다양해.	The price range varies.
□	비싸다고 다 좋은 것은 아니야.	It's not always good just because it's expensive.
□	등산복의 기능성이 강화됐어.	Mountain clothes are more functional than before. *mountain = hiking
□	방수, 방풍 효과가 뛰어나.	They have excellent resistance against rain and wind.
□	장비를 하나씩 사 모으고 있어.	I'm buying the equipment one by one. *buying = collecting
□	화려한 옷이 필요해.	I need colorful clothes. *colorful = vivid-colored, multi-colored
□	가족과 함께 등산 갈 거야.	I'm going to the mountains with my family.
□	직원들과 함께 등산할 거야.	I'm going hiking with colleagues from work.
□	등산은 칼로리 소모가 많아.	Climbing really burns up calories.
□	올라갈 때 많이 힘들어.	Climbing up is very difficult.
□	이 고생을 왜 하고 있지?	Why am I doing this?
□	정상에서의 경치가 아름다워.	The view from the mountain top is absolutely breathtaking.
□	간식 먹는 재미가 있어.	It's fun to have snacks.

DIALOGUE

A It's the perfect season for mountain-climbing. Let's go climbing today.
B Sounds great. But I don't even have any mountain clothes.
A Do you have a wind breaker and sneakers?
B Sure, I do. Is there anything else I need?

A 등산하기 좋은 계절이야. 오늘 등산 가자.
B 좋은 생각이야. 하지만 난 등산복도 없는 걸.
A 스포츠용 점퍼와 운동화 있어?
B 물론이지. 그 밖에 또 필요한 것이 뭐야?

08 자전거 타기

자전거는 eco-friendly transportation(친환경적 교통수단)으로, 여가 시간에 즐기거나 출퇴근용으로 이용하는 사람들이 부쩍 늘면서 자전거에 대한 관심도 커지고 있습니다. 하지만 여전히 수요에 비해 bike rack(보관대)이 부족하고 휴대에 번거로움이 있다는 문제가 있죠.

원어민 발음 듣기 ☑□ 회화 훈련 □□ 듣기 훈련 □□

□ 요즘은 자전거가 큰 인기야.
Biking is very popular these days.
*biking = cycling

□ 자전거 종류가 다양해.
There are many different kinds of bicycles.

□ 자전거 멋지다!
What a cool bike!

□ 출근할 때 자전거 타.
I ride my bike to work.

□ 아침에 상쾌한 공기를 즐겨.
I enjoy the fresh air in the morning.

□ 교통 체증 없이 출근해.
I go to work without a traffic jam.
I don't need to be stuck in a traffic jam.

□ 나는 운동 삼아 자전거를 타.
I ride a bike for exercise.

□ 자전거 타러 가자.
Let's go for a bike ride.
Shall we go for a bike ride?

□ 나는 아직 자전거가 없어.
I don't have a bike yet.

□ 나는 자전거를 못 타.
I don't know how to ride a bike.

□ 10분이면 배워.
It takes only ten minutes to learn.

□ 자전거 안 탄 지 오래됐어.
I haven't ridden a bike for a long time.

□ 자전거를 빌리면 돼.
You can rent a bike.

□ 자전거는 어디에서 빌려?
Where can I rent a bike?

□ 2인용 자전거를 어디에서 빌려?
Where can I rent a tandem bike?

□ 자전거 선택 요령은 뭐야?
How do you choose your bike?

□ 자전거 가게는 어디에 있어?
Where is the bicycle shop?

□ 중고 자전거는 저렴해.
A used bike is cheaper.

☐	자전거는 친환경적 교통수단이야.	A bike is an eco-friendly way to transport.
☐	자전거 여행을 떠나려고 해.	I'm going to take a bike trip.
☐	자전거는 어디에 세워?	Where do you keep your bike?
☐	자전거 보관대에 체인으로 묶어 놨어.	I chained my bike to the bike rack.

*bike = bicycle

☐	내 자전거 벽에 기대어 놨어.	I just leaned my bike against the wall.
☐	자전거를 세워둘 곳이 없어.	There's no place to keep my bike.
☐	자전거를 가지고 버스 타기가 힘들어.	It's difficult to get on the bus with my bike.
☐	자전거 도난 사고가 빈번해.	There have been many cases of bike burglary.
☐	자전거가 고장 났어.	My bike is broken.
☐	자전거 브레이크가 고장 났어.	My bike brake broke down.
☐	바퀴에 바람이 빠졌어.	My bike has a flat tire. I've got a flat tire.
☐	체인을 바꿔야 해.	I have to replace the bike chain.
☐	엉덩이가 아파.	My buttocks hurt. I have a pain in my buttocks.
☐	심한 경적소리를 삼가도록 하세요.	Try not to blow a horn too much.

Chapter 18 취미

 Notes

be stuck in ~에 끼여 꼼짝 못하다 ride a bike 자전거 타다 transport 교통수단 bike rack 자전거 보관대
lean against ~에 기대다, 기대어 놓다 break down 기계가 고장 나다 flat tire 바퀴에 바람이 빠짐 replace
교체하다, 바꾸다 buttocks 사람이나 동물의 엉덩이, 둔부 blow a horn 경적을 울리다

09 전시회 관람

계절마다 다양한 exhibitions(전시회)가 개최됩니다. 요즘은 직접 만지고 체험할 수 있는 전시회가 큰 인기를 끌고 있죠. 전시회와 함께 열리는 events(행사)에 참여하는 것도 또 다른 재미가 있습니다. 관람 전에 관람 시간, 휴관일을 미리 확인하고 가면 더욱 좋습니다.

원어민 발음 듣기 ☑□ 회화 훈련 □□ 듣기 훈련 □□

□ 가 볼 만한 전시회가 있어?

Are there any exhibitions we have to check out?

□ 전시회 정보는 어디에서 얻어?

Where do you get information of exhibitions?

□ 전시회 정보 무료 어플은 없나?

Is there any free application to give us information about exhibitions?

□ 디자인 관련 전시회를 찾고 있어.

I'm looking for design-related exhibitions.

□ 가을엔 전시회가 많아.

There are many exhibitions during fall.

□ 방학엔 전시장이 아이들로 붐벼.

The exhibition is filled with children during vacation.

□ 전시회에 딸린 행사도 다양해.

Other events are also held with the exhibition.

□ 난 꽃 박람회에 관심 있어.

I'm interested in the flower exhibition.

□ 특별한 전시회가 열리고 있어.

The museum's putting on the very special exhibition.
*exhibition = display, show

□ 처음 소개되는 전시회야.

They're exhibited for the first time here.
We've never seen this kind of exhibition before.

□ 이곳에서 최대 규모의 전시회야.

This is the biggest exhibition ever here.

□ 만지고 체험하는 전시회야.

This is the experience-oriented exhibition.

□ 어른과 아이가 모두 좋아해.

Both adults and children can enjoy it.

□ 이 많은 것을 언제 다 보지?

How do we look around all these?

□ 천천히 보자.

Let's take (our) time.

□ 안내문을 챙겨야지.	Let's get a brochure.
□ 기념품 가게에 들러볼까?	Shall we stop by the gift shop?
□ 입장료가 아깝지 않아.	The exhibition was worth spending money.
□ 입장료가 아까워.	It's not worth spending money.
□ 볼 것이 하나도 없어.	There's nothing much to see.
□ 광고만 요란했네.	The exhibition has promoted with media hype, but actually it's boring.
□ 전시회 초대권이 생겼어.	I've got invitation tickets for the exhibition.
□ 같이 갈 사람을 구하고 있어.	I'm looking for a person to go with.
□ 초대권 드릴게요.	Let me give you invitation tickets.
□ 친구와 함께 가세요.	Why don't you go with your friends?
□ 관람 기간은 언제까지예요?	What are your admission hours? *admission = opening
□ 오전 9시부터 오후 6시까지입니다.	It's from 9 am to 6 pm.
□ 휴관일은 언제예요?	When is the museum closed?
□ 월요일마다입니다.	Every Monday. On Mondays.

Notes

be held 열리다, 개최되다 take time 시간을 갖다, 천천히 하다 stop by 잠시 들르다 worth ~할 가치가 있는
promote 홍보하다, 널리 알리다 hype 과대 선전

Chapter 18 취미

10 콘서트 관람

콘서트에 가면 가수들의 열정적인 performances(공연)와 세련된 stage manners(무대 매너), fantastic stage setting(화려한 무대 장치) 등으로 콘서트장이 열광의 도가니가 됩니다. 콘서트에서 쓸 수 있는 표현들에 대해 알아보겠습니다.

원어민 발음 듣기 ☑□   회화 훈련 □□   듣기 훈련 □□

□ 오늘 밤 콘서트 구경 가.	I'm going to the concert tonight.
□ 학수고대하던 콘서트야.	I'm looking forward to this concert.
□ 스타들이 한 자리에 모여.	All super stars will be on the stage.
□ 어디에서 열려?	Where is it held?
□ 실내 공연이야, 야외 공연이야?	Is this the indoor or outdoor concert?
□ 야외 공연이 더 재미있어.	I have more fun at the outdoor concert.
□ 불꽃놀이도 한대.	There will be fireworks, too.
□ 그 전설적인 그룹이 드디어 한국에 온대.	The legendary group is finally coming to Korea.
□ 공연이 언제야?	When is the concert?
□ 두 달 뒤야.	The concert will be held in two months.
□ 예매는 언제부터야?	When does the ticket sale begin?
□ 다음 주부터야.	It begins from next week.
□ 표 구했어?	Did you get the tickets?
□ 가까스로 두 장 구했어.	I got them at the last minutes.
□ 암표 구했어.	I've got illegal tickets. I got tickets from a scalper.
□ 정상 가격의 두 배를 지불했어.	I paid twice more than a regular price.
□ 표가 일주일 만에 매진됐어.	The tickets were sold out in a week.
□ 표를 구할 방법이 없어.	There's no way to get tickets.
□ 이제야 그들의 인기를 실감하겠어.	Now I realize how popular they are.

열광의 도가니였어.	People went mad with wild excitement.
열정적인 공연이었어.	It was a spectacular and passionate performance.
가수들의 무대 매너가 좋았어.	The singers have such great stage manners.
무대 장치가 환상적이었어.	The stage setting was fantastic.
일부 열성팬은 너무 흥분해서 기절했어.	Some fans were overexcited and passed out.
목이 터져라 노래했어.	He sang his heart out.
가장 신나는 콘서트였어.	It was the best concert ever.
가장 형편없는 콘서트였어.	It was the worst concert ever.
선곡이 뛰어났어.	Their repertoire was great.

DIALOGUE

A It was a spectacular performance, wasn't it?
B Yeah, people went mad with wild excitement.
A Did you see some fans overexcited and passed out?
B Of course, I did. I realized how popular the band is.

A 정말 끝내주는 공연이었어, 그렇지 않니?
B 맞아. 정말 열광의 도가니였어.
A 일부 열성팬들이 너무 흥분해서 기절하는 거 봤어?
B 물론 봤지. 그 밴드가 얼마나 인기가 많은지 실감했어.

Notes

illegal 불법의, 비합법적인 scalper 매매 차익을 챙기는 사람, 암표상 overexcited 지나치게 흥분한 pass out 기절하다, 졸도하다 sing one's heart out 목이 터지도록 큰 소리로 노래 부르다 repertoire 레퍼토리, 상영(연주) 목록

11 동호회 활동

club 혹은 society라고 불리는 동호회에 가입하면 회원들과 친목을 도모할 수 있을 뿐 아니라 관심 분야에 관련된 유익한 정보도 얻을 수 있습니다. learning clubs(배우는 것을 목적으로 하는 동호회)의 경우 개인적으로 배우는 것에 비해 돈을 훨씬 절약할 수도 있죠.

원어민 발음 듣기 ☑□   회화 훈련 □□   듣기 훈련 □□

☐ 동호회에 가입하고 싶어.	I'd like to join a club. *club = society
☐ 이색적인 동호회를 찾고 있어.	I'm looking for a unique club. I'm looking for something different.
☐ 동호회 종류가 매우 다양해.	There are many different kinds of clubs.
☐ 직장 내 동호회는 어때?	How about joining a club at workplace? *how = what
☐ 회원들과 친목 도모를 할 수 있어.	You can socialize with members.
☐ 유용한 정보를 얻을 수 있어.	You can get useful information.
☐ 일상생활의 활력소가 될 거야.	Joining a club will be full of fun in life.
☐ 어떤 동호회가 좋을까?	What club should be good for me?
☐ 어떤 분야에 관심 있어?	What are you interested in?
☐ 마라톤에 관심이 있어.	I'm interested in marathon.
☐ 전통 음악에 관심이 있어.	I'm interested in our traditional music.
☐ 재테크에 관심이 있어.	I'm interested in financial investments.
☐ 동호회 가입 자격이 있나요?	What are the qualifications to join a club?
☐ 달리기를 좋아하는 사람이면 됩니다.	Anyone who likes running can be a member.
☐ 전통 음악을 사랑하는 사람이면 됩니다.	Anyone who loves our traditional music can be a member.
☐ 친구와 함께 가입해도 되나요?	Can I join with my friends? Can I bring my friends?
☐ 완전 초보자인데요.	I'm an absolute beginner.

□ 가르쳐 주시나요?	Do you guys teach me?
	Do you guys give me lessons?
□ 동호회 회원 전체가 선생님입니다.	All members can be your teachers. *teachers = instructors
□ 가입비가 따로 있나요?	Is there membership fee? *membership = admission
□ 모임은 얼마나 자주 갖나요?	How often do you guys meet?
□ 주말마다 모입니다.	We meet every weekend.
□ 대회에도 참가하나요?	Do you participate in competitions? *competitions = contests
□ 매년 대회에 참가합니다.	We take part in contests once a year.

📑 **Notes**

workplace 직장, 작업장, 일터   socialize with ~와 친하게 지내다, 사귀다   financial investments 금융투자, 재태크   absolute 절대적인, 완전한   instructor 강사, 교관   take part in ~에 참여(참가)하다

12 배우기, 자격증 취득

요즘에는 단순히 hobby(취미)로 시작했다가 starting own company(창업)을 하는 경우도 많습니다. 뭔가를 배우거나 certificates(자격증)를 취득하는 활동을 영어로는 어떻게 표현하는지 알아봅시다.

원어민 발음 듣기 ☑□　　회화 훈련 □□　　듣기 훈련 □□

□ 나 요즘 뭐 배우러 다녀.
I attend a class.
*attend = take
*class = course, lesson
I go to an institute.

□ 뭐 배우는데?
What class?
*class = institute

□ 나 요가 학원 다녀.
I take a yoga class.

□ 나 요리 학원 다녀.
I take a class in cookery.
I go to a cooking school.

□ 천연 비누와 화장품 만드는 것을 배워.
I take a natural soap and cosmetics class.

□ (너무) 어렵지 않아?
Isn't it (too) difficult?

□ 이해하기 어려운 전문 용어가 많아.
There are many buzzwords that I don't understand.

□ 할 만해.
It's okay.
It's not so bad.

□ 수강료가 얼마야?
How much (do you) pay for the class?
How much is the tuition?
*tuition = fee

□ 수강생은 몇 명이나 돼?
How many people in the class?

□ 한 반에 20명 정도야.
About 20 people in a class.

□ 이게 가장 인기 있는 강좌야.
This is the most popular class.

□ 초급, 중급, 고급 3개 레벨이 있어.
There are three levels: beginning, intermediate, and advanced.
*levels = courses
*advanced = certificated

☐ 준비물은 뭐야?	What do I need for a class?
	What do I need to prepare for a class?
☐ 재료비는 얼마나 들어?	How much for the class materials?
☐ 재료비가 많이 들어.	The materials for a class cost a lot.
☐ 나도 배워 보고 싶어.	I'd like to take a class, too.
☐ 얼마나 배웠어?	How long have you been learning?
☐ 자세히 설명해 줘.	Can you explain to me in detail?
	Details, please.
☐ 왜 배우는 거야?	Why are you taking a class?
☐ 취미로 배워.	I take a class as a hobby.
	I take a course for fun.
☐ 창업하려고.	To start my own company.
☐ 교사가 되려고 배워.	To be an instructor.
☐ (뭔가를) 배우는 것이 좋아.	I really enjoy learning (something).
☐ 그냥 교실에 있는 게 좋아.	I just like being in a classroom.
☐ 자격증 취득이 재미있어.	I enjoy getting certificates.

*certificates = certifications

DIALOGUE

A Hey, stranger. I haven't seen you for a while.
B I'm sorry. I've been busy to take a class.
A What class?
B I take a natural soap class. It's a certificate course.
I have lots of things to study.

A 너무 오랜만이다. 못 본 지 한참 됐어.
B 미안해. 뭐 좀 배우러 다니느라 요즘 바빠.
A 뭘 배우러 다니는데?
B 천연 비누 강좌야. 자격증반 과정을 듣고 있거든. 공부할 게 많아.

📋 **Notes**

buzzwords 이해하기 어려운 전문 용어 tuition 수업료, 수강료 intermediate 중간의, 중급의 advanced 상급의, 고급의 certificated 자격(면허)를 가진 materials 재료, 소재 for fun 재미로, 재미 삼아

Chapter 19

교통
Transportation

01 교통수단

public transportation(대중교통)은 도시 생활을 원활하게 만드는 핵심 수단입니다. 교통 체증 없이 달리는 subway(지하철), 군데군데 닿지 않는 곳이 없는 town bus/city bus(버스), 장거리 여행 시 발이 되어 주는 express bus(고속버스) 등 다양한 교통수단이 있습니다.

원어민 발음 듣기 ☑☐   회화 훈련 ☐☐   듣기 훈련 ☐☐

☐ 출근 시에는 지하철을 타.	I go to work by subway.
☐ 지하철이 가장 빠르니까.	The subway is the quickest way to work.
☐ 지하철이 사람들로 꽉 찼어.	The subway is packed with people.
☐ 바쁠 때는 택시를 타.	When I'm in a hurry, I take a cab. *cab = taxi
☐ 어떻게 출퇴근(통학)해?	How do you commute?
☐ 한 번에 가는 버스가 있어.	There's a bus to get there without change. *change = transfer
☐ 강릉까지 어떻게 갈까?	How do we go to Gangneung?
☐ 고속버스 타자.	Let's take the express bus.
☐ 여행갈 때는 고속버스나 기차를 타.	I take the express bus or train when I go travel.
☐ 출장 갈 때는 KTX를 타.	I take KTX when I travel on (company) business.
☐ 난 내 차를 운전해.	I drive my own car.
☐ 난 내 차 없이 아무 데도 안 가.	I don't go anywhere without my car.
☐ 그 섬까지는 배를 타고 가.	We take the ferry to the island.
☐ 하루에 두 번 운행하는 배가 있어.	There's the ferry that runs twice a day.
☐ 일본까지 배 타고 가 본 적 있어?	Have you traveled to Japan by ship?
☐ 여기서부터는 대중교통 수단이 없어.	There's no public transportation from here.
☐ 히치하이크 하자.	Let's hitchhike.
☐ 택시를 부르자.	Let's call a cab.

02 교통 상황

월요일 아침 rush hour(출퇴근 시간)이면 traffic jam(교통 체증)이 유난히 더 심합니다. 라디오에서는 연신 Cars are moving slowly.(차들이 서행합니다.), There's been an accident.(사고가 났습니다.), Please take other roads.(우회하세요.) 등과 같은 보도를 하죠.

원어민 발음 듣기 ☑☐ 회화 훈련 ☐☐ 듣기 훈련 ☐☐

☐ 지금 교통 상황이 어때?	How are the traffic conditions?
	How's the road?
☐ 지금 도로가 많이 붐빌 거야.	The road must be busy now.
	There must be a huge traffic jam.
	*jam = congestion
	There must be bumper-to-bumper.
☐ 출퇴근 시간이잖아.	It's the rush hour.
	It's the morning rush.
	*the morning rush → the evening rush(저녁 때 러시아워)
☐ 월요일 아침이잖아.	It's Monday morning.
☐ 지금쯤이면 교통 상황이 괜찮을 거야.	I think the traffic conditions are much better now.
☐ 교통 방송 확인해 보자.	Let's check out the traffic report.
☐ 차들이 서행하고 있습니다.	Cars are moving slowly.
	Cars are crawling.
☐ 오늘 교통 체증이 매우 심합니다.	The traffic is heavily congested today.
☐ 교통 체증이 유난히 심합니다.	The traffic is heavier than usual.
☐ 교통 체증이 극심합니다.	There have been major delays.
☐ 다른 길로 우회하세요.	Please detour.
	Please take other roads.
☐ (대형) 교통사고가 났습니다.	There has been an (major) accident.
☐ 도심에서는 대규모 집회가 있겠습니다.	There will be a big demonstration in downtown.
☐ 오늘은 교통 통제 구간이 많습니다.	There are many traffic control sections today.

Chapter 19

교통

311

☐ 오늘은 공사 구간이 많습니다.	There are many construction sections today.
☐ 오늘은 막히는 구간이 많습니다.	There are many blocking areas today.
☐ 길이 매우 미끄럽습니다.	The roads are very slippery.
☐ 길이 얼었습니다.	The roads are very icy.
☐ 현재는 소통이 원활합니다.	Now cars are moving okay. Now the traffic is looking good. The road is much lighter now.
☐ 길이 차로 꽉 막혔네.	The road is packed with cars. *packed = chocked *cars = traffic
☐ 사고가 났었던 게 분명해.	There must be an accident. It's probably because of an accident.
☐ 이유 없이 차가 막히네.	The traffic is jammed without any particular reason.
☐ 도로가 한가하다.	The traffic is light.
☐ 오늘처럼 늘 한가했으면 좋겠어.	I wish the traffic was always light as today.

Notes

bumper-to-bumper 자동차가 꽉 들어찬 crawl 기다, 차가 서행하다 detour 우회하다, 돌아가다 block 막다, 못 들어오게 하다 slippery 미끄러운, 잘 미끄러지는 icy 얼음으로 뒤덮인 light 통행이나 상거래가 한산한

03 지하철과 버스 타기

신촌에서 동대문 시장까지 찾아가는 상황을 가정하여 getting on(버스나 지하철 타기), getting off(내리기), transferring(갈아타기) 등의 표현을 정리했습니다. 안내 방송을 듣고 제대로 하차하기, interval(배차 간격), running hours(운행 시간)를 확인하는 표현도 함께 알아보겠습니다.

원어민 발음 듣기 ✔□   회화 훈련 □□   듣기 훈련 □□

□ 여기서 동대문 시장까지 어떻게 가죠? How do we go to the Dongdaemun Market?

□ 일단 마을버스를 타세요. First, take a local bus.
*local bus = town bus

□ 신촌 지하철역에서 하차하세요. Get off at the Sinchon subway station.

□ 지하철 2호선을 타세요. Take the subway Line No. 2.

□ 다음은 동대문역사문화공원역입니다. The next station is Dongdaemun History & Culture Park station.

□ 동대문역사문화공원역에서 내리세요. Get off at Dongdaemun History & Culture Park station.

□ 동대문역사문화공원역은 환승역입니다. It's the interchanges.
*interchange = transfer station, junction

□ 4호선으로 갈아타세요. Transfer to Line No. 4.
*transfer = change

□ 동대문역까지 몇 정거장이죠? How many stations to Dongdaemun station?

□ 몇 정거장이나 더 가야 하나요? How many more stations (should we go)?

□ 한 정거장만 더 가면 됩니다. We have to go one more station.
Just one more station.

□ 지하철에서 내려서 6번 출구를 찾으세요. Get off the subway, find the exit No.6.

□ 6번 출구로 나가세요. Take the exit No. 6.

□ (시장으로 가는) 다른 방법은 없나요? Is there any other way (to get to the market)?

□ 신촌 지하철역에서 시내버스를 타세요. Take a (town) bus at the Sinchon subway station.

313

☐ 종로6가역에서 하차하세요.	Get off at Jongro-6-ga (bus) stop.
☐ 노선 안내 방송을 잘 들으세요.	Pay attention to the route announcements.
☐ 안내 방송이 잘 안 들려요.	I can't hear what the conductor's saying.
☐ 버스가 왜 이렇게 안 오지요?	Why isn't the bus coming? Why is the bus late?
☐ 배차 간격이 몇 분인가요?	How often do they run? What's the interval between buses?
☐ 5~8분 간격이에요.	They run every 5~8 minutes.
☐ 들쑥날쑥 다녀요.	They run irregularly.
☐ 첫차 시간이 언제입니까?	When is the first bus?
☐ 막차 시간이 언제입니까?	When is the last bus?
☐ 버스를 잘못 탔어요.	I've got on the wrong bus. I took the wrong bus.
☐ 반대편에서 탔어야 했는데.	I should've taken the bus in the opposite side.
☐ 그 버스는 더 이상 운행하지 않나 봐요.	I don't think the bus runs any more.
☐ 버스 도착 알림판에 그 번호가 없네요.	I can't find the bus (number) on the bus arrival time board.
☐ 며칠 전에도 그 버스를 탔었는데요.	I took the bus even a few days ago.
☐ 번호가 바뀌었나 봐요.	The number might have been changed.
☐ 노선표를 확인해 봅시다.	Let's check the (bus) route map.
☐ 그 정류장은 항상 복잡합니다.	The bus stop is always busy and crowded.
☐ 정류장이 너무 길어요.	The bus stops are too long.
☐ 버스를 놓쳤어요.	I missed the bus.
☐ 서두르지 않으면 버스를 놓쳐요.	If you don't hurry up, you'll miss the bus.
☐ (버스 기사의 말) 꼭 잡으세요.	Hold on tight, please.

📑 **Notes**

local bus 마을버스 junction 갈아타는 역, 환승역 route 노선, 루트 conductor (버스, 열차) 차장 irregularly 불규칙적으로 hold on tight 단단히 붙들다, 꽉 잡다

314

택시 타기

택시를 타면 기사에게 원하는 길로 가 달라고 말하거나, 속도나 차내 온도 조절을 부탁하는 경우가 있죠. 또 원하는 장소에 내릴 때는 Pull over here, please.(여기서 세워 주세요.) 또는 Let/Drop me off at the crosswalk, please.(횡단보도에서 내려 주세요.)라고 하면 됩니다.

원어민 발음 듣기 ☑☐　회화 훈련 ☐☐　듣기 훈련 ☐☐

☐ 택시!	Taxi, taxi!
☐ 택시가 잘 안 잡히네요.	I can't get a cab.
☐ 택시 기사들이 다들 점심 먹으러 가는 중이에요.	Most cab drivers are on their way to having lunch.
☐ 동대문 시장으로 가 주세요.	Take me to the Dongdaemun market, please. Go to the Dongdaemun market, please.
☐ 어느 길로 갈까요?	Which route would you prefer? *route = way
☐ 다니시던 길이 있나요?	Do you have usual route to go there?
☐ 신촌 지하철역 쪽으로 가 주세요.	I'd like you to go through the Sinchon subway station.
☐ 기사님이 알아서 가 주세요.	Take any route you like, please.
☐ 지금 교통 체증이 없는 길을 아세요?	Do you know which road is open now?
☐ 이 시간대에는 그 길이 많이 막혀요.	The traffic is heavy around this time.
☐ 다른 길로 가 주세요.	Why don't you take another way?
☐ 빨리 가 주세요.	Please hurry. Would you please speed up?
☐ 너무 빨리 달리시네요.	You're driving too fast.
☐ 속도를 늦춰 주세요.	Please slow down.
☐ 멀미가 나요.	I feel nauseous.
☐ 너무 더워요. 에어컨을 켜 주시겠어요?	It's too hot. Can you please turn the air conditioner on?

☐ 너무 추워요. 에어컨 좀 줄여 주세요.	It's too cold. Turn the air conditioner down, please.
☐ 히터를 꺼 주시겠어요?	Do you mind if you turn off the heater?
☐ 히터 세기를 높여 주시겠어요?	Could you please turn up the heater?
☐ 창문 좀 열게요.	I'd like to open the window.
☐ 라디오 소리가 너무 커요.	The radio is too loud.
☐ 아직인가요?	Are we there yet? How much further should we go?
☐ 거의 다 왔습니다.	We're almost there.
☐ 저기 횡단보도에서 내려 주세요.	Please let me off at the crossing. *let ~ off = drop ~ off *crossing = crosswalk
☐ 유턴해서 바로 세워 주세요.	Why don't you make a U-turn and pull over?
☐ 교차로 건너서 세워 주세요.	Cross the intersection and stop, please.
☐ 요금이 얼마죠?	What's the fare? How much do I owe you?
☐ 7,000원입니다.	It's 7,000 won.
☐ 카드로 계산할게요.	I'll pay by (credit) card.
☐ 기계에 카드를 대세요.	Put your card on the card machine.
☐ 영수증 주시겠어요?	Can I have the receipt?

📝 Notes

usual route 자주(늘) 가는 노선(길)   speed up 속도를 높이다. 속도 내다   slow down 속도를 낮추다
nauseous 메스꺼운, 멀미가 나는 turn on ~을 켜다 turn down ~의 세기를 낮추다, 줄이다 turn up ~의 세
기를 높이다, 세게 하다 let ~ off ~을 내려주다 pull over 차를 세우다, 멈추게 하다 fare 교통수단의 요금, 운임
owe 빚지다, 지불해야 하다

05 대중교통 티켓 요금

대중교통 요금은 흔히 fare라고 합니다. 한국 지하철의 경우 일회용 티켓 사용 후 내릴 때 ticket deposit(티켓 보증금)을 돌려받을 수 있습니다. 또한 한국과 미국 모두 일정 기간 동안 사용할 수 있는 metro card/pass(정기 승차권)가 있습니다.

원어민 발음 듣기 ☑☐   회화 훈련 ☐☐   듣기 훈련 ☐☐

☐ 지하철 요금은 얼마죠?	How much is the train fare?
☐ 기본요금은 얼마죠?	How much is the basic fare? *fare = charge
☐ 일반 성인 요금은 얼마죠?	How much is the fare for general people?
☐ 어린이 요금은 얼마죠?	How much is the children's fare?
☐ 구간별로 다릅니다.	The fare depends on where you go. It depends on how far you go.
☐ 멀리 갈수록 요금이 추가됩니다.	The further you go, the more you have to pay.
☐ 어디까지 가십니까?	Where is your destination?
☐ 티켓 발매기를 이용하세요.	Please use the ticket machines.
☐ 3개의 외국어 서비스가 제공됩니다.	It provides three different foreign languages.
☐ 티켓 보증금을 찾는 것 잊지 마세요.	Don't forget to get your ticket deposit back.
☐ 지하철 요금이 인상됐어.	The train fare has increased.
☐ 버스 요금이 얼마죠?	How much is the bus fare?
☐ 교통카드 이용 시 1,050원입니다.	If you use your traffic card, the fare is 1,050 won.
☐ 광역버스는 더 비쌉니다.	The red bus fare is more expensive.
☐ 서울-부산 사이 KTX 요금은 얼마죠?	How much is the KTX train fare from Seoul to Pusan?
☐ 5만 원 안팎입니다.	It's 50,000 won more or less.
☐ 정기 승차권 주세요.	Metro pass, please.

Chapter 19

교통

317

06 면허 따기, 운전하기

운전을 능숙하게 잘 하는 사람을 good driver라고 합니다. 한편 driving/driver's test(운전면허 시험)을 준비할 때는 written test(필기시험)과 performance test(실기시험)의 시험 양식을 잘 파악해야 합니다.

원어민 발음 듣기 ☑☐   회화 훈련 ☐☐   듣기 훈련 ☐☐

☐ 내 차를 갖고 싶어요.
I'd like to have my own car.
I want to own a car.

☐ 차를 구입할 여유가 생겼어요.
I have extra money to buy a car.
I think I can afford a car.

☐ 12개월 할부로 사려고요.
I'm going to buy a car in 12 month installments.

☐ 자동차 면허는 땄어요?
Did you get your driver's license?

☐ 장롱면허입니다.
I have a driver's license, but I don't drive.

☐ 운전을 별로 안 좋아해요.
I don't like driving.

☐ 드라이브를 즐겨요.
I enjoy driving.
I love to go for a ride.

☐ 운전을 잘하시네요.
You're good at driving.
You're a good driver.
You drive well.

☐ 길을 잘 아시네요.
You have a good sense of direction.

☐ 운전을 잘 못해요.
I'm not a good driver.

☐ 나도 운전을 잘하고 싶어요.
I want to drive well.

☐ 연습을 계속 하세요.
Keep practicing.

☐ 운전 학원에서 연수 받으세요.
Get a lesson at driving school.

☐ 실력이 늘 거예요.
You'll get better.
You'll improve soon.

☐ 운전에 자신감이 생길 때 더 조심하세요.
Be more careful when you feel confident of driving.
*confident → comfortable (편안한)

☐ 운전면허 시험에 대해 알려 주세요.	Tell me about the driving test. *driving test=driver's test
☐ 필기시험과 실기시험을 치러야 해요.	You have to take a written and practical test. *practical test=performance test
☐ 운전면허 시험에서 또 떨어졌어요.	I failed my driving test again.
☐ 운전면허 시험을 한 번에 붙었어요.	I passed my driving test on the first try.
☐ 운전을 잘하나요?	Do you drive well? Are you a good driver? Are you good at driving? *be good at=be good with
☐ 나는 완전 초보 운전자야.	I'm a complete beginner.
☐ 나는 10년 무사고 운전자야.	I've been driving my car for 10 years without a single accident. I have a perfect driving record for 10 years.
☐ 항상 앞을 봐.	Keep your eyes on the road.
☐ 운전 중에는 휴대폰을 사용하지 마.	Don't use your cell phone while driving.
☐ 졸음운전은 금물이야.	Don't drive while you feel sleepy. *sleepy=drowsy Don't do sleepy driving. Don't be a sleepy driver.
☐ 음주 운전은 금물이야.	Don't drink and drive. Don't do drunk driving. Don't be a drunk driver.
☐ 음주 운전은 매우 위험해.	It's very dangerous to drink and drive.
☐ 운전면허를 취소당해.	Your driver's license will be revoked.
☐ 음주 운전 단속 중이야.	There's a crackdown on drinking and driving. *crackdown=clampdown
☐ 경찰관이 음주 측정기를 불라고 했어.	The policeman asked me to blow into the breathalyzer.

07 주유, 세차하기

"휘발유가 리터당 얼마입니까?"라고 물을 때는 How much is the gas/gasoline price per a liter?라고 합니다. 요즘은 알뜰한 운전자가 늘어서 직접 주유하는 self-service gas station(셀프 주유소)도 많아지고 있는 추세입니다.

원어민 발음 듣기 ☑□　회화 훈련 □□　듣기 훈련 □□

□ 이 근처에 주유소가 어디 있죠?　Where is the gas station near here?

□ 휘발유가 리터당 얼마죠?　How much is the gas price per a liter?
　*gas = gasoline

□ 리터당 2,000원입니다.　It's 2,000 won a liter.

□ 경유가 리터당 얼마죠?　How much is the diesel price per a liter?

□ 주유소마다 가격이 달라요.　Every gas station has a different price.
　The cost varies in every station.

□ 서울의 기름 값이 한국에서 제일 비싸요.　The gas price in Seoul is the most expensive in Korea.

□ 기름 값 비교 사이트가 있어요.　There're oil price comparison websites.

□ 기름 값이 계속 오르고 있어요.　The gas prices are continuously increasing.

□ 기름 값이 계속 내리고 있어요.　The gas prices are continuously decreasing.

□ 주유소에 들릅시다.　Let's stop for gas at the (gas) station.
　We have to stop for gas at the station.

□ 차에 기름을 넣어야 해요.　We need to fill the fuel tank.
　We need to refuel.

□ 연료가 거의 바닥이에요.　The fuel tank is almost empty.

□ 5번 주유기에 차를 세우세요.　Pull up to the number 5 gas pump, please.

□ 연료 주입구를 열어 주세요.　Open your fuel cap, please.

□ 10,000원어치 넣어 주세요.　Refuel 10,000 won, please.
　*refuel = fill

□ 가득 채워 주세요.　Fill her up.

	Tank up.
	Fill up the tank.
□ 여기 사은품입니다.	Here's the free gift for you.
□ 여기는 셀프 주유소입니다.	This is the self-service gas station.
□ 세차하기 좋은 날이네요.	It's a perfect day for washing my car.
□ 오늘 세차했더니 내일 비 온대요.	I washed my car today and it will rain tomorrow.
□ 여기서 세차할 수 있나요?	Can I wash my car here?
□ 자동 세차기를 이용하고 싶어요.	I'd like to use an automatic car wash.
□ 이 쿠폰을 사용할 수 있나요?	Can I use my free coupon?
□ 손 세차 해 주세요.	Can you hand wash my car?
□ 소형차는 2만 5천 원입니다.	It costs 25,000 won for a small car. *small = compact
□ 차 안팎을 다 닦아 주세요.	I'd like you to hand-wash my car inside and out.
□ 제가 직접 손 세차를 하고 싶어요.	I'd like to hand-wash my car.
□ 물은 어떻게 해야 나오나요?	How can I get water from the hose?
□ 동전을 투입하세요.	Insert coins into the slot.
□ 시간제한이 있어요.	There's a time limit.

DIALOGUE

A I think we have to stop for gas at the next station.
B Sure. If it's the self-service station, you pump the gas and I get sodas.
A No problem.

A 다음 주유소에서 기름 넣어야 할 것 같아.
B 좋아. 셀프 주유소면 네가 기름 넣어. 내가 음료수 사 올게.
A 문제없어.

📒 **Notes**

fill the fuel tank 연료 탱크를 채우다, 기름 넣다, 주유하다 refuel 연료를 다시 채우다 pull up 차를 세우다, 멈추다
gas pump 주유 펌프기 fuel cap 차 연료 주입구 tank up 연료 탱크에 연료를 가득 채우다 hand-wash 손으
로 닦다 slot 자판기의 동전 구멍 pump the gas 주유하다

08 주차장에서

parking(주차)은 주차가 허용된 건물 주차장이나, 유료 주차장, 공용 주차장 등에만 해야 합니다. 아무 데나 주차했다가 be towed(견인되다)되거나 get a parking ticket(주차 위반 딱지를 떼다) 할 수도 있습니다. parking charge(주차 요금)는 동네마다 천차만별입니다.

원어민 발음 듣기 ☑□   회화 훈련 □□   듣기 훈련 □□

☐ 주차 요금은 얼마죠?	How much do you charge for parking?
☐ 주차장은 만차입니다.	The parking lot is full.
☐ 30분에 2,000원입니다.	It's 2,000 won per 30 minutes.
☐ 주차장은 어디 있나요?	Where is the parking lot? Can you tell me where the parking lot is?
☐ 근처에 다른 주차장은 없나요?	Is there any other parking lot around here?
☐ 이 건물 뒤편에 주차장 입구가 있습니다.	There's the parking entrance behind this building.
☐ 공용 주차장을 이용하세요.	Why don't you use the public parking lot?
☐ 백화점 지하 주차장을 이용하세요.	Use the department store's parking lot, please.
☐ 여기에 주차하시면 됩니다.	You can park here. Park here, please.
☐ 여기에 주차하시면 안 돼요.	You're not allowed to park here.
☐ 불법 주차하지 마세요.	Don't park illegally.
☐ 불법 주차된 차량은 견인됩니다.	An illegally parked car will be towed.
☐ 주차할 곳을 못 찾겠어요.	I can't find a parking spot.
☐ 주차 공간이 너무 좁아요.	The parking space is too narrow.
☐ 차를 당장 옮기세요.	Move your car immediately.
☐ 주차 위반 딱지를 떼겠습니다.	I'll give you a parking ticket. *give ~ a ticket = write ~ a ticket
☐ 나 주차 위반 딱지를 뗐어.	I got a parking ticket.

09 교통사고, 사고 처리

traffic accident(교통사고)에는 정차한 차를 scratch(긁다)하거나 차끼리 부딪히는 fender-bender(가벼운 접촉 사고), 심하게는 사람을 다치게 하고 여러 대의 차가 충돌하는 car chain-collision(연쇄 추돌 사고) 등이 있습니다.

원어민 발음 듣기 ☑□   회화 훈련 □□   듣기 훈련 □□

☐ (교통)사고가 났어요.	There was an (car) accident. *car = traffic There was a car crash.
☐ 차들이 심하게 찌그러졌어요.	Cars are totally crashed. *crashed = dented, wrecked
☐ 10중 연쇄 추돌 사고예요.	It's a ten-car chain collision. It's a ten-car rear-ends collision. It's a ten-car pileup.
☐ 끔찍해라.	It's horrible.
☐ 가벼운 접촉 사고예요.	It's a fender-bender.
☐ 정차한 차를 받았어요.	I hit a parked car. *hit = dump I drove into a parked car. *drove into = ran into
☐ 정차한 차를 긁었어요.	I scratched a parked car.
☐ 내 차를 벽에 처박았어요.	I rammed my car into the wall.
☐ 누군가 내 차를 긁었어요.	Somebody scratched my car. *scratched = nicked, keyed
☐ 사람을 치었어요.	I hit someone.
☐ 사람을 칠 뻔했어요.	I almost hit someone.
☐ 사람이 차에 치였어요.	Someone was hit by a car.
☐ 사고로 사람이 다쳤어요.	She has been injured in the accident.
☐ 트럭이 사람을 치고 달아났어요.	A truck hit someone and ran away.
☐ 차가 자전거 탄 사람을 치었어요.	A car hit someone on a bike. A car hit a cyclist.

Chapter 19

교통

□	그는 의식이 없어요.	He is not conscious.
□	상대편이 내게 고함을 질러요.	He is yelling at me.
□	나를 여자라고 함부로 대해요.	He treated me bad because I'm a woman.
□	사람이 다친 경우 119를 부르세요.	When you hit someone, call 119 right away.
□	부상자를 흔들지 마세요.	Don't shake the injured. *the injured = the wounded
□	다친 사람과 함께 병원에 가세요.	Go to the hospital with the injured.
□	보험 회사에 전화하세요.	Call your insurance company.
□	보험 회사에서 알아서 처리해 줍니다.	Your insurance company will take care of everything.
□	현장 사진을 찍으세요.	Take pictures of the accident scene. *pictures = photos
□	현장에 스프레이를 뿌리세요.	Spray the accident scene.
□	서로 연락처를 주고받으세요.	Exchange each other's contact numbers.
□	경찰에게 침착하게 설명하세요.	Explain what happened to the police calmly.

DIALOGUE

A You look a little upset. Is there something wrong?
B Well, I had a fender-bender today.
   And the driver got out of his car and started yelling at me.
A Was it totally your fault?
B No, he is the one ran a red light.

A 너 기분이 약간 언짢아 보인다. 무슨 일 있어?
B 그게 말이야. 오늘 가벼운 접촉 사고가 있었거든.
   상대편 운전자가 차에서 나오더니 다짜고짜 내게 소리를 지르는 거야.
A 네 잘못으로 사고가 난 거야?
B 아니. 정작 신호를 위반한 사람은 그 사람이야.

📄 Notes

crash 찌그러뜨리다 dent 움푹 들어가게 하다 wreck 망가뜨리다, 파괴하다 collision 충돌 rear end 자동차 후미의 pileup 연쇄 추돌 bump 충돌하다, 들이받다 ram 심하게 부딪히다, 처박다 nick 날카로운 자국을 내다

10 수리, 점검 받기

car tune-up(자동차 점검)을 받으려면 auto repair shop(자동차 정비소)에 가야 합니다. estimate (견적서)를 받아 수리의 정도를 가늠하죠. I hear sounds from the brake.(브레이크에서 소리가 나요.), I can't start my car.(시동이 안 걸려요.) 등 이상 현상을 말하는 표현을 알아보겠습니다.

원어민 발음 듣기 ✔☐   회화 훈련 ☐☐   듣기 훈련 ☐☐

☐ 근처에 자동차 정비소가 어디에 있지?

Where is a car repair shop near here?
*car repair shop = auto repair shop

Where is the car service center?
*car service center = car service station

☐ 자동차 수리해 주세요.

Could you please fix my car?

Repair my car, please.

☐ 수리비가 얼마나 나올까요?

How much will it cost for the repairs?

How much will you charge for the repairs?

☐ 견적서 내 주세요.

Give me an estimate, please.

☐ 수리비가 너무 많이 나왔어요.

You charge me too much for repairing my car.

☐ 자동차 점검해 주세요.

Could you check my car?

☐ 브레이크에서 소리가 나요.

I hear sounds from the brake.

☐ 시동이 안 걸려요.

I can't start my car.

I can't get my car started.

My car won't start.

☐ 와이퍼를 바꿀 때가 됐어요.

I think it's time to change the wipers.
*wipers = windshields

☐ 타이어 마모 상태를 확인하세요.

Check how much the tires are worn out.

☐ 엔진 오일을 확인하세요.

Check the engine oil.

☐ 배터리의 색깔을 확인하세요.

Check the car battery color.

☐ 자동차 정기 점검을 받으세요.

Have your car tuned up routinely.

☐ 정기 점검을 안 하면 벌금을 내야 해요.

If you don't do it, you have to pay a penalty.
*penalty = fine

Chapter 19

교통

325

11 자동차 보험

차를 운전하는 사람에게 car insurance(자동차 보험)은 필수적입니다. 종류가 워낙 많으니 monthly premium(월 보험료), coverage(보상금), insurance policy(보험 약관), special contract(특약 사항) 등을 잘 비교해서 선택해야 합니다.

원어민 발음 듣기 ☑□   회화 훈련 □□   듣기 훈련 □□

☐ 자동차 보험이 필요해요.
I need a car insurance.
*car insurance = auto insurance, motor insurance

☐ 자동차 보험에 가입하고 싶어요.
I'd like to get a car insurance.
*get = take out

☐ 좋은 자동차 보험 추천해 주세요.
Can you recommend me a good one?

☐ 자동차 보험 회사가 너무 많아요.
There are so many car insurance companies.
*companies = insurers

☐ 월 보험료가 얼마예요?
How much is the monthly premium?

☐ 최고 보상금이 얼마예요?
How much is the maximum coverage?

☐ 이 보험의 장점은 뭐가요?
What are the benefits of this car insurance?

☐ 보험료가 가장 싼 보험을 찾고 있어요.
I'm looking for a car insurance with the cheapest premium.

☐ 교통사고가 나면 보험료가 올라갑니다.
If you have an accident, your insurance premium will go up.

☐ 보험 약관을 잘 읽어 보세요.
Read your insurance policy carefully.

☐ 자동차 보험 특약을 잘 활용하세요.
Use your special contract wisely.

☐ 자동차 보험이 곧 만기돼요.
My car insurance will expire soon.
*expire = mature

☐ 보험 특약에 가입하고 싶어요.
I'd like to buy a special contract.

☐ 보험 증권은 언제 받을 수 있죠?
When can I get my insurance policy?

☐ 우편으로 발송됩니다.
You'll get it by mail.

☐ 이메일로 발송됩니다.
It will be emailed.

12 교통 법규

traffic laws(교통 법규)에 위반이 되는 행동으로는 speeding(과속), run(go through) a red light(신호 위반), ignoring the stop lines(정지선 무시) 등이 있습니다. 적발되면 traffic ticket(딱지)을 떼고 fine/penalty(범칙금)를 내야 하죠. 특히 위반 사항이 심할 경우 운전자 penalty points(벌점)를 받을 수도 있습니다.

원어민 발음 듣기 ☑□   회화 훈련 □□   듣기 훈련 □□

□ 과속하셨습니다.   You were speeding.

□ 신호를 위반하셨습니다.   You ran a red light.
You went through a red light.

□ 운전면허증, 차량 등록증을 제시하세요.   Can I see your driver's license and car registration?
Your license and car registration, please.

□ 전 교통 법규를 한 번도 어긴 적이 없어요.   I've never broken any traffic laws.

□ 교통경찰에게 적발됐어요.   I got pulled over by the traffic police.
*police=cop
I was stopped by the policemen.

□ 딱지를 뗐어요.   I've got a traffic ticket.
I was ticketed.

□ 범칙금을 내야 해요.   I have to pay a fine.
*fine=penalty

□ 교통 신호를 잘 지키세요.   Pay attention to traffic signals.
*signals=lights

□ 정지선을 잘 보세요.   Don't violate the stop lines.

□ 과태료 7만 원을 내야 돼요.   I have to pay 70,000 won for a fine.

□ 범칙금은 어디에 납부해야 하죠?   Where do I go to pay for a fine?

□ 벌점을 받았어요.   I received penalty points.
*received=got

□ 면허를 취소당했어요.   My driver's license was suspended.
*suspended=revoked

□ 항상 안전벨트를 매세요.   Keep your seat belt on.

Chapter 20

각종 신고
Report

01 소매치기 · 분실 · 실종 신고

소매치기를 당하거나 물건을 분실하면 경찰에 꼭 신고해야 합니다. 지갑을 도난당한 경우라면 신용 카드 회사에 신용 카드 분실 신고를 해야겠죠. 지하철에 물건을 두고 내리면 lost and found center(유실물 센터)를 확인해 보아야 합니다.

원어민 발음 듣기 ☑☐   회화 훈련 ☐☐   듣기 훈련 ☐☐

☐ 지갑을 소매치기 당했어요.	I got my pocket picked.
	I was robbed by a pickpocket.
☐ 가방이 찢겨져 있어요.	My bag was torn.
☐ 지갑 안에 뭐가 들었죠?	What did you have in your bag?
	What items did you have in your bag?
☐ 약간의 현금과 신용 카드가 있었어요.	I had some cash and credit cards.
☐ 요즘 소매치기가 극성입니다.	There are a lot of pickpockets lately.
	Be aware of pickpockets.
☐ 이상한 낌새는 없었나요?	Did you sense anything?
	*sense = feel
☐ 다친 데는 없나요?	Are you hurt?
	Are you all right?
☐ 눈 깜짝할 사이였어요.	It happened in a second.
	It happened so quickly.
	It happened before I knew it.
☐ 지갑이 없어진 것조차 몰랐어요.	I didn't even realize that my wallet's gone.
☐ 신용 카드를 분실했어요.	I lost my credit card(s).
☐ 카드 회사에 분실 신고하세요.	You'd better report your card(s) missing.
☐ 분실된 카드를 신고하려고요.	I'd like to report a lost card.
☐ 여권을 잃어버렸어요.	I lost my passport.
☐ 부주의로 분실했어요.	I lost it because of my carelessness.
☐ 어디에 신고해야 하죠?	Where should I report to?

☐ (국내) 가까운 파출소에 신고하세요.	Report your loss to the police station nearby.
☐ (국외) 한국 영사관 콜 센터로 전화하세요.	Call the Korean Consulate office.
☐ 지갑을 택시에 두고 내렸어요.	I left my purse in the cab.
☐ 가방을 지하철에 두고 내렸어요.	I left my bag on the subway.
☐ 휴대폰을 버스에 두고 내렸어요.	I left my cell phone on the bus.
☐ 이 탁자 밑에 가방을 뒀는데요.	I put my bag under this table.
☐ 어느 회사 택시인지 기억하세요?	Do you remember the name of the taxi company?
☐ 차 번호를 기억하세요?	Do you remember the (license) plate number?
☐ 택시 회사에 전화해 보세요.	You should call the taxi company.
☐ 지하철 유실물 센터에서 확인해 보세요.	Check the lost-and-found (center) in the subway.
☐ 아이가 실종됐어요.	My child is missing. *child → son(아들), daughter(딸)

DIALOGUE

A I got my pocket picked yesterday.
B Oh no. Did you call the police?
A Yes, but I haven't called my credit card company yet.
B You'd better hurry.

A 나 어제 소매치기 당했어.
B 세상에. 경찰에 신고했어?
A 응, 그런데 아직 카드 회사에는 전화 안 했어.
B 서두르는 것이 좋겠어.

Notes

get pocket picked 소매치기 당하다 **be robbed** 강탈(약탈) 당하다 **be torn** 뜯기다, 찢기다 **be aware of** ~에 대해 잘 알고 있다, 인지하고 있다 **sense** 느끼다, 감지하다 **had better** ~하는 편이 낫다, ~해야 한다 **leave** 내버려 두다, 방치하다 **(license) plate** 금속판, 차량번호판

02 도난 · 주거 침입 · 해킹 신고

집에 break-in(침입)의 흔적이 있으면 바로 경찰에 신고해야 하죠? 요즘 큰 문제가 되고 있는 인터넷상의 information leakage(정보 누출)이나 voice phishing(전화 사기)는 발생 즉시 경찰에 신고하는 것이 좋습니다. 개인 컴퓨터에 security program(보안 프로그램)을 꾸준히 업데이트하는 것도 잊지 마세요.

원어민 발음 듣기 ☑☐   회화 훈련 ☐☐   듣기 훈련 ☐☐

☐ 경찰서죠?	Hello, is this the police station? Hello, is this 112?
☐ 빨리 좀 와 주세요.	Please come quickly. Could you please come over here?
☐ 도난을 신고하려고요.	I'd like to report the theft. I'm going to report the theft.
☐ 누군가가 집에 침입했어요.	Somebody broke into my house.
☐ 침입한 흔적이 있어요.	There are some signs of a break-in.
☐ 문이 열려 있어요.	My front door is wide open.
☐ (누군가) 문을 억지로 열고 들어왔어요.	My door was forced open.
☐ 유리창이 깨져 있어요.	The windows are broken.
☐ 집 안을 엉망으로 만들었어요.	The burglar made my house a mess. My house is a mess.
☐ 도난당한 물건이 있나요?	Do you have any stolen goods? What did the burglar take from your house?
☐ 현금과 귀금속이 없어졌어요.	Cash and jewelry are gone. Cash and jewelry were stolen.
☐ 당신 일과를 잘 아는 사람이 있나요?	Is there anyone who is aware of your daily routine?
☐ 당신 말고 열쇠를 가진 사람이 있나요?	Does anybody else have the house key besides you?
☐ 이웃이 허락 없이 함부로 들어와요.	My neighbor bursts into my house without knocking. *knocking = permission

☐ 집을 비운 사이 집주인이 들락거려요.	My landlord keeps coming in and out of my room while I'm out.
☐ 제 개인 정보를 도난당한 것 같아요.	I think my Internet ID was stolen. *ID = identification, identity의 준말
☐ 인터넷 뱅킹 정보가 유출됐어요.	My private Internet banking information has been leaked.
☐ 전화 사기 당했어요.	I was swindled by voice phishing. *swindled = cheated My private information has been used for voice phishing.
☐ 돈이 무단으로 인출됐어요.	My money was withdrawn without my permission.
☐ 이상한 메일이 와요.	I often get strange emails. Strange emails come in my email box all the time.
☐ 사이버 공간은 안전하지 않아요.	Cyberspace is not safe.
☐ 낯선 메일은 열람하지 마세요.	Don't open unfamiliar emails.
☐ 개인 PC에는 백신을 설치하세요.	Install anti-virus software on your personal computer. *anti-virus software = virus checker
☐ 스팸 방지 소프트웨어를 설치하세요.	Install anti-spam software on your computer.
☐ 보안 프로그램을 자주 업데이트하세요.	Update your security program regularly.
☐ 공용 PC에서 개인 정보를 쓰지 마세요.	Don't use your personal information on the public computers.
☐ 공인 인증서는 따로 보관하세요.	Keep your (Internet) certificate separate from your computer.

📝 **Notes**

come over 찾아오다, 오다 break into ~에 침입하다 break-in 불법 침입 mess 엉망진창, 뒤죽박죽 burst into 갑작스럽게 집에 뛰어들다 come in and out ~에 들락날락 하다 leak 새다, 누출하다 swindle 속여서 빼앗다 cheat 속이다, 사기 치다 withdraw 돈을 빼다, 인출하다 anti-virus 컴퓨터의 항 바이러스 프로그램 anti-spam 스팸 메일을 막는 프로그램 internet certificate 인터넷상에서 이용되는 공인 인증서 separate from ~에서 분리하다, 따로 두다

03 사고 · 범죄 목격 신고

사고나 범죄가 일어날 만한 상황을 목격하면 바로 112에 신고합니다. 이때 '~을 목격했어요.'는 I witnessed ~. 또는 I saw ~.라고 말하면 됩니다. 현재 벌어지고 있는 상황을 전할 때는 be동사+-ing(현재 진행)를 써서 말합니다. 이밖에 신고가 필요한 상황은 또 어떤 경우일까요?

원어민 발음 듣기 ☑□   회화 훈련 □□   듣기 훈련 □□

☐ 본 것을 정확히 말해 주시겠어요?	Could you tell me exactly what you saw? Tell me what you witnessed, please.
☐ 목격자가 누구입니까?	Who is an eyewitness?
☐ 교통사고를 목격했어요.	I witnessed the traffic accident.
☐ 뺑소니차를 목격했어요.	I witnessed a hit-and-run accident.
☐ 추돌 사고를 목격했어요.	I witnessed a rear-end collision.
☐ 범인의 얼굴을 봤어요.	I saw the criminal's face.
☐ 살인을 목격했어요.	I witnessed a homicide. *homicide = murder
☐ 범죄 현장을 목격했어요.	I witnessed a crime scene.
☐ 끔찍한 광경을 봤어요.	I saw a horrible scene.
☐ 내 눈으로 직접 봤어요.	I saw it with my own eyes.
☐ 부부 싸움이 났어요.	There's a fight between a husband and wife.
☐ (고등) 학생들이 패싸움을 하고 있어요.	Students are having a gang fight. High-schoolers are fighting in groups.
☐ 여러 명이 남자애를 괴롭히고 있어요.	A boy is being bullied by a bunch of other boys.
☐ 학생들이 칼을 가지고 놀고 있어요.	Students are playing with a knife. *knife = pocket knife, razor
☐ 여성이 추행 당하고 있어요.	A couple of men are assaulting a girl.
☐ 낯선 사람이 따라와요.	A stranger keeps following me.
☐ 누가 따라오는 것 같아요.	I feel like I'm being followed.

☐ 집 밖에 수상한 사람이 있어요.	There's a stranger outside my house.
☐ 아이가 공원에 혼자 앉아 있어요.	A child is sitting alone in the park.
☐ 노인이 길을 헤매고 있어요.	An old man is wandering around.
☐ 남자가 개를 발로 차고 있어요.	A man is kicking a dog.
☐ 취객이 행패를 부리고 있어요.	A drunken man is attacking other people.
☐ 남자가 아이에게 치근대고 있어요.	A man is bothering a child. *bothering = annoying, harassing, molesting
☐ 누군가가 이웃집 담을 넘고 있어요.	Someone is climbing over my neighbor's wall.
☐ 친구 몸에 항상 멍 자국이 있어요.	My friend is black and blue all over his body.
☐ 산에서 고기를 구워 먹고 있어요.	Some people are having a barbecue party in the mountain.
☐ 건물에서 연기가 나요.	There is smoke coming out of the building.
☐ (큰)불이 났어요.	There's a (big) fire.

DIALOGUE

A This is 112.

B Yes. A bunch of students are having a gang fight.
   It looks pretty serious.

A Where is your exact location?

A 112입니다.

B 네. 한 무더기의 학생들이 모여서 지금 패싸움을 벌이고 있어요. 상당히 심각해 보여요.

A 지금 계신 곳이 정확히 어디입니까?

📑 **Notes**

hit-and-run 치고 달리기, 뺑소니   rear-end 후미의   collision 충돌, 추돌   homicide 살인, 살인행위
with one's own eyes ~의 눈으로 직접   gang fight 패싸움   high-shoolers 고등학교 학생들   bully
~을 못살게 굴다, 따돌리다, 왕따 시키다   a bunch of 한 무더기(덩어리, 다발, 송이, 무리)   assault 폭행하다, 강간하다
wander around 이리저리 돌아다니다   molest 괴롭히다, 여성이나 아이에게 짓궂게 굴다, 성희롱하다   climb over
~를 타고 올라가다   black and blue 멍(자국)

04 민원 신고

My neighbor is making too much noise.(이웃집이 너무 시끄러워요.), People throw garbage everywhere.(쓰레기를 아무 데나 버려요.), I got overtreated. (과잉 진료 받았어요.) 등 불편한 사항들은 어떻게 표현하는지 알아봅시다.

원어민 발음 듣기 ☑☐ 회화 훈련 ☐☐ 듣기 훈련 ☐☐

☐ 관공서 직원이 (아주) 불친절했어요. A public official was (very) rude to me.

☐ 동사무소 직원들이 다 불친절해요. The officials of Dong office are rude.

☐ 이웃집이 너무 시끄러워요. My neighbor is making too much noise.
I'd like to make a noise complaint.

☐ 공사장 소음이 심해요. There's too much noise from the construction site.

☐ 이웃집에서 악취가 풍겨요. A bad smell is coming from my neighbor.
*bad = nasty

☐ 버스가 급정거해서 넘어졌어요. The bus stopped suddenly and I fell (down).
A sudden bus stop made me fall.

☐ 버스가 정류소를 그냥 지나쳤어요. The bus didn't stop at the bus stop.
The bus just passed the bus station.

☐ 택시가 승차를 거부했어요. The taxi refused passengers.
The taxi declined to pick up passengers.

☐ 신호등이 고장 났어요. The traffic light is broken.
*broken = out of order

☐ 인도가 울퉁불퉁해요. The sidewalk is not even.
*sidewalk = walkway

☐ 어떤 남자에게 돈을 떼였어요. I was cheated by him.
*be cheated = be bilked

☐ 월급이 석 달간 체납됐어요. I haven't got paid for three months.
My payment has been delayed for three months.

☐ 사기 당했어요. I was swindled out of money.
*be swindled = be cheated

He defrauded me.

I fell for his trick.

☐ 그 식당 음식을 먹고 식중독에 걸렸어요.　I got food poisoning (after having meal) at that restaurant.

I was poisoned by rotten food at that restaurant.

☐ 사람들이 침을 아무 데나 뱉어요.　People spit on the streets.

People spit everywhere.
*everywhere = anywhere

☐ 금연 구역에서 담배를 피워요.　People are smoking in non-smoking areas.

☐ 쓰레기를 아무 곳에나 배출해요.　People throw garbage everywhere.
*garbage = trash

☐ 쓰레기 분리를 안 해요.　People don't recycle their garbage.

☐ 과잉 진료(치료) 받았어요.　I got overtreated by my doctor.

I got overmedicated by my doctor.

☐ 병원이 불필요한 검사를 강요했어요.　The hospital forced me to take unnecessary exams.

☐ 우리 집 앞에 항상 차가 주차되어 있어요.　There is always a car parked in front of my house.

☐ 애니멀 호더가 있어요.　I'd like to report an animal hoarder.

📋 **Notes**

sudden bus stop 버스의 급정거　refuse 거절(거부)하다(= decline)　passenger 승객　even 평평한, 고른　bilk ~을 떼어먹다, 속여서 빼앗다, 사기 치다　defraud 속여서 빼앗다, 사취하다　fall for ~에 빠지다, 속다　food poison 음식의 독, 식중독　overtreated 과도하게 치료받은(= overmedicated)　force someone to 강제로 ~하게 하다　take exam(s) 검사 받다　hoarder 동물을 모아 놓고 전혀 돌보지 않는 사람

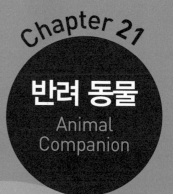

Chapter 21

반려 동물
Animal Companion

01 반려 동물 입양하기

요즘 반려 동물로 개나 고양이 등을 입양하려는 사람들이 많습니다. 개는 man's best friend(사람의 좋은 친구)로 다정하고 믿음직합니다. 고양이는 독립적이고 손이 많이 가지 않는다는 장점이 있죠. 입양을 보내야 할 경우라면 someone trustworthy(믿을 만한 사람)을 찾아 안정된 곳으로 보내야 합니다.

원어민 발음 듣기 ☑☐   회화 훈련 ☐☐   듣기 훈련 ☐☐

☐ 어떤 동물을 입양할까?	What (kind of) animal should we adopt?
☐ 고양이를 입양하고 싶어.	I'd like to adopt a cat.
☐ 집이 좁으니 작은 동물로 하자.	We have a small house. Let's adopt a small animal.
☐ 마당이 있으니 큰 동물로 하자.	We have a yard. Let's adopt a bigger animal. *yard → rooftop (옥상)
☐ 개는 사람의 좋은 친구야.	Dogs are man's best friend.
☐ 개는 믿음직해.	Dogs are very faithful.
☐ 개는 혼자 있으면 불안해 해.	Dogs can suffer from separation anxiety. Dogs are anxious when they are alone.
☐ 개는 불안하면 물건을 물어뜯어.	When a dog is nervous, he bites things.
☐ 고양이는 독립적이야.	Cats are independent.
☐ 고양이는 손이 별로 안 가.	Cats are low maintenance.
☐ 강아지, 아니면 성견을 입양할까?	Should we adopt a puppy or an adult dog? *puppy = pup
☐ 노견을 입양할까?	How about an old dog? *how about = what about
☐ 장애견을 입양하자.	Let's adopt a disabled dog. *disabled = handicapped
☐ 어디에서 입양하지?	Where do we adopt a dog? Where should we go to adopt an animal?
☐ 애견 숍에 가자.	Let's go to the pet shops.
☐ 애견 숍은 가지 마.	Don't go to the pet shops.

□ 동물 보호소에서 입양하자.	Let's adopt a dog from the animal shelter.
□ 친구네 개가 한 번에 8마리를 낳았어.	My friend's dog had a litter of eight pups.
□ 특별히 좋아하는 견종이 있어?	What kind of dogs do you like?
□ 난 대형견을 좋아해.	I love big dogs.
□ 난 대형견이 무서워.	I'm afraid of big dogs. *afraid = scared
□ 대형견이 더 점잖고 온순해.	Big dogs are more gentle and milder.
□ 그녀의 개는 다정다감해.	Her dog is very sweet.
□ 활발한 성격의 개가 좋아.	I like energetic dogs.
□ 개들마다 성격이 달라.	Every dog has different personality.
□ 개에게 배변 훈련을 시켜야 해.	We need to train our dog to be housebroken.
□ 입양하기 전에 다시 한번 생각해 봐.	Think again before you adopt an animal.
□ 내 고양이를 더 이상 돌봐줄 수 없어.	I can't take care of my cat any more. I have to give up my cat.
□ 입양처를 알아보고 있어.	I'm looking for a new home for my cat.
□ 믿을 만한 사람을 찾고 있어.	I'm looking for someone trustworthy. *trustworthy → responsible (책임감 있는)
□ 동물은 장난감이 아니야.	Animals are not toys.
□ 인터넷에 입양 공고했어.	I've posted my cat information on the Internet adoption sites.

📋 **반려 동물**(animal companions)

개 dog, canine	이구아나 iguana
고양이 cat, feline	수달 otter
새 bird	고슴도치 hedgehog
토끼 rabbit	기니피그 guinea pig
거북이 tortoise	물고기 fish
햄스터 hamster	

📝 **Notes**

adopt (사람, 동물을) 입양하다   separation anxiety 분리 불안(증)   disabled 몸이 부자유스러운, 신체 장애의
(= handicapped)   litter 동물의 한 배에서 난 새끼   housebroken (개, 고양이, 아이가) 집안에서 대소변을 가리는

02 동물 병원에서

animal companion(반려 동물)이 아프면 animal clinic(동물 병원)에 데려가서 veterinarian(수의사)에게 symptoms(증상)를 설명합니다. 동물 병원에서는 dewormer(구충제) 등의 예방약은 물론 반려 동물에게 필요한 다양한 물품을 구입할 수 있습니다.

원어민 발음 듣기 ☑□ 회화 훈련 □□ 듣기 훈련 □□

☐ 고양이 예방 주사 맞히러 왔어요.	I'm here to get my cat shot.
	Can you give my cat a shot?
	I'd like you to vaccinate my cat.
☐ 개 구충제 주세요.	Can I have dog dewormer?
	I'd like to buy dewormer chewables for dogs.
☐ 벼룩과 진드기 약 주세요.	Do you have flea and tick treatment for dogs?
☐ 이 약은 닭고기 맛이 나요.	This medicine has a chicken flavor.
	It's chicken-flavored.
☐ 한 달에 한 번씩 먹이세요.	Administer once a month, please.
☐ 이 약은 구충과 외부 기생충을 없앱니다.	This medicine kills intestinal worms and parasites.
☐ 우리 고양이가 아파요.	My cat is sick.
☐ 증상이 어떤가요?	What are the symptoms?
	What seems to be the problem?
☐ 사료를 안 먹어요.	He doesn't eat food.
	He barely eats food.
☐ 토해요.	She vomits.
☐ 설사를 해요.	She has diarrhea.
☐ 하루 종일 웅크리고 있어요.	She crouches all day.
☐ 코가 바싹 말랐어요.	His nose is dry.
☐ 오줌에 피가 섞여 나와요.	There's blood in his urine.
☐ 귀에서 냄새가 나요.	Her ears smell.

□ 눈에 눈곱이 잔뜩 끼었어요.	My dog gets a lot of gunk in his eyes. *gunk = mucus My dog's eyes are very gummy. *gummy = mattery
□ 피부에 빨간 점이 잔뜩 있어요.	There are lots of red rashes on his skin. My dog has many red rashes on his skin.
□ 다리를 (약간) 절어요.	My dog limps (slightly). My dog has a bad limp.
□ 왼쪽 다리를 절어요.	He is lame in his left leg.
□ 얼굴이 부었어요.	Her face is (all) swollen up. *face → foot (발)
□ 다른 개에게 물렸어요.	My dog was bit by another dog. *bit = bitten
□ 개가 화초를 뜯어 먹어요.	My dog eats plants.
□ 개가 이불에다 오줌을 싸요.	My dog wet my blanket.
□ 개가 털이 너무 날려요.	My dog hair is everywhere. There is too much dog hair at home.
□ 개가 너무 많이 짖어요.	My dog barks too much.
□ 요즘 예민해요.	She is sensitive these days.
□ 털을 자주 곤두세워요.	He erects his hair quite often.
□ 스케일링 때문에 왔어요.	I'm here for teeth cleaning for my dog. *cleaning = scaling My dog needs to get her teeth cleaned. *cleaned = scaled
□ 몇 가지 검사를 하겠습니다.	I'm going to run some tests. We need to run some tests on your cat.
□ 이 개 보호자가 누구시죠?	Who's the owner of this dog?
□ 여기서 잠시 기다리세요.	Wait here for a minute, please.
□ 개를 데리고 이쪽으로 오세요.	Come this way with your dog.
□ 체중을 잴게요.	Let me weigh your cat. I need to take his weight.

□ 채혈할게요.	I'll take your dog's blood.
□ 주사를 놓겠습니다.	I'm going to give him a shot.
□ 약을 지어 드릴게요.	I'll give you medicines for your cat. Your cat needs to take some medicines.
□ 연고를 드릴게요.	Why don't I give you an ointment for your cat?
□ 수술을 해야 해요.	Your dog needs a surgery.
□ 개에게 사람 음식을 주지 마세요.	Don't give any human food to your dog.
□ 개를 잃어버렸어요.	I lost my dog. My dog ran away.
□ 개를 찾고 있어요.	I'm looking for my dog.
□ 병원 입구에 전단지를 붙여 주세요.	Could you please post this flyer on the front gate?
□ 개를 찾아 주시는 분께 사례금을 드려요.	There's a reward for finding my dog.
□ 길에서 개를 발견했어요.	I found this dog on the street.
□ 유기견 같아요.	She looks like an abandoned dog. She seemed lost.
□ 털이 엉망이에요.	The dog's hair is a mess.
□ 건강 상태를 체크해 주세요.	Can you check his vital signs, please?
□ 건강 상태가 어떤가요?	How's his health condition?
□ 피부병이 심해요.	The dog has a serious skin disease.
□ 영양실조예요.	She is malnourished. *malnourished = undernourished She is suffering from malnutrition.

📑 **Notes**

get shot 예방 주사를 맞다 give ~ a shot 예방 주사를 놓다 vaccinate 예방 접종을 하다 dewormer 구충제 chewable 씹을 수 있도록 만들어진 것(약) administer 약을 먹이다, 투약하다 intestinal worms 체내에 사는 내부 기생충 parasites 체외에 사는 외부 기생충 vomit 구토하다 crouch 쭈그리다, 웅크리다 gunk 끈적끈적한 물질, 점액(= mucus) gummy 끈적끈적한, 진득진득한(= mattery) rash 발진, 뾰루지 limp 절다, 절뚝거리다 lame 절름발이의 wet blanket 이불을 적시다, 이불에 오줌 싸다 erect 곧추세우다 run test 검사를 실시하다 flyer 전단지, 광고지(= flier) reward 보상(금) abandoned 버려진, 버림 받은 vital signs 맥박, 호흡, 체온 등 생명의 징후 malnourished 영양실조의, 영양 장애의(= undernourished)

03 애견 미용 숍, 애견 호텔에서

pet grooming shop(애견 미용 숍)에서는 dog groomer(애견 미용사)들이 개의 털을 예쁘게 깎아 줍니다. 혼자서 개를 키우는 사람들이 많아지면서 pet boarding(애견 호텔)도 증가하고 있는데, 개를 맡길 때는 '맡기다', '하숙시키다'의 의미인 동사 board를 써서 I'd like to board my dog.이라고 하면 됩니다.

원어민 발음 듣기 ☑□   회화 훈련 □□   듣기 훈련 □□

☐ 어떻게 해 드릴까요?	How would you like to cut your dog's hair? What kind of hair style do you want for your dog?
☐ 아주 짧게 깎아 주세요.	I'd like you to cut his hair very short.
☐ 꼬리 끝의 털은 남겨 주세요.	Cut his hair very short except the tail.
☐ 발과 얼굴만 미용해 주세요.	Can you groom my dog's feet and face?
☐ 가위로 잘라 주셨으면 해요.	I prefer (haircutting) scissors.
☐ 귀 세정해 주세요.	Could you please clean her ears?
☐ 이빨을 닦아 주세요.	Could you please brush her teeth?
☐ 발톱 깎아 주세요.	Clip her nails, please.
☐ 항문낭을 짜 주세요.	Squeeze his anal sack, please.
☐ 목욕 시켜 주세요.	Can you give him a bath?
☐ (모두) 끝나는 데 얼마나 걸릴까요?	How long does it take to finish (all this)?
☐ 두 시간 정도 걸립니다.	It will take about two hours. About two hours to get through.
☐ 저희 개를 잠시 맡길 수 있을까요?	Can I leave my dog here for a short time? Can you dog-sit for a minute? Could you watch my dog for a while?
☐ 세 시간 후에 오겠습니다.	I'll be back in three hours.
☐ 미용이 끝났습니다.	Your dog's grooming is done. Your dog is ready to go home.
☐ 얼굴 털 모양이 마음에 안 들어요.	I don't like the way you cut my dog's face hair.

반려 동물

345

☐ 미용 중에 상처가 났어요.	Your dog got a cut during grooming. *grooming = clipping
☐ 살짝 긁혔어요.	Your dog got slightly scratched.
☐ 미용 중에 개가 자꾸 움직여요.	Your dog moves a lot while grooming.
☐ 개가 이발기(클리퍼) 소리를 싫어해요.	She doesn't like clipper sound. Clipper sound makes your dog nervous.
☐ 조심하셨어야죠.	You should've been more careful. You should've been extra cautious.
☐ 상처가 심하지 않아요.	It doesn't look so bad. It's not that serious.
☐ 신경 쓰지 마세요.	Don't worry about it. Never mind.
☐ 저희 개를 호텔에 맡기려고요.	I'd like to board my dog.
☐ 하루에 얼마죠?	How much do you charge for a day? How much for a day?
☐ 내일 모레 올게요.	I'll be back the day after tomorrow to pick up my dog. I'll be back in two days.
☐ 잘 돌봐 주세요.	Please take good care of my dog.

Notes

groom 다듬다, 몸단장하다 clip nails 손톱이나 발톱을 깎다 anal sack 항문 주변에 있는 분비물 낭, 항문낭 get through 겪다, 경험하다 leave 맡기다, 잠시 두다 dot-sit 개를 돌봐 주다 way 방식, 방법 get a cut 베이다, 상처 입다 get scratched 긁히다, 생채기가 나다 clipper 이발기 day after tomorrow 내일 모레, 이틀 후 pick up (사람, 물건, 동물)을 가져오다, 데려오다

04 (반려 동물을 위한) 물품 구입

반려 동물을 위한 supplies(물품)의 종류는 매우 다양합니다. 가장 기본적으로 사료에서 간식, 옷, 목줄 등이 있습니다. '~을 주세요.'는 I'd like to have ~. 혹은 Can I have ~?, I need ~. 등의 표현을 씁니다.

원어민 발음 듣기 ☑□   회화 훈련 □□   듣기 훈련 □□

☐ 개 사료 주세요.	I'd like to have dog food. Can I have dog food?
☐ 건조 사료 아니면 캔 사료 드릴까요?	(Would you like) Dry or can food?
☐ 비만 견용 사료 있나요?	Do you have reduced fat food for dogs?
☐ 유기농 사료는 없나요?	Don't you have organic cat food?
☐ 애견 간식 주세요.	I need dog biscuits and treats.
☐ 우리 개는 육포를 좋아해요.	My dog loves jerky treats.
☐ (훈련용) 개 장난감 있나요?	Do you have dog (training) toys?
☐ 강아지 겨울옷을 찾고 있어요.	I'm looking for winter clothes for my dog.
☐ 목걸이와 줄을 사려고요.	I want to buy a collar and leash for my dog.
☐ 중형 견용 몸줄 주세요.	I'd like a harness leach for a middle-sized dog.
☐ 개 귀 세정제가 있나요?	Do you have an ear cleaner for dogs?
☐ 영양제가 필요해요.	I need supplements for my dog.
☐ 어항 주시겠어요?	Can I get a fish tank? *tank = bowl
☐ 물고기 사료 주세요.	Fish food, please.
☐ 새장이 다양하네요.	You have quite a variety of bird cages.
☐ 햄스터는 주로 무엇을 먹죠?	What do hamsters live on?
☐ 햄스터는 씨앗을 좋아해요.	Hamsters love seeds.
☐ 고슴도치는 벌레를 좋아해요.	Hedgehogs love worms.

Chapter 21

반려 동물

347

애견과 산책하기

개를 산책시킬 때는 toilet paper(휴지)나 plastic bag(비닐봉지)을 가지고 다니면서 개의 오물을 반드시 치워야 합니다. 공공장소의 경우 목줄이나 몸줄을 착용해야 벌금을 물지 않죠. 요즘은 개 전용 공원인 dog park가 있어 허용된 공간에서는 개들이 마음껏 뛰어놀 수 있습니다.

원어민 발음 듣기 ☑☐   회화 훈련 ☐☐   듣기 훈련 ☐☐

□ 너 개 키우니?	Do you have a dog?
□ 개 세 마리 키우고 있어.	I have three dogs. I live with three dogs.
□ 둘은 수놈이고 하나는 암놈이야.	Two are boys and one is a girl.
□ 우리 개를 하루에 두 번씩 산책 시켜.	I walk my dog twice a day.
□ 주로 공원이나 길을 걸어.	I usually walk them in the park or street.
□ 개 전용 공원이 있으면 좋겠어.	I wish there was the dog park.
□ 개를 얼마 동안 산책 시켜?	How long do you walk your dog(s)?
□ 1시간 정도 산책 시켜.	I walk my dog(s) about an hour.
□ 개들도 때때로 스트레스를 받아.	Dogs can be stressful sometimes.
□ 산책 시 목줄이 필요해.	You need a collar and leash while walking.
□ 차들을 조심해.	Watch out for cars.
□ 휴지를 항상 가지고 다녀.	Always carry toilet paper. *paper = tissue
□ 오물 치우는 것 잊지 마.	Don't forget to pick up after your dog(s). Clean up your dog droppings.
□ 다른 사람에게 폐가 되지 않도록 해.	Try not to trouble other people.
□ 개를 만지기 전에 주인의 허락을 받아.	Get permission first from a dog's owner before you touch a dog.

📋 **Notes**

stressful 스트레스가 많은, 긴장하는 watch out 조심하다. 주의하다 droppings 동물의 똥, 오물 trouble 번거롭게 하다. 폐를 끼치다 touch 만지다. 쓰다듬다

동물 보호 단체에서

각국의 동물 보호 단체에서는 volunteer workers(자원봉사자)들의 도움으로 위기에 처한 동물들을 구조하고, 청결한 animal shelter(동물 보호소) 운영을 하고 있습니다. 때로는 대규모 adoption campaign(입양 행사)나 donation campaign(기부금 행사)를 벌이기도 합니다.

원어민 발음 듣기 ☑️☐　회화 훈련 ☐☐　듣기 훈련 ☐☐

☐ 동물 보호 단체에 대해 들어봤어?	Have you heard of animal protection groups? Do you know any animal rights groups?
☐ 우리나라에 몇몇 단체가 있어.	We have several animal protection groups in Korea.
☐ 보호소에 500마리가 넘는 동물이 있어.	There're more than 500 animals in the animal shelter.
☐ 우리 모두 동물 보호가가 될 수 있어.	We all can be an animal activist.
☐ 대부분 버려진 동물들이야.	Most of the animals were abandoned. *abandoned → abused (학대 받은)
☐ 자원봉사 할래?	Are you interested in volunteer works? Are you up for any volunteer works?
☐ 보호소에서 자원봉사 했어.	I volunteered at the animal shelter.
☐ 우리는 동물들을 목욕 시켜.	We bathe animals. *bathe → feed (밥을 주다)
☐ 우리는 견사를 청소해.	We clean dog cages.
☐ 기부금을 내려고요.	I'd like to donate some money.
☐ 보호소에 물품을 기증하려고요.	I'd like to donate some items to the animal shelter.
☐ 동물 옷, 담요, 사료 등이 필요해요.	We (usually) need clothes, blankets, and food.
☐ 입양 신청하려고요.	I'd like to adopt a cat. I'd like to apply for an animal adoption.
☐ 임시 보호 신청하려고요.	I'd like to apply for a temporary custody for a dog.

Chapter 22

전화
Telephone

01 전화 받기, 바꿔 주기

보통 Hello.(여보세요.), It's ~'s residence.(~네 집입니다.), It's ~'s cell phone.(~의 휴대폰입니다.)과 같이 전화 통화를 시작합니다. 다른 사람에게 전화를 바꿔 줄 때는 One moment, please.(잠시만요.)라고 말합니다.

원어민 발음 듣기 ☑☐　회화 훈련 ☐☐　듣기 훈련 ☐☐

☐ 전화벨이 울려.	The phone is ringing.
☐ 전화 안 받을 거야?	Aren't you going to answer that?
☐ 나 지금 전화 받을 수 없어.	I can't pick up the phone now.
☐ 대신 받아 줄래?	Would you pick it up for me? Answer the phone, please.
☐ 나 찾으면 없다고 해.	Tell whoever it is, I'm not here.
☐ 메모만 받아 줄래?	Would you take a message for me?
☐ 다시 건다고 말해 줄래?	Tell her I'll call back. Would you tell him that I'll call back?
☐ 여보세요.	Hello.
☐ 김 씨네 집입니다.	(This is) Kim's residence.
☐ 크리스털 휴대폰입니다.	(It's) Crystal's cell phone.
☐ 제가 크리스털인데요.	It's Crystal. Crystal speaking. This is she (speaking).
☐ 예, 바꿔드릴게요.	Sure. I'll get her for you.
☐ 예, 잠시만요.	Sure. One moment, please.
☐ 크리스털, 네 전화야.	Crystal, it's for you.
☐ 웬 남자가 널 찾아.	It's a guy.
☐ 네 어머니야.	It's your mom.
☐ 화난 목소리야.	She sounds upset.
☐ 기분 좋은 목소리야.	She sounds pleasant.

□ 다급한 목소리야.	She sounds urgent.
□ 나 좀 바꿔 줘.	Let me talk to her.
□ 그는 지금 전화를 받을 수 없어요.	He can't talk to you right now.
□ 그는 지금 여기 없어요.	He is not in.
□ 그는 잠깐 외출했어요.	He is out for a minute.
□ 그는 통화 중이에요.	His phone line is busy.
□ 그는 잠시 자리를 비웠어요.	He is not into the office right now.
	He is out of the office right now.
□ 금방 돌아올 거예요.	She will be back soon.
□ 돌아올 때가 됐는데.	She should be back by now.
□ 아직 학교에서 안 왔어요.	She hasn't come back from school.
□ 아직 퇴근 안 했어요.	She is not back from work yet.
□ 사무실로 전화해 보세요.	Call him at his office.
	Why don't you try his office?
□ 그는 아직 출근 안 하셨습니다.	He hasn't come to work yet.
	He hasn't come in the office yet.
□ 그는 휴가 중입니다.	He is on his vacation.
	*vacation = holiday
	He is away on leave.
	He has been off work.
□ 그녀는 출산 휴가 중입니다.	She is on her maternity leave.
□ 누구시죠?	Who's speaking?
	Who's calling?
	May I ask who this is?
	Who is this?
□ 'N' 회사입니다. 무엇을 도와드릴까요?	N Company. What can I help you?
	N Company. How may I help you?
□ 내선으로 연결해 주세요.	Could you connect me with extension?
□ 내선으로 연결해 드리겠습니다.	I'll connect you with her extension.

02 전화 걸기, 전화 끊기

전화를 걸 때 "~와 통화하고 싶은데요."는 I'd like to talk to ~. 또는 Can I speak
to ~?라고 표현합니다. 찾는 사람이 자신이 맞다면 This is she/he (speaking).라고
하면 됩니다. 전화를 끊을 때도 I gotta go.(끊어야겠다.), I'm hang up.(끊을게.) 등
여러 가지 표현이 있습니다.

원어민 발음 듣기 ☑□   회화 훈련 □□   듣기 훈련 □□

☐ 크리스털과 통화하고 싶은데요.	I'd like to talk to Crystal. *talk = speak Can I talk to Crystal?
☐ 안녕하세요, 크리스털 있나요?	Hello, is Crystal there? Hello, is Crystal around? Hello, is Crystal available now?
☐ 그녀가 전화했다고 들었어요.	I heard (that) she called. I believe (that) she called me earlier.
☐ 전화하려고 했어.	I've been meaning to call you. I was going to call you.
☐ 좀 더 빨리 전화하려고 했는데.	I was going to call you sooner.
☐ 잠깐만. 다른 전화가 왔어.	Hold on a second. I've got another call. Hold on. I've got someone on another line. Hold on. I have a call on the other line.
☐ 문자 메시지 좀 확인할게.	Let me check my text. I've got to check my text.
☐ 끊지 마.	Don't hang up.
☐ 수 전화번호 좀 알려 줘.	Let me have Sue's phone number. Can I have Sue's number? Do you know Sue's number?
☐ 전화번호가 있는지 잘 모르겠어.	I'm not sure that I have her number. I'm not sure whether I have it.
☐ 전화번호부 좀 확인할게.	I'll check my phone book. Let me check my phone book.

□ 그만 끊어야겠다.	I gotta go.	
	I've got to go.	
	Let's hang up.	
□ 자주 통화하자.	Let's call each other often.	
□ 자주 좀 전화해.	Call me more often.	
	*call = ring	
□ 내일 전화할게.	I'll call you tomorrow.	
□ 조만간 전화할게.	I'll call you soon.	
□ 도착하자마자 전화할게.	I'll call you as soon as I arrive.	
	I'll ring you when I get there.	
□ 내일은 통화 못 해.	I can't call you tomorrow.	
	I can't talk to you on the phone tomorrow.	
□ 언제 통화할 수 있어?	When can I call you?	
	When can I talk to you on the phone?	
	When are you available to talk?	
□ 시간 나면 전화해.	Call me when you have time.	
	*when = if	
	Give me a call whenever you have time.	
□ 전화 끊을게.	I'm going to hang up.	
	I'm hanging up.	
□ 네가 먼저 끊어.	You hang up first.	
□ 안녕. 들어가.	Bye.	

 Notes

mean ~하려고 하다, ~하려는 의도가 있다   hang up 수화기를 놓다, 전화를 끊다   gotta ~해야 한다(= have got to)   ring 전화 걸다   have time 시간 나다, 여유가 생기다

메모 받기, 메모 남기기

전화로 메모를 받을 때는 Can I take a message?(메모를 남겨 드릴까요?), 메모를 남기고 싶을 때는 Could you leave a message for me?(메모를 남겨 주시겠어요?)라고 말하면 됩니다. 보통 메모 내용은 전화 건 사람의 이름과 연락처, 걸려온 시간 등과 같은 간단한 사항입니다.

원어민 발음 듣기 ☑□ 회화 훈련 □□ 듣기 훈련 □□

☐ 메모를 남겨 드릴까요?	Can I take a message? Do you want to leave a message? Do you want me to take a message for you?
☐ 예, 그래 주시면 감사하겠습니다.	Yes, I'd appreciate if you do that. Yes, it would be appreciated.
☐ 아니요, 됐습니다.	No, thanks. That won't be necessary.
☐ 성함이 어떻게 되시죠?	May I have your name? Can I have your full name, please?
☐ 이름 철자를 불러 주세요.	Could you spell your name, please? Spell your name, please.
☐ 성은 어떻게 되시죠?	What's your last name? May I ask what your last name is? *may=can
☐ 제 성은 김입니다.	My last name is Kim. It's Kim.
☐ 그와 어떤 사이시죠?	Can I ask about your relationship with him?
☐ 그와 친구 아니면 회사 동료인가요?	Are you his friend or colleague from work?
☐ 대학 동창입니다.	We went to college together. We were at the same college.
☐ 성함이 귀에 익어요.	Your name sounds familiar. Your name rings a bell.
☐ 어디에서 들어본 이름이에요.	I think I've heard your name before.

연락처는 어떻게 되시죠?	What's your phone number? *phone = contact Can I have your phone number? Your phone number, please.
그가 당신의 연락처를 알고 있나요?	Does he know your phone number? How can he reach you? What number can he call?
휴대폰 번호를 알려 드릴게요.	I'll give you my cell number.
이 번호로 전화 주시면 됩니다.	You can contact me at this number. Call this number.
그녀에게 전화하라고 할까요?	Shall I have her call you? Do you want me to have her call you back?
전화하라고 전할게요.	I'll tell her to call you back.
제가 몇 시쯤 전화하면 될까요?	When should I call her?
몇 시쯤 전화하신다고 전해 드릴까요?	What time should I tell him to expect your call?
메모를 남겨 주시겠어요?	Could you leave a message for me?
메모를 꼭 전해 주세요.	Make sure he gets the message.
전화했었다고 전해 주세요.	Tell him that I called. Would you please tell him that I called?
전화 기다린다고 전해 주세요.	Tell her that I'll be waiting for her returning call. Please tell her that I'll be expecting her call.
급한 일이라고 전해 주세요.	Tell him that it's urgent. Tell him that it's an urgent matter.
그가 방금 전화했었어요.	He just called.
국제 전화가 왔었어.	There was an international call for you.
그가 왜 전화했지?	I wonder why he called. I wonder why he is calling me.

357

04 용건 묻고 말하기

전화 건 사람의 용건을 물을 때는 친한 사이가 아닌 이상 예의 있게 May I ask what this is about?(무슨 일인지 여쭤봐도 될까요?)라고 하면 됩니다. 대답할 때는 I'm calling (you) about ~.(~때문에 전화했어요.)라고 합니다. 전화상에서 용건을 묻고 대답하는 표현을 살펴보겠습니다.

원어민 발음 듣기 ☑□   회화 훈련 □□   듣기 훈련 □□

☐ 잠시 통화 괜찮으세요?

Do you have a moment?

Can I talk to you for a second?

☐ 무슨 용건이시죠?

May I ask what this is about?

What is this about?

What is this regarding?
*regarding = concerning

May I ask what this is in regard to?
*in regard to = with regard to

☐ (친한 사이에) 무슨 일이야?

What's up?

☐ 무슨 일 있어?

What's going on?

What's wrong?

☐ 네 목소리가 듣고 싶어서.

I just want to hear your voice.

☐ 네 생각이 나서.

I miss you.

I was thinking about you.

☐ 방금 네 꿈을 꿔서.

I dreamt about you just now.

☐ 할 말이 있어서 전화했어.

I'm calling because I want to talk to you about something.
*talk = speak

☐ 궁금한 것이 있어서 전화했어.

I'm calling because I want to ask you (about) something.

☐ 중요한 용건이 있어서 전화했어.

I'm calling because I have an important thing to say.

☐ 급한 일이라서 전화했어.

I'm calling because it's urgent.

☐ 그것 때문에 전화한 거야?

Are you calling me because of that?

☐ 그와 연락할 방법이 있을까?

Is there any way that I can contact him?

☐ 아침까지 기다릴 수가 없었어.	I couldn't wait until the morning.
	It can't wait till the morning.
☐ 전화 기다리고 있었어.	I've been waiting for your call.
	I'm expecting you to call.
	I was anticipating your call.
☐ 메모 받자마자 전화했어요.	I'm calling you as soon as I got your message.
☐ 일전에 전화 드렸던 크리스탈입니다.	This is Crystal. I called you a couple of days ago.
☐ 이 건으로 전화 드렸습니다.	I'm calling (you) about this.
	I'm calling because of this.
	This is about this.
	*about = regarding, concerning
	What I'm calling about is this.
	I'll explain why I'm calling.

A Hi, what's up?
B I'm calling because I want to ask you something.
  Do you happen to know Crystal's cell number?
A No, I don't. What's going on?
B It's urgent. Is there any way that I can contact her?

A 안녕, 어쩐 일이야?
B 뭐 물어볼 것이 있어서 전화했어. 혹시 크리스탈 휴대폰 번호 알아?
A 아니, 모르는데. 무슨 일 있어?
B 급한 일이야. 그녀와 연락할 수 있는 방법이 있을까?

 Notes

dream about ~에 대해 꿈꾸다 anticipate 기대하다, 예견하다 regarding ~에 관해서, ~에 대해서, ~인 점에서
(= in/with regard to, concerning)

05 전화 상태, 통화 시 상황

전화 통화를 할 때에는 잡음이 심하거나, 주위가 시끄럽거나, 양손에 물건이 있는 등
여러 가지 상황이 있을 수 있습니다. 그러니 통화가 연결되자마자 Is it okay to talk
now?(지금 통화 괜찮아?)라며 상대편에게 전화를 받아도 괜찮은 상황인지를 먼저
묻는 것이 좋겠죠.

원어민 발음 듣기 ☑☐ 회화 훈련 ☐☐ 듣기 훈련 ☐☐

☐ 여보세요, 여보세요.	Hello, hello!
☐ 소리가 (전혀) 안 들려요.	I can't hear you (at all).
☐ 좀 더 크게 말씀해 주시겠어요?	Can you speak up?
	Speak loudly, please.
☐ 듣고 있어요?	Are you (still) there?
	Are you listening to me?
☐ 잡음이 심해요.	There's lots of static on the line.
	My phone has lots of static.
☐ 주변 소음이 심해요.	It's too noisy around you.
	There's too much noise out there.
☐ TV 소리가 너무 커요.	Your TV is too loud.
	Could you turn down the TV (volume)?
☐ 혼선이 됐나 봐요.	The lines are mixed.
	*mixed = crossed
	The lines are all messed up.
	There's some interference.
☐ 통신 장애가 있어요.	There's some communication problems.
	There's a communication breakdown.
☐ 전화가 안 걸려요.	I can't get through (on the phone).
	My call won't go through.
☐ 메시지 전송이 잘 안 돼요.	I can't send my text message.
	My text message won't be transmitted.
☐ 전화가 갑자기 끊겼어요.	The phone was suddenly cut off.
	The phone was suddenly disconnected.

	I was suddenly cut off.
	*was = got
	The line went dead suddenly.
□ 배터리가 다 됐어요.	My phone battery is dead.
	The battery has run down.
□ 전화기가 곧 꺼질 거예요.	My phone will be dead soon.
□ 전화기가 꺼져 있어요.	My phone has gone dead.
	My phone is turned off.
□ 전화선이 빠져 있어요.	Your (home) phone is off the hook.
□ 자동 응답기가 받네요.	Your answering machine picks up.
□ 음성 사서함으로 넘어갔어요.	It's his voice mail.
□ 음성 메시지를 남겨야 할까요?	Should we leave a message on his voice mail?
□ 지금 통화 괜찮아?	Is it okay to talk now?
	Is this a bad time to talk?
□ 지금 전화하기 곤란해.	I can't talk to you right now.
	This is not a good time to talk.
□ 전화로 말하긴 좀 그렇다.	I can't talk to you about this on the phone.
□ 나 지금 뭐 좀 하는 중이야.	I'm in the middle of something.
□ 지금 가스 불 위에 뭐 올려놨어.	I've got something on the stove.
□ 지금 샤워하는 중이야.	I'm taking a shower.
□ 지금 버스에서 내리는 중이야.	I'm getting off the bus.
□ 지금 저녁 먹는 중이야.	I'm having dinner.
□ 저 지금 회의 중인데요.	I'm in the meeting.
□ 저 누구와 면담 중인데요.	I'm talking with someone.
	I'm having a meeting with someone.
□ 저 지금 통화 중인데요.	I'm on the phone.
□ 지금 어디에서 거는 거야?	Where are you calling from?
□ 사무실에서 걸고 있어.	I'm calling from my office.

□ 공중전화로 걸고 있어.	I'm calling from the pay phone.
□ 나중에 내가 다시 걸게.	Can I call you back later?
	Let me call you again.
□ 내가 다시 걸까?	Do you want me to call back?
	Should I call you back later?
□ 바로 다시 걸게.	I'll call you back right away.
□ 그가 전화를 안 받아.	He won't pick up the phone.
	He doesn't answer the phone.

DIALOGUE

A (On the phone) Hi, Michael, It's Crystal.

B Hey, Crystal.

Listen! I'm in the middle of something.

Can I call you back a little later?

A Sure.

B Thanks. I'll call you in 10 minutes.

A (전화상에서) 안녕 마이클. 나 크리스털이야.

B 안녕, 크리스털. 있잖아. 나 지금 뭐 하는 중이거든.

내가 잠시 후에 다시 걸어도 될까?

A 물론이지.

B 고마워. 10분 후에 다시 걸게.

📑 **Notes**

speak up 큰 소리로 말하다 **static** 전파 장애 **mixed** 혼선된, 뒤섞인(= crossed) **mess up** 엉망으로 만들다, 뒤죽박죽이 되다, 망쳐놓다 **interference** 장애, 방해, 혼선 **breakdown** 파손, 전기의 절연 **get through** 전화를 연결해 주다, 전화 걸다 **go through** 겪다, 통과하다 **transmit** 보내다, 전송하다 **cut off** 자르다, 절단하다, 끊다 **go dead** 죽어가다, 죽다, 꺼지다 **off the hook** 전화선이 빠진 **in the middle of** 한창 ∼하는 중인

06 통화 예절

전화를 걸고 받을 때는 반드시 지켜야 할 telephone etiquettes(통화 예절)가 있습니다. 늦은 시간에 전화하지 않는 것 혹은 통화 중에 음식을 먹으면서 말하지 않는 것 등을 들 수 있습니다.

원어민 발음 듣기 ☑☐ 회화 훈련 ☐☐ 듣기 훈련 ☐☐

☐ 늦은 시간에 전화해서 미안해. I'm sorry I called you so late (at night).

☐ 너무 이른 시간에 전화해서 미안해. I'm sorry I called you so early (in the morning).

☐ 자꾸 전화해서 미안해. I'm sorry I keep calling you.

☐ 너무 오랜 시간 통화해서 미안해. I'm sorry I talked such a long time.

☐ 한 가지만 물어보고 끊을게. I'll ask one thing, and hang up.

☐ 방해한 건 아니지? Am I interrupting anything?
Is this a bad time?

☐ 자는 데 깨운 건 아니지? I hope I'm not waking you up.
Did I wake you up?

☐ 괜찮아. 이야기 해. No, you're not. What's up?

☐ 언제든지 전화해. Call me anytime.

☐ 내일 아침에 전화해. Call me in the morning.
Why don't you call me in the morning?

☐ 밝은 때에 전화해. Call me at more civilized hour.

☐ 이게 무슨 소리야? What is that noise?

☐ 뭐 먹어? Are you eating?
What are you eating?

☐ 과자 먹고 있어. I'm eating crackers.
*crackers=cookies

☐ 통화 중에는 음식 먹지 마. Don't eat while you're on the phone.

☐ 누구에게 소리치는 거야? Who are you yelling at?

□ 통화 중에 크게 소리 지르지 마.	Don't yell while you're on the phone.
□ 할 말 더 있어?	Do you have more things to say?
	Anything else you want to talk about?
□ 할 말 없으면 끊자.	If you have nothing to say, let's hang up.
□ 전화는 용건만 간단히 하자.	Let's cut it short.
	Let's make short.
	Keep it short and sweet.
	*keep = make
	Just short and sweet.
□ 전화 잘못 거셨어요.	You've got the wrong number.
	You've dialed the wrong number.
□ 그런 사람 없습니다.	There's no one here by that name.
□ 자꾸 전화하지 마세요.	Stop calling me.
□ 장난 전화하지 마세요.	Stop making a prank call.
	*prank = hoax, crank
□ 지하철에서 통화할 때는 조용히 하세요.	Keep your voice down when you talk on the phone in the train.
□ 전화 좀 빌려 써도 될까요?	May I use your phone?
□ 전화 주셔서 고맙습니다.	Thank you for calling.
	I appreciate your call.

Notes

civilized hour 너무 이르거나 늦지 않은, 예의에 어긋나지 않은 시간대 **cut it short** 간단히 하다, 짤막하게 하고 끝내다(= make short) **short and sweet** (전화 통화에서) 짧지만 명쾌하게 **prank** 짓궂은 장난(= hoax, crank) **keep one's voice down** 목소리를 낮추다, 조용히 말하다

07 집 전화 설치하기

집 전화를 설치하려면 전화국에 electrician(설치 기사)의 방문을 예약해야 합니다. 보통 전화번호의 area code(국번)는 정해져 있고, 뒷자리 네 개 번호는 사용자가 정하게끔 되어 있습니다. 설치가 끝난 후 언제 전화가 개통되는지도 알아 두는 것이 좋겠죠.

원어민 발음 듣기 ☑□ 회화 훈련 □□ 듣기 훈련 □□

집 전화 설치하려고요.	I'd like to install a telephone. I want to have a phone put in.
어떻게 해야 하죠?	What should I do?
날짜를 정해 주시겠어요?	Would you set a date? *set a date = schedule a date
설치 기사가 방문할 겁니다.	Our electrician will visit your house to install it. We'll send one of our electricians to your home to install it.
기본요금은 얼마죠?	What is the basic charge?
월 기본료는 5,000원입니다.	The basic charge is 5,000 won every month.
3년 약정 계약입니다.	You'll have our phone service under a three-year contract.
번호는 어떻게 받죠?	How can I receive my phone number?
새 번호를 받고 싶어요.	I'd like to get a new phone number.
이 지역은 국번이 몇 번이죠?	What's the area code here?
뒷자리 번호만 정하세요.	You decide the last four digits. *digits = numbers Why don't you decide the rest of your phone number?
전화가 언제 개통되죠?	When can I expect my phone to be working?
바로 사용하시면 됩니다.	You can use it right away.
이 전화기는 무료입니다.	This telephone is free.

📑 **Notes**

put in (기계 등을) 설치하다 **electrician** 전기 기술자, 전기공 **~ year contract** ~년간 약정

Chapter 22 전화

365

휴대폰 서비스 센터 이용하기

휴대폰이 고장 나면 customer service center(고객 서비스 센터)를 찾죠? The display screen is broken.(액정이 깨졌어요.), I can't turn on my cell phone.(전원이 켜지지 않아요.), The sound goes on and off.(소리가 들렸다 안 들렸다 해요.) 등의 문제점을 설명해야 합니다.

원어민 발음 듣기 ☑□ 회화 훈련 □□ 듣기 훈련 □□

☐ 가까운 휴대폰 서비스 센터가 어디죠?
Where is the nearest customer service center for the cell phone?

☐ 휴대폰이 고장 났어요.
My cell phone isn't working (properly).
My cell phone broke.

☐ 어떤 문제가 있죠?
What are the problems?

☐ 액정이 깨졌어요.
The display screen on my cell phone is broken.
*broken = cracked

☐ 소리가 들렸다 안 들렸다 해요.
The sound goes on and off.

☐ 전원이 켜지지 않아요.
I can't turn on my cell phone.

☐ 저절로 꺼져요.
My cell phone is turned off by itself.

☐ 접촉 불량인 것 같아요.
There seems to be loose contact.

☐ 휴대폰을 얼마나 쓰셨어요?
How long have you been using your cell phone?

☐ 떨어뜨린 적이 있나요?
Have you dropped your cell phone?

☐ 물에 빠뜨렸나요?
Have you dropped your cell phone in water?

☐ 1년간 무상 수리됩니다.
Your cell phone has a one-year warranty.
Your cell phone will get free repairs for a year.

☐ 지금은 무상 수리 기간입니다.
Your cell phone is still under warranty.

☐ 무상 수리 기간이 지났습니다.
Your cell phone is not under warranty.
Your warranty period for free repairs is expired.

□ 간단한 고장입니다.	It's a simple problem.
	It's nothing serious.
□ 부품을 교체해야 합니다.	We need to replace some parts of your cell phone.
	Some parts need to be replaced.
□ 3일 후에 오세요.	Come back in three days.
	Stop by in three days.
□ 요금은 5만 원입니다.	The repair charge will be 50,000 won.
□ 휴대폰 평균 수명은 얼마나 되죠?	What's the average life of cell phones?
□ 수리하면 얼마나 더 쓸 수 있죠?	If it gets repaired, how much longer can I use my cell phone?
□ 새로 사는 게 나을까요?	Do you think it would be better to get a new one?
	hould I buy a brand-new one?

 Notes

go on and off 됐다 안됐다 하다, 오락가락하다 loose contact 접촉 부위가 헐거워진, 접촉 불량인 drop 떨어뜨리다 warranty 품질 보증(서), 무상 수리 (기간) parts 부품, 부속품 average 평균, 보통, 표준 brand-new 아주 새로운, 신제품의